Anthropology and Nostalgia

ANTHROPOLOGY AND NOSTALGIA

Edited by

Olivia Angé and David Berliner

berghahn
NEW YORK · OXFORD
www.berghahnbooks.com

Published in 2015 by
Berghahn Books
www.berghahnbooks.com

Library of Congress Cataloging-in-Publication Data
Anthropology and nostalgia / edited by Olivia Angé and David Berliner. – First
edition.
pages cm
Includes bibliographical references and index.
ISBN 978-1-78238-453-3 (hardback : alk. paper) – ISBN 978-1-78238-454-0 (ebook)
1. Nostalgia–Cross-cultural studies. 2. Nostalgia–Social aspects. I. Angé, Olivia.
II. Berliner, David.
BF575.N6A67 2014
302'.1–dc23

2014016266

British Library Cataloguing in Publication Data
A catalogue record for this book is available from the British Library

ISBN: 978-1-78238-453-3 hardback
ISBN: 978-1-78238-454-0 ebook

Contents

Illustrations

Acknowledgements

Special thanks are due to all the authors of this volume for their participation in this editorial project and their contribution to the discussion on nostalgia-related questions: Jonathan Bach, Rebecca Bryant, Chris Hann, Gediminas Lankauskas, Joseph Levy, Maya Nadkarni, Petra Rethman and Olga Shevchenko; as well as William Bissel for his generous afterword. Our anonymous readers for Berghahn Books helped us to improve the manuscript and we are indebted to them for reading it so cautiously. We also appreciate the editorial support of Mikaëla Le Meur and Maria Sigutina. We finally wish to express our gratitude to Marion Berghahn for her interest in our collection of essays and for rendering its publication possible.

Introduction

Anthropology of Nostalgia – Anthropology as Nostalgia

Olivia Angé and David Berliner

La pensée d'un homme est avant tout sa nostalgie.

Camus, *Le mythe de Sisyphe.*

This book explores how nostalgic discourses and practices work concretely in different social and cultural environments. Since the rediscovery of memory by social scientists (Berliner 2005), and in particular its emotionality (White 2006), nostalgia has increasingly attracted anthropologists' attention. Terms including 'structural' (Herzfeld 2004), 'synthetic' (Strathern 1995), 'armchair' (Appadurai 1996), 'colonial' (Bissel 2005), 'imperialist' (Rosaldo 1989), 'practical' (Battaglia 1995), 'resistant' (Stewart 1988) and 'for the future' (Piot 2010) have been applied to it in order to deal with its complexity, at the intersection of the individual, the social and the political. Scholars have realized that nostalgia constitutes a fascinating site for studying contemporary issues of identity, politics and history.

However, fine-grained ethnographies of nostalgia and loss are still scarce (Berliner 2012, Bissel 2005, Graburn 1995, Ivy 1995, Metcalf 2012, Schneider 2000). Most of the topical literature focuses on post-socialist contexts (Berdahl 1999, Boyer 2006, Todorova and Gille 2012). As much as the Holocaust has become a paradigm for research in memory studies (Lapierre 2007), works on nostalgia are paradigmatically 'Eastern European'. This book intends to expand on this research, ethnographically and theoretically. Drawing on disparate fieldwork around the globe (Argentina, Germany, Cyprus, Spain, Lithuania, Russia and Hungary), the contributors explore the fabric of nostalgia, by addressing its places, interactions, agents, institutions, objects, rituals, politics, codes, critical moments, gestures, banal temporalities and media. They investigate nostalgic feelings, discourses and practices in the fields of heritage and tourism, exile and diasporas, economic exchange and consumerism, politics and nationalism. Although the bulk of the texts are ethnographic in essence, the book gathers a gamut of works based on classical as well as unconventional empirical cases and brings together insights from history, literature, museology and political sciences. Analytically, they all contribute to a better understanding of how individuals and groups remember, commemorate and revitalize their pasts, and the crucial role played by nostalgia in the process of remembering.

Nostalgia, in the sense of a 'longing for what is lacking in a changed present . . . a yearning for what is now unattainable, simply because of the irreversibility of time' (Pickering and Keightley 2006: 920), is a central notion that permeates present-day discourses and practices. Theorists see in it a distinctive attitude towards the past inherent to contemporary culture, 'a reaction against the irreversible' (Jankélévitch 1983: 299) to be found everywhere and now often commodified, the result of 'a new phase of accelerated, nostalgia-producing globalization' (Robertson 1992: 158). Whilst, in *L'ignorance*, Milan Kundera describes his hero, Josef, a Czech man who feels only disinterest towards his past, as suffering from 'a lack of nostalgia' (2005: 87), in many parts of the world there seems to be a current overdose of nostalgia, a reaction to the modern 'accelerism' (the acceleration of modern temporality coined by Robert Musil in *The Man Without Qualities*) and deployed in universes as diverse as nationalism, heritage policies, vintage consumerism, the tourism industry and religious and ecological movements.

Nostalgia, however, has a long history. Reviewing past literature on the subject would be an impossible task, far beyond the reach of this introduction. Psychiatrists and psychoanalysts, historians, literary critics, scholars of cultural studies and philosophers have abundantly discussed such history, from Odysseus's homesickness, yearning for his return to Ithaca, to the medicalization of nostalgia (as a physical trouble) by Johannes Hofer in the seventeenth century (Bolzinger 2007, Jankélévitch 1983, Starobinsky 1966). The nineteenth century saw nostalgia lose its clinical connotations and started to take the metaphorical meaning of longing for a lost place and, especially, a vanished time. In Europe, at that period, nostalgia for past times indeed blossomed. Massive changes, such as those induced by industrialization and urbanization but also by the French Revolution, fostered a 'perception of history as decline' (Turner 1987: 150), 'a dramatization of discontinuity' (Fritzsche 2001: 1610) and a desire to recapture what life was before. A sense of temporal acceleration prompted by unprecedented social and economic transformations produced, among many European elites, a sense of loss and distance from the past that nurtured their wish to patrimonialize and museumify it, but also boosted their scientific and literary interest in memory and loss (Terdiman 1993). This massive deployment of historiographical and patrimonial consciousness is brilliantly grasped by historian Pierre Nora in his voluminous *Lieux de mémoire* (1984, 1986, 1992) where he explores the impact of the 'acceleration of history' on the social fabric of memory in France. Although Nora's writing is imbued with nostalgia for a time when memory was spontaneous, warm and absolute rather than cold and relative history ('there are *lieux de mémoire*, sites of memory, because there are no longer *milieux de mémoire*, real environments of memory' [1989: 7]), his work cogently teases out the emergence of a modernist posture towards the past, and the role of material culture as quintessential mediation for collective remembering. What historians name the nineteenth century 'memory boom' or 'heritage crusade' in Europe was undoubtedly a result of this modernist nostalgia, yet it was only by the second half of the twentieth century that the notion entered popular vocabulary. In the West, a 'culture of nostalgia' arose in the 1960s and 1970s, a time of great social transformations accompanied by a growing media culture and the commercialization of nostalgia through popular culture (Davis 1979, Grainge 2002, Jameson 1991). 'Why so much nostalgia *now*?' writes Davis in the late 70s. 'Why the almost frenetic preoccupation of nearly every postpubescent age group with fads and fashions from the past?' (Davis 1979: 105). Even more today, a nostalgic craze glorifying past ways and objects is pervasive in the West and can be observed in the growing success of flea markets and antiques, organic food, 'natural' childbirth techniques, eco-museums, vintage consumption, and so forth, such *retromania* invading modern day new technologies (think of 'Instagram' that makes your present pictures look 'instantly nostalgic' [see Bartholeyns 2014]). A whole field of research about the contemporary forms of nostalgia remains to be investigated, and this book is a commencement only, both theoretical and ethnographic.

To begin with, it is worth noting that, for anthropologists and sociologists, studying nostalgia today resembles a return of the repressed. The foundation of sociology as an academic discipline was built upon a conception of modernity imbued with nostalgia (Shaw and Chase 1989). Durkheim, Weber, Tönnies and Simmel's theories involve a critical stance towards the emergent Western industrial society, framed by a moral opposition between tradition and modernity. As compared to the former, they share a view of the latter as characterized by cultural and political breakdown, in a rhetoric permeated with a sense of social degradation (Berlan 2012). Primitivist nostalgia played a crucial role in the formation of anthropology as well, with the first ethnographies by Franz Boas, Bronislaw Malinowski, Edward Evans-Pritchard and Marcel Griaule, among many others, fuelled with a longing for vanishing societies and ruptured equilibriums (Metcalf 2012, Rosaldo 1989). While anthropologists in the West were building a science on nostalgia for disappearing distant Otherness, an ethnographic interest for the popular and the rural led to the institutionalization of folklore studies in the second half of the nineteenth century in Western Europe (Bendix 1997). David Berliner opens the volume with a chapter on anthropologists' disciplinary nostalgia, which he terms exo-nostalgia, i.e., feelings and discourses about other people's (cultural) loss. Such nostalgia rested on combined ideas about the fragility of traditional societies and the impact of colonialism, all wrapped in a pre-apocalyptic tone. Berliner argues that this posture persists to this day, albeit under different expressions. Anthropologists' favourite others are now the local, the particular and the poor, versus the global, the heterogeneous and the dominant, an attitude deeply rooted in their disciplinary exo-nostalgia.

For some time, nostalgia has thus been a structuring temporal framework for the social sciences, when many anthropologists were blind to their own usage of time (Fabian 1983). This probably explains why it only became an object of study in the late 1970s, with the rise of postmodernism and the deconstruction of the *méta-récits*. Long seen as a malaise, as 'bad history', nostalgia was often attacked for its sentimentalism and historical falsification, and it still is. Historian David Lowenthal (1989), for instance, apprehends nostalgia as a modern symptom of memory distortion. For some, nostalgia is regarded as a dangerous misuse of history, trading on 'comfortable and conveniently reassuring images of the past, thereby suppressing both its variety and its negative aspects' (Shaw and Chase 1989: 1). Such distortions make nostalgia prone to instrumentalization by conservative strata of the society, striving to legitimate their privileges and to impede social changes (Natali 2004, Tannock 1995). However, in the wake of the literary turn, researchers paid more attention to the past as it is lived by social agents and to concepts closer to human experience (Ricoeur 2000). Anthropologists and sociologists left the suspicious attitude towards memory that previously characterized many histories for a more phenomenological approach, capturing the way people remember, forget and reinterpret their own past. They became as interested in the reliability of memory as in the memory work itself (sometimes more), and nostalgia found its way in the emerging field of memory studies. Published in 1979, Fred Davis' pioneering *Yearning for Yesterday* provides the first in-depth discussion on the social aspects of nostalgia. Analysing 1960s' social ruptures in American society (mostly challenges to beliefs around what was seen as 'natural' in terms of race, gender, sexualities and lifestyles) and the 'nostalgia orgy' in the following decade, Davis argued that nostalgic reactions originate in perceived threats to continuity of identity in the context of present fears, discontents and uncertainties, when identities have been 'badly bruised by the turmoil of the times' (Davis 1979: 107). Against the idea of retrospective yearnings as politically regressive and emotionally disturbed, Davis approached nostalgia as an act anchored in present context that says a lot more about contemporary social configurations than about the past itself, as it plays a crucial role in 'constructing, maintaining, and reconstructing our identities' (1979: 31). Recent anthropological literature has confirmed that nostalgia as affect, discourse and practice mediate collective identities, whether they are social, ethnic or national (Bissell 2005, Bryant 2008, Cashman 2006, Herzfeld 2004). Far from only being an evasion towards an irretrievable past, or politically non-subversive (Rethmann 2008), nostalgic laments can involve both moral critique of the present and an alternative to deal with social changes (Parla 2009, Yang 2003). Sometimes, nostalgia is 'a weapon', as Berdahl nicely puts it (1999: 201). Similarly, Atia and Davies emphasize that nostalgia is 'a potent form of such subaltern memory', underlining 'nostalgia's empowering agency' and 'critical potential' (2010: 181). As a matter of fact, nostalgia is mostly approached today as a narrative of loss by way of such 'power/resistance' paradigm.

* * *

The texts that follow push the discussion around nostalgia in four directions. While all the texts engage, by and large, in these ways, some add more focus on one point rather than another. First, it is time to clarify the notional fog surrounding the label 'nostalgia' and to meticulously describe the multiple cognitive and emotional investments that lie behind it. Nostalgia has become a catch-all notion used to refer to an array of memory discourses and practices that sometimes share little commonalities. Katherine Stewart already warned us that if 'nostalgia ... is everywhere', 'it is a cultural practice, not a given content; its forms, meanings, and effects shift with the context – it depends on where the speaker stands in the landscape of the present' (1988: 227). Although rooted in the idea that the past is no longer available, nostalgic longings are indeed multiple. William Bissell invites anthropologists to look at how 'nostalgia takes on very different forms and dimensions, engaging an array of social agents, interests, forces, and locations' (Bissell 2005: 239). In the same vein, Dominic Boyer remarks that nostalgia is not only 'indexical', but also 'heteroglossic', a 'dialogical gossamer of idiosyncratic references, interests, and affects that are channelled through nostalgic discourse' (Boyer 2012: 20). Some authors have highlighted the need to operate distinctions between different types of nostalgia. Svetlana Boym distinguishes between nostalgias that are 'restorative', aiming at the 'transhistorical reconstruction of lost home' (Boym 2001: xviii), and those that are 'reflective', ironic and longing for the longing itself. Whereas Davis separated 'private' and 'collective' nostalgias (1979: 122), Jameson (1991) suggested a discrimination between the 'nostalgic mood', caused by a feeling of loss, and the 'nostalgic mode', i.e., the consumable style that does not involve memory per se (for an elaboration on Jameson's typology, see Grainge 2002). More generally, the latter designates these 'fragments of the past [that] are energetically manufactured and avidly consumed but do not necessarily correspond to the evidence of experience' (Fritzsche 2001: 1617).

This raises important questions for anthropologists: what forms can nostalgia take and, when identified, how to grasp them in thick description? Is nostalgia an effect (positive or negative?), a social practice, a form of discourse? How to distinguish it from other past-oriented states (such as non-nostalgic reminiscences)? Does nostalgia bring into play a temporality of its own? Nostalgia's psychological mechanisms are habitually left in the shadow by anthropologists, albeit Bloch (1998) and Wertsch (2009) have recommended one take into account the complex workings of mnemonic fixation. A bouquet of studies examines the psychological triggers, contents and functions of nostalgia, demonstrating its ability to generate positive affects (Routledge et al. 2011, Wildschut et al. 2006). Although the present volume does not constitute an exploration into the mental processes of nostalgia, such research (that draw on methods many anthropologists might find irrelevant) opens fascinating avenues for further anthropological enquiries. In his article for this volume, David Berliner calls for an ambitious but nonetheless rigorous use of the notion. A consuming feeling born of the realization that human temporality is irreversible, mostly embodied in the Proustian madeleine experience (that of *In Search of Lost Time* which triggers the author's involuntary memories of Combray), nostalgia can be disconnected from intense emotional feelings and sometimes from personal experiences altogether. Berliner recommends that one disentangles its multiple attachments, some of which are not always nostalgic. Likewise, Gediminas Lankauskas regrets that the conceptual fuzziness surrounding nostalgia and the dominant paradigm of *nostalgification* in post-socialist studies wipes out the very complexity and ambiguity of memory practices that we should strive to describe. His chapter forcefully illustrates an expression of post-socialist nostalgia within an interactive theme park in a bunker of the Lithuanian capital where, guided by professional actors, visitors experience conditions of life under communism, such as KGB interrogations, medical examinations, civil defence training and so forth. Lankauskas regards these shows (the 'survival drama') as commemorative performances where the period of communist rule is represented using memorial media ranging from visual imagery and discourse to acoustic and gustatory effects. Meanwhile, social memories are also contested by participants. Although, in Eastern Europe, many people historically and biographically represent socialism as a 'vanished home', in the Bunker, the performances that recall the austerity and harshness of the Soviet era are better comprehended as non-nostalgic recollections, a past to be remembered and forgotten. According to the participants' glosses on their experience, Lankauskas differentiates between nostalgic longings and 'memories of bygone' where the relationship with the past is one of dissociation rather than affective continuity. His article offers several insightful vignettes from the Bunker 'survival drama', and argues that after socialism there is more to individual and collective memory than nostalgia.

The same quest for conceptual clarification underlies the important contribution by Olga Schevchenko and Maya Nadkarni. Whereas Lankauskas disentangles diverse memory works in the Bunker, Schevchenko and Nadkarni discriminate among different kinds of references to the past, stressing that not all of them are nostalgic. Comparing the relationship of nostalgia to politics in post-socialist Hungary and Russia in the 1990s and 2000s, they stress the analytical confusion that surrounds many discussions about nostalgia. Often, nostalgia has been associated with a priori political meanings (either progressive or reactionary) and reified into an essentialized object with a given and stable content. Their chapter convincingly shows that there is a multiplicity of meanings to nostalgia, many of which depend on who mobilizes the desire to renew a relationship to the past. Portraying the heterogeneity of nostalgic practices, they argue that similar forms of longing carry very different meanings depending on the political agendas in which they were enmeshed. For instance, expressions of nostalgia in Hungary were considered less subversive than in Russia, because the geopolitical context of Hungary at that time made it impossible to exploit nostalgia politically. A longing for something no longer attainable, nostalgia thus arises relationally. It is precisely these indexical relations that need to be elucidated in the studies of nostalgia.

*   *   *

Second, the contributions gathered in this book aim at describing the concrete fabric of nostalgia in interactions, facts of communication, places and times, and through texts, objects and technologies (see also Todorova 2012).

Who are the different protagonists of nostalgia? In which social networks and political ideologies does it take place? What are the sites and contexts in which it is expressed? Are words and objects the most powerful vehicles for longing? How is nostalgia transmitted to younger generations? Like Schevchenko and Nadkarni, Chris Hann's chapter advocates a treatment of nostalgia that takes into consideration the larger sociohistorical context, with a focus on its contemporary politicization. Assembling private and public strands of Hungarian nostalgia, he emphasizes the complex entanglement of private and collective memories. Drawing on his long-term research in the village of Tazlar, Hann shows the persistence of nostalgia for socialism in the private sphere, although the prevailing ideology of private property nowadays obstructs public appreciation of the socialist decades. Furthermore, his multi-level ethnography demonstrates how private dissident memories persist in the domestic space, while political elites strive to shape a collective nostalgia rooted in the pre-socialist *mythomoteur* of Hungarian nationalism. We discover how Hungarian politicians today manipulate such pre-communist mythology from which the villagers are largely estranged.

In the fabric of nostalgia, physical objects play an important role. Not unlike the famous madeleine cake of Proust, materialities mediate people's relationship to their past and, often, they trigger powerful mnemonic responses (Parkin 1999, Radley 1990). A literary and dramatic example of this is found in Orhan Pamuk's *Museum of Innocence* (2010), the shattering tale of a young Turkish man who builds a museum to honor the nostalgic memories of his impossible love story. A somehow similar spirit animates the text by Jonathan Bach, who explores the workings of post-socialist nostalgia in the former German Democratic Republic. His chapter revisits the well-known phenomenon of *Ostalgie* (a German neologism meaning nostalgia for the former socialist East [see also Berdhal 1999 and Boyer 2006]) in contemporary Germany. More than two decades after the demise of the GDR, nostalgia for communism remains a contentious semantic space. Bach examines the symbolic and economic appreciation of everyday life objects that came to epitomize the socialist era, emphasizing how they have been transfigured into what he terms 'nostalgia-objects'. Focusing on the material culture of nostalgia expressed in private museums of everyday life under socialism, he argues that massive purchase of socialist objects by local collectors, today obsolete as compared with newly imported Western goods, constitutes a mourning for some aspects of their past. These privately run museums claim historical authenticity in addition to commercial attraction, and coexist in a vexed relationship with scholarly and state archival practices. On the other hand, one finds among Easterners a wide consumption of goods once produced under socialist brands. Consumer objects occupy the border between a longing for a style of life under communism, and a capitalist nostalgia organized around an aesthetic of kitsch. Rather than a desire to revive the socialist regime itself, consumption of both these kinds of products should be interpreted as a political device for Easterners to position themselves in a field of cultural production dominated by the West. Bach's study of the re-evaluation and re-appropriation of GDR objects further teases out the complex process by which nostalgia intervenes as a vector of cultural transmission.

The relationship existing between objects of nostalgia, cultural transmission and trauma lies at the heart of Joseph Josy Lévy and Inaki Olazabal's chapter. Taking as case the traumatic exile of Spanish Jews in 1492 after the Catholic kings religiously unified the kingdom, they return to the very first meaning of nostalgia as a longing for a lost geographical home. Scattered, Jewish exiles reorganized their communities in new countries and kept over centuries a rich heritage by which nostalgia for Spain was maintained alive and reactivated in daily and ritual occasions. In memoirs, historical texts, folklore and contemporary novels (like Marcos Aguinis' *Gesta del marrano*, Eliette Abécassis' *Sefarad* and Jorge Semprun's *Twenty Years and One Day*), Levy and Olazabal scrutinize the persistent presence of *La llave*, the key of the lost house that Sephardic Jews are said to have carried throughout their exile, a powerful symbol of their ancestral house, evoking a longing for Spain. And the key continues its social life, 'formalized as heritage' producing 'legitimacy through aestheticization' (Roy 1994). It is now a cultural icon publicly mobilized by Spanish politicians to restore relationships with Jewish communities around the world and used by national and international agencies to develop tourism.

*   *   *

Third, far from being a feeling hidden in the confines of the self only, nostalgia is 'a force that does something' (Dames 2010: 272). Such a transformative aspect of nostalgia is elegantly captured by Milan Kundera in *The Unbearable Lightness of Being* when he writes: 'In the sunset of dissolution, everything is illuminated by the aura of nostalgia, even the guillotine' (1984: 4). Therefore, anthropologists must investigate its pragmatic conditions and effects. What and how do nostalgic memories make act? How may nostalgic longings constitute operators for social transformations? When used for social and political concerns, nostalgic discourses and practices do not necessarily involve the melancholy with which it is usually associated. In some cases, they bond diverse categories of actors and constitute a source of mnemonic convergence. Such convergence remains relatively under studied by anthropologists, in favour of stories of clashes and misunderstandings between multiple pasts. For instance, in Luang Prabang (Lao PDR), David Berliner has observed the flourishing of a mnemonic community centred on nostalgia for the Indochinese past among Western experts, expatriates, travellers and some Lao from the diaspora, whilst frictions about meaningful heritage opposed UNESCO experts and locals (Berliner 2012). In her text for this volume, Rebecca Bryant forcefully highlights one function of nostalgia, namely the reification of social identities and the production of cultural boundaries in context of important changes. Her article examines discourses of nostalgia in north Cyprus that have emerged in the past decade, after almost thirty years of relative silence regarding the pre-conflict past. With the division of Cyprus in 1974, more than two hundred thousand persons were displaced from their homes. Almost fifty thousand Turkish Cypriots moved from the island's south to a new, ethnically cleansed homeland in the island's north, where they engaged in practices of forgetting their former homes. Bryant describes a new emphasis by Turkish Cypriots on their displacement and life before conflict, evident in a flood of books, television programs and newspaper articles that document homes and villages left behind. Non-recognition of the Turkish Cypriot state, a flood of immigration and the 2003 opening of the border have resulted in doubts about gains and a new discovery of loss. But unlike many other forms of nostalgia that emphasize a prelapsarian moment and longing for its return, these nostalgic productions are non-utopian, pointing to the 'fall from grace' of coexistence with one's former Greek Cypriot neighbours. In certain cases, nostalgia may be used to facilitate forgetting and to stress irretrievability. Furthermore, she discusses how nostalgia is strategically deployed to define thresholds, boundaries and hence orientations towards the future. Her ethnography reveals that nostalgia constitutes a longing for an idealized and stereotyped self image that one believes is irremediably lost. A 'longing for essentialism', as she terms it, it fosters a well-defined representation of oneself that has irretrievably gone.

Olivia Angé adopts a similar angle and looks at the efficacy of nostalgic discourses in economic exchanges between Highland and Lowland peasants in Argentina. Studying barter fairs in the Argentinean cordillera, in a way that is reminiscent of Cretan shepherds' 'structural nostalgia' (Herzfeld 2004), she examines how the trope of a vanishing balanced reciprocity is mobilized during barter haggling in order to increase rewards, without necessarily involving affective attachment to the past. Angé suggests that one distinguishes between 'nostalgic dispositions', implying emotional investment, and 'nostalgic discursive devices', strategic utterances targeting present benefits. Through the use of these nostalgic devices, fairs' transactions manifest a moral and symbolic continuity with an ancestral past. It is by lamenting its loss and denunciating its violation that barter between Highlanders and Lowlanders is displayed as a normative ideal. Moreover, corroborating Bryant's statement, repeated allusions to the ancestors' code of exchange and its vanishing contribute to essentializing ethnic identities in a context of social liminarity.

* * *

Fourth, and finally, nostalgia reveals relationships that exist between the past, the present and the future. As Dominic Boyer lucidly puts it, 'nostalgia always carries with it a politics of the future' (2012: 25). 'Nostalgia', writes Boym, 'is not always about the past. It can be retrospective as well as prospective' (2001: xvi). Following the historian Koselleck (2004 [1979]), one must consider nostalgic discourses and feelings about the passing of time as *always already* framed within the 'horizons of expectations' in the present. Comparing Greek-Cypriot and Turkish-Cypriot histories of their island's partition, Bryant has lucidly shown how visions of lost homelands are also visions of 'homelands yet to be realized' (Bryant 2008: 399). The women's narratives that Bryant analyses 'complicate our notions of nostalgia through a longing for a homeland that is not absent but rather apocalyptic – a homeland not of the past but of the future' (2008: 404). Nostalgia is being crafted within such horizons of expectations and anxieties about the future. And hope is never far from nostalgia, as shown by recent ethnographies of hope and the politics of future (Cole 2010, Piot 2010). The final chapter by Petra Rethmann discusses the defeat and promise of communism in GRD. Since socialism has been declared an 'extinction event', its structure, shape and configuration can only be imagined as ruin. In inverse relation, leftist ideologists such as Fredric Jameson, Slavoj Zizek and Jodi Dean hold on to the idea of socialism as utopia and dream, a political horizon to which contemporary critical and leftist thinkers should aspire. In her article, Rethmann studies if and how socialism can still constitute a meaningful horizon in Germany today. Building on her research in a conference entitled *Kommunismus* organized in Berlin in 2010, she approaches two manifestations of 'left-wing nostalgia' and their attempt to reimagine a fair future.

This last point brings us to a key question on nostalgia, that of temporality. Since the foundation of the discipline, anthropologists have been interested in the cultural constructions of time (Gell 1992, Munn 1992). If nostalgia implies a specific positioning towards the past seen as irreversible, an awareness of something which has disappeared or is disappearing, it is reasonable to ask whether it is universal. Without giving a definitive answer to such a riddle, it is fair to point out that every society around the world has faced breaches and crises and that all human groups have experienced some reflexive distancing from their past, often taking the form of long-ings for a lost past. In that regard, we follow Maurice Bloch in his famous discussion of Geertz's appraisal of time: people, he claims, can hold different conceptions of duration depending on the context (Bloch 1977), a point that is made clear about nostalgia by some of our contributors to this volume (Lankauskas, Schevchenko and Nadkarni). As a matter of fact, nostalgia takes place within very specific ontological temporalities (see also Naumescu 2010 on schismatic Orthodox Old Believers in Romania). As anthropologists, our intellectual endeavours consist of grasping the expressions of such nostalgic laments in the midst of historical contingencies. But studying nostalgia not only invites us to refine our understanding of the experience of temporality. As social representations and practices undergo constant mutations, but still persist in time, it also directs our attention to operations of continuity and discontinuity. Atia and Davies underline that 'whatever its object, nostalgia serves as a negotiation between continuity and discontinuity' (Atia and Davies 2010: 184). An anthropological exploration of nostalgia (as well as other mnemonic states) indeed nurtures such a reflection upon the durability of human societies in the face of the ruptures of history. For the anthropologist, this born nostalgist, nostalgia constitutes a fascinating angle to explore the creative persistence and the disappearance of cultural forms. Even more importantly, it allows a number of important reconciliations: between the anthropological, the historical and the psychological; the continuous and discontinuous; the persistent and the mutable; but also between the past, the present and the future.

References

Appadurai, A. 1996. *Modernity at Large: Cultural Dimensions of Globalizations.* Minneapolis: University of Minnesota Press.

Atia, N. and J. Davies. 2010. 'Nostalgia and the Shapes of History', *Memory Studies* 3 (3): 81–186.

Bartholeyns, G. 2014. 'Nostalgia and Digital Retro Photography', in K. Niemeyer (ed.), *Media and Nostalgia: Yearning for the Past, Present and Future.* Basingstoke: Palgrave Macmillan.

Battaglia, D. 1995. 'On Practical Nostalgia: Self-Prospecting among Urban Trobrianders', in D. Battaglia (ed.), *Rhetoric of Self-Making.* Berkeley: University of California Press, pp. 76–96.

Bendix, R. 1997. *In Search of Authenticity: The Formation of Folklore Studies.* Madison: The University of Wisconsin Press.

Berdahl, D. 1999. '"Ostalgie" for the Present: Memory, Longing, and East German Things', *Ethnos* 64 (2): 192–211.

Berlan, A. 2012. *La Fabrique des derniers hommes. Retour sur le présent avec Tönnies, Simmel et Weber.* Paris: La Découverte.

Berliner, D. 2005. 'The Abuses of Memory: Reflections on the Memory Boom in Anthropology', *Anthropological Quarterly* 78 (1): 197–211.

———. 2012. 'Multiple Nostalgias: The Fabric of Heritage in Luang Prabang (Lao PDR)', *The Journal of the Royal Anthropological Institute* (N.S.) 18 (4): 769–86.

Bissel, W. 2005. 'Engaging Colonial Nostalgia', *Cultural Anthropology* 20 (2): 215–48.

Bolzinger, A. 2007. *Histoire de la nostalgie.* Paris: Editions Campagne Première.

Bloch, M. 1977. 'The Past and the Present in the Present', *Man* 12 (2): 278–92.

———. 1998. *How We Think They Think: Anthropological Approach to Cognition, Memory and Literacy.* Boulder, CO: Westview Press.

Boyer, D. 2006. 'Ostalgie and the Politics of the Future in Eastern Germany', *Public Culture* 18 (2): 361–81.

———. 2012. 'From Algos to Autonomos: Nostalgic Eastern Europe as Postimperial Mania', in M. Todorova and Z. Gille (eds), *Post-Communist Nostalgia.* Oxford: Berghahn, pp. 17–28.

Boym, S. 2001. *The Future of Nostalgia.* New York: Basic Books.

Bryant, R. 2008. 'Writing the Catastrophe: Nostalgia and Its Histories in Cyprus', *Journal of Greek Modern Studies* 26: 399–422.

Camus, A. 1942. *Le mythe de Sisyphe.* Paris: Gallimard.

Cashman, R. 2006. 'Critical Nostalgia and Material Culture in Northern Ireland', *The Journal of American Folklore* 119 (472): 136–60.

Cole, J. 2010. *Sex and Salvation: Imagining the Future in Madagascar.* Chicago: University of Chicago Press.

Dames, N. 2010. 'Nostalgia and Its Disciplines', *Memory Studies* 3 (3): 269–75.

Davis, F. 1979. *Yearning for Yesterday: A Sociology of Nostalgia.* New York: Free Press.

Fabian, J. 1983. *Time and the Other: How Anthropology Makes Its Object.* New York: Columbia University Press.

Fritzsche, P. 2001. 'Specters of History: On Nostalgia, Exile, and Modernity', *The American Historical Review* 106 (5): 1587–618.

Gell, A. 1992. *The Anthropology of Time: Cultural Constructions of Temporal Maps and Images.* Oxford: Berg.

Graburn, N. 1995. 'The Past in the Present in Japan: Nostalgia and Neo-Traditionalism in Contemporary Japanese Domestic Tourism', in R. Butler and D. Pearce (eds), *Change in Tourism: People, Places, Processes.* London: Routledge, pp. 47–70.

Grainge, P. 2002. *Monochrome Memories: Nostalgia and Style in Retro America.* Westport, CT: Praeger.

Herzfeld, M. 2004. *Cultural Intimacy: Social Poetics in the Nation-State*, second edition. London: Routledge.

Ivy, M. 1995. *Discourses of the Vanishing: Modernity, Phantasm, Japan.* Chicago: University of Chicago Press.

Jameson, F. 1991. *Postmodernism, or, the Cultural Logic of Late Capitalism.* Durham: Duke University Press.

Jankélévitch, V. 1983. *L'irréversible et la nostalgie.* Paris: Flammarion.

Koselleck, R. 2004 [1979]. *Futures Past: On the Semantics of Historical Time*, trans. K. Tribe. New York: Columbia University Press.

Kundera, M. 1984. *The Unbearable Lightness of Being*, trans. M.H. Heim. New York: Harper & Row.

———. 2005. *L'ignorance*. Paris: Gallimard.

Lapierre, N. 2007. 'Le cadre référentiel de la Shoah', *Ethnologie Française* 37 (3): 475–82.

Lowenthal, D. 1989. 'Nostalgia Tells It Like It Wasn't', in C. Shaw and M. Chase (eds), *The Imagined Past: History and Nostalgia*. New York: Manchester University Press, pp. 18–32.

Metcalf, P. 2012. 'Nostalgia and Neocolonialism', in S. Howell and A. Talle (eds), *Return to the Field: Multitemporal Research and Contemporary Anthropology*. Bloomington: Indiana University Press, pp. 123–52.

Munn, N. 1992. 'The Cultural Anthropology of Time: A Critical Essay', *Annual Review of Anthropology* 21: 93–123.

Musil, R. 2011. *The Man Without Qualities*. New York: Picador.

Natali, M. 2004. 'History and the Politics of Nostalgia', *Iowa Journal of Cultural Studies* 4: 10–25.

Naumescu, V. 2010. 'Le vieil homme et le livre. La crise de la transmission chez les vieux croyants', *Terrain* 55: 72–89.

Nora, P. (ed.) 1984. *Les lieux de mémoire. La République*. Paris Gallimard.

———. (ed.) 1986. *Les lieux de mémoire. La Nation*. Paris Gallimard.

———. (ed.) 1992. *Les lieux de mémoire. Les Frances*. Paris Gallimard.

———. 1989. 'Between Memory and History: Les Lieux de Mémoire', *Representations* 26: 7–25.

Pamuk, O. 2010. *The Museum of Innocence*. New York: Vintage International.

Parla, A. 2009. 'Remembering Across the Border: Postsocialist Nostalgia among Turkish Immigrants from Bulgaria', *American Ethnologist* 36 (4): 750–67.

Parkin, D. 1999. 'Mementoes as Transitional Objects in Human Displacement', *Journal of Material Culture* 4 (3): 303–20.

Pickering, M. and E. Keightley. 2006. 'The Modalities of Nostalgia', *Current Sociology* 54: 919–41.

Piot, C. 2010. *Nostalgia for the Future: West Africa after the Cold War*. Chicago: Chicago University Press.

Proust, M. 2003. *In Search of Lost Time*. New York: Modern Library.

Radley, A. 1990. 'Artefacts, Memory and a Sense of the Past', in D. Middleton and D. Edwards (eds), *Collective Remembering*. London: Sage Publications, pp. 46–59.

Rethmann, P. 2008. 'Nostalgie à Moscou', *Anthropologie et Sociétés* 32 (1–2): 85–102.

Ricoeur, P. 2000. *La mémoire, l'histoire, l'oubli*. Paris: Editions du Seuil.

Robertson, R. 1992. *Globalization. Social Theory and Global Culture*. London: Sage Publications.

Rosaldo, R. 1989. 'Imperialist Nostalgia', *Representations* 26: 107–22.

Roy, A. 1994. 'Nostalgias of the Modern', in A. Nezar (ed.), *The End of Tradition?* London: Routledge.

Routledge, C., Arndt, J., Wildschut, T., Sedikides, C., Hart, C.M., Juhl, J., Vingerhoets, A.J.J.M. and Schlotz, W. 2011. 'The Past Makes Present Meaningful: Nostalgia as an Existential Resource', *Journal of Personality and Social Psychology* 101: 638–52.

Schneider, A. 2000. *Futures Lost: Nostalgia and Identity among Italian Immigrants in Argentina*. Oxford: Peter Lang.

Shaw, C. and M. Chase. 1989. 'The Dimensions of Nostalgia', in C. Shaw and M. Chase (eds), *The Imagined Past: History and Nostalgia*. New York: Manchester University Press, pp.1–17.

Starobinski, J. 1966. 'Le Concept de Nostalgie', *Diogène* 54: 92–115.

Stewart, K. 1988. 'Nostalgia – A Polemic', *Cultural Anthropology* 3 (3): 227–41.

Strathern, M. 1995. 'Nostalgia and the New Genetics', in D. Battaglia (ed.), *Rhetorics of Self-making*. Berkeley: University of California Press, pp. 97–120.

Tannock, S. 1995. 'Nostalgia Critique', *Cultural Studies* 9 (3): 453–64.

Terdiman, R. 1993. *Present Past: Modernity and the Memory Crisis*. Ithaca, NY: Cornell University Press.

Todorova, M. 2012. 'Introduction: From Utopia to Propaganda and Back', in M. Todorova and Z. Gille (eds), *Post-Communist Nostalgia*. New York: Berghahn, pp. 1–13.

Todorova, M. and Z. Gille (eds). 2012. *Post-Communist Nostalgia*. New York: Berghahn.

Turner, B. 1987. 'A Note on Nostalgia', *Theory, Culture and Society* 4 (1): 147–56.

Wertsch, J. 2009. 'Collective Memory', in P. Boyer and J. Wertsch (eds), *Memory in Mind and Culture*. Cambridge: Cambridge University Press, pp. 117–37.

Wildschut, T., Sedikides C. and Arndt J. 2006. 'Nostalgia: Content, Triggers, Functions', *Journal of Personality and Social Psychology* 91: 975–93.

White, G. 2006. 'Epilogue: Memory Moments', *Ethos* 34 (2): 325–41.

Yang, G. 2003. 'China's Zhiqing Generation: Nostalgia, Identity and Cultural Resistance in the 1990s', *Modern China* 29 (3): 267–96.

Chapter 1

Are Anthropologists Nostalgist?

David Berliner

The past assailed him savagely ... Now, every chair, every table gently moved its lips and, all, they spoke to him, inaudible whispers, understandable and clear to himself only. I lived in that house, he could not help thinking, something of me remained.

Zweig, *Journey into the Past.*[1]

Diagnoses of cultural loss are everywhere today. Losing culture, identity, traditions and roots and its corollary – the need to pass down – are tropes mobilized by individuals and groups throughout the world, although differently within diverse social and cultural contexts. This phenomenon is what I call the contemporary *tout-perdre* (losing everything), a specific posture vis-à-vis the past seen as irreversible. Suffice it to think of the heated debates on the Christian roots of Europe, the success of *Roots* by Alex Haley in the United States, the craze of heritage tourism and the genealogical obsession, but also the claims addressed by many to preserve their culture (from *Peuples Premiers* in Canada to indigenous communities in South America and passing by Jewish and Muslim families in Europe).[2] Evidence suggests that cultural loss has become a politicized issue, as the concept is regularly used by politicians, local elites, UNESCO experts and some anthropologists. In Europe, right-wing politicians invoke the trope of the crisis in cultural transmission for nationalistic purposes, to reaffirm a sense of shared national *ethos*, to castigate so-called uprooted young immigrants, but also to patronize other countries (remember former French President Sarkozy in his memorable speech on Africa).[3] Often, the theme of the 'disappearing culture' is deployed by ordinary men and women in a world perceived as globalizing and uprooting. In a troubling example for a European audience, two deaf Americans looked for a deaf donor in order to maximize their chance to have a deaf child. Interviewed by the press, they expressed their desire to transmit deaf culture to their child, seen here not as a handicap, but rather as a cultural identity of its own (Renaut 2010). This extreme case makes sense in the multiculturalist atmosphere prevailing in the US, but, to a larger scale, it reveals the current attachment of countless individuals to notions of 'culture', 'transmission', 'traditions' and 'roots', which are even more precious now that they are said to be threatened and to be disappearing.

As a matter of fact, many of those who desire to transmit and patrimonialize their culture today are historical victims and their descendants. Nicole Lapierre brilliantly shows how the Jews of Plock survived the Holocaust between impossible words and intolerable forgetting, and that it is precisely this 'painful in-between' which 'is transmitted' (Lapierre 2001: 31).[4] For some decades now, former colonized, discriminated and exterminated populations, whether they are Aboriginal Australians, African *anciens colonisés*, post-Holocaust Jews or Native Americans, have sought to unveil their traumatic memories and, at the same time, to rediscover their culture before it was subject to destruction. However, such aspiration to remember and preserve far exceeds these groups of victims. In our time, anxieties about 'losing culture' are part of a general discourse about crisis, 'a crisis that never ends' (Revault d'Allonnes 2012). 'This general crisis … has struck across the modern world and to almost all branches of human activity', assumed Hanna Arendt (Arendt 1972: 223). Motivated by a '*désir de catastrophe*' (Jeudy 2010), a new moralism unfolds where ethical choices and political decisions are posed a priori in reference to a concern for future generations, with a pre-apocalyptic tone. In contemporary catastrophism, the present time is already invaded by a terrible future; the worst-case scenario is not a fantasy anymore but 'a universal category of experience' (Foessel 2012: 7). For the children of the future, one must preserve forms of life, values, identities, roots, languages, rites, know-hows and so forth. This heritage 'crusade' (as David Lowenthal (1998) has put it) is not recent. In nineteenth-century Europe, conservation policies have been deployed concurrently to nationalistic projects. Combined with a sense of loss in the face of growing industrialization (Poulot 2006), they were effectively exported to the colonies. Nowadays, such global institutionalization of the preservation attitude continues via the existence of international organizations like UNESCO (Berliner 2012). Although they are much more fragmented than one might expect (between different delegations and regional offices), UNESCO policies significantly contribute to the dissemination of the trope of vanishing heritage around the world. The Intangible Cultural Heritage (ICH) paradigm itself is an institutionalized response to the worldwide diagnosis of crisis in cultural transmission. Interestingly, such booming is not only geographical, but it also colonizes new ontological areas. As clearly shown by Jean-Louis Tornatore (2010), the sense of loss and the need for transmission are not limited to past monuments and human traditions anymore, but they now encompass natural spaces and biological entities (genes, for instance) that humans seek to protect and pass on to future generations. This current entanglement of biology and heritage is highlighted, in an exemplary manner, by an internet user on a forum when asking 'Do you get sick when you lose your roots?'

For anthropologists, although many have become increasingly uncomfortable with it, there is nothing new in this patrimonialist rhetoric. Losing culture is a nostalgic figure as old as anthropology. As much as continuity is a key idea for social scientists (Berliner 2010, Robbins 2007), our discipline has, from its birth, held on to nostalgia for disappearing worlds, far away or close to home, as in the case of folklorists (Bendix 1997).[5] This article suggests, as others have already pointed out, that one considers the existence of a nostalgia that lies at the very foundation of our discipline and concerned the major anthropological traditions.[6] I call it a disciplinary *exo-nostalgia*. In the conclusive part, I show that, often under new clothes, such nostalgic proclivity still permeates anthropologists' postures. Obviously, the present landscape of anthropology is diverse and fragmented. Even within national traditions, there are multiple paradigmatic orientations and I do not pretend to be exhaustive in this domain.[7] Yet, here, I would like to propose some avenues to explore the entanglement of anthropology and nostalgia. Although many refuse to be associated with the trope of vanishing culture, I argue that anthropologists hardly escape nostalgic forms of thinking and writing.

*   *   *

In a thought-provoking article, Holly High has recently suggested the existence of a 'disciplinary melancholia' in anthropology (High 2011). Based on the experience of mourning one of her main Lao interlocutors, Suaay, and a reading of Freud's perspective on melancholy, High invites us to pay a particular attention to these self reproaches that very often interfere with anthropologists' thoughts when they return from the field. She sees

the anthropologist as 'an abandoner (through withdrawal)' who 'calls for
redemption through ethical engagement' (ibid.: 230). Such disciplinary
melancholy is indeed ubiquitous among present-day anthropologists. Post-
colonial studies and the postmodern turn have certainly contributed to the
spread of feelings of guilt and other moral anxieties, as Marcus and Fischer
(1999) themselves admitted. However, I tend to think that such melancholy
is quite a recent phenomenon. Few anthropologists voiced it before the
'symmetrical turn' and its ethical need for reciprocity (Scheper-Hughes
1995). On the contrary, if there is a posture that has characterized early
anthropologists, it is undoubtedly 'nostalgia'.

First, I must give some precision about the concept of nostalgia that
I will use in this text. Like many other notions in the social sciences (Berliner
2005a), 'nostalgia' has become a catch-all to describe, in general terms, an
attitude of regret for the past. In his article (this volume), Lankauskas lucidly
shows, among scholars of post-communism, the tendency to gather together
all discourses about the past under the label 'nostalgia'. Dominique Boyer
makes the same remark when he writes, with a certain irony, that 'Eastern
Europe is nostalgic; it yearns' (2012: 17). He suggests that one looks at the
'the dialogical gossamer of idiosyncratic references, interests and affects
that are channeled through nostalgic discourse' (ibid.: 20). I agree with both
and suggest that we clarify the fog surrounding the notion, as I myself have
tried elsewhere by revealing the multiple forms – cognitive and emotional –
that nostalgia takes in a World Heritage Site of Northern Laos (Berliner
2012).

Following French philosopher Jankélévitch, who has produced one of
the major texts to grasp the nostalgic experience, *L'irréversible et la nostalgie*,
I believe that 'the nostalgic man [is] absorbed in the auscultation of a dead
past that can never be revived' (1974: 185). At first glance, nostalgia constitutes a consuming and painful feeling born of the realization that human
temporality is irreversible, that return is impossible. Obviously, I refer here
to the Proustian madeleine, a perfect example of the entanglement between
the involuntary resurgence of the past and a strong emotional intensity.[8]
However, there is a variety of nostalgic tones, with multiple cognitive and
emotional investments. Some longings are more or less disconnected from
intense emotional feelings. Others are slightly pleasurable, like the bitter-
sweet *rêverie* I have for some unique moments of my childhood that I do
not particularly want to resuscitate. Nostalgia can also be disconnected
from personal experiences altogether. I am thinking here at my regret for
an idealized May '68 intellectual era that I have not lived personally. All
over the world, young patriots are longing for a country they have usually
not known, and that probably never existed (see Herzfeld on 'structural

nostalgia' [1997]). Broadly speaking, one can treat nostalgia as a specific posture vis-à-vis the past seen as irreversible, a set of publicly displayed discourses, practices and emotions where the ancient is somehow glorified and considered lost forever, without necessarily implying the experience of first-hand memories. Such vicariousness goes as far as to be lamenting the vanishing of other people's past and culture. Appadurai has coined the word 'armchair nostalgia' (Appadurai 1996: 78) to describe such vicarious yearning for the past, reminiscent of 'that nostalgia for an unknown land' (*cette nostalgie du pays qu'on ignore*) evoked by Baudelaire in *L'invitation au voyage* (1869: 49). Nowadays, the latter attitude is common among Western tourists whose externalist discourses about cultural loss do not refer to their own historical past. During my research in Luang Prabang (in Lao PDR), I remember hearing three Dutch tourists in front of a Buddhist temple who exclaimed with a disappointed tone: 'It's a shame. Locals do not even wear their traditional clothes anymore. Too bad. It is too late'. Is this an expression of nostalgia? I think so. Although vicarious and lower in emotional intensity, such an exclamation carries with it the idea of regret for a world imagined as disappearing, the feeling of losing something important. Often, it leads to heated conversations about cultural loss in the tropics once the tourists return home.

In short, as noted by Dominic Boyer, nostalgia is heteroglossic. It can take many forms, from the Proustian cake to the contemporary tourist experience. Thus, in order to clarify this fuzzy theoretical situation, I propose that one distinguish between two fundamental nostalgic postures: nostalgia for the past one has lived personally (what I would term 'endo-nostalgia'), the Proustian madeleine being the reference for this kind of experience; and nostalgia for a past not experienced personally, a vicarious nostalgia that I would term 'exo-nostalgia', which encompasses discourses about loss detached from the direct experience of losing something personal, nonetheless triggering a whole array of affects such as indignation, anger or pain. Let us now see how this latter notion applies to the perspective of our disciplinary founders.

*   *   *

Undoubtedly, many anthropologists have nostalgic memories of their fieldwork. The ethnographic experience produces a great deal of endo-nostalgia for intense social events and encounters, but also for the banalities of everyday life once lived by the researcher in the field. This is not the nostalgia that I will discuss here. In this chapter, I will focus on a specific emotional and cognitive posture informing the production of anthropological knowledge in the academy. Nostalgia for disappearing 'unknown lands', a form of exo-nostalgia, has played a primary role in the history of anthropology. Several authors (e.g., Bendix 1997, Clifford 1986, de L'Estoile 2010, Kuklick 2008, Rosaldo 1989) have highlighted the nostalgic presuppositions of the fathers of the discipline vis-à-vis the societies they studied, from the mid nineteenth century until the Second World War and even later in some cases (France, for instance). It is risky to regroup diverse anthropological traditions under a common paradigmatic umbrella (to tackle such diversity, see Barth et al. 2010). Yet many American, British, German or French anthropologists, conducting fieldwork in the early twentieth century, used nostalgic tropes to describe so-called traditional societies. Suffice it to read Malinowski's *Argonauts* (1922) or Lévi-Strauss' *Tristes Tropiques* (1955) to have examples of ethnographies deploying what French ethnologist Daniel Fabre termed the '*paradigme des derniers*' (Fabre 2008). Under the assault of Western colonialism, traditional societies were losing much of their authenticity rooted in pre-colonial times. Witnessing the end of an era, often battling against a dominant rhetoric that indigenous people had always been 'savage' and had nothing interesting to say to the world, anthropologists of the time emphasized the fragility of these communities in the face of new cultural contacts, imported religions and technologies. As Henrika Kuklick reminds us, 'these peoples were destined to become extinct in cultural, if not necessarily physical terms. Thus, their distinctive characteristics must be recorded for posterity' (Kuklick 2008: 5). This was the dominant romantic episteme through which the young Franz Boas, Bronislaw Malinowski, Edward Evans-Pritchard and Marcel Griaule described the cultures they studied. Their ethnographies quickly became 'cultural obituaries' (Metcalf 2002: 115) and most of their students went to the field accustomed to the idea that it might be 'too late' already.

Several points are to be discussed here. First of all, I wish not to minimize the historical fact that human groups were annihilated and their culture gone forever. Around the world, the Western colonial enterprise was a deadly one. Among others, the ethnocide perpetrated against Native American populations in the United States and the brutal colonization of the Aboriginal Australians constitute two telling examples of such cruelty. However, many diagnoses of cultural loss posed by ethnologists at the time proved wrong. Johannes Fabian (1983) has shown that a 'denial of coevalness' was central to the manner in which early anthropologists approached the native Other. Besides their denial of a common temporality, our founders also shared a specific conception of the fragility of traditional groups and cultural transmission's mechanisms. Traditional societies were a priori treated as unable to resist changes to which they were exposed. Such assumption was based on the idea that these cultures were supposed to be in essence conservative. Marcel Mauss notes that archaic societies 'live in a way that is so well adapted to their internal and external milieu that they only need one thing: to continue what they have always done' (Mauss 1968: 119). In these societies, cultural transmission occurs without a hitch, Mauss emphasizing that, there, 'the transmission of things and practices, and of collective representations, goes smoothly' (ibid.: 144), in contrast with what happens with us, Moderns, who do not know anymore 'how to smoothly transmit our culture over generations', as Lévi-Strauss was later to write (1975: 100). In 'uncivilized worlds', the adherence to tradition was considered instinctive. The primitive man had 'conservative dispositions' (Lévy-Bruhl 1976 [1922]: 369), an idea already supported by social Darwinist Herbert Spencer, who characterized primitive societies by the 'fixity of habit' and their 'aversion to change' (2002 [1898]: 71), their *misonéisme*. Lévy-Bruhl summarizes very well the theoretical stance that underlies most anthropological reflections at the time: 'Primitive societies, in general, are hostile to anything that comes from outside ... They form closed systems where anything penetrating might trigger a process of decomposition. They are like organisms that live a long time, if the external environment varies little, but if new elements burst in, they quickly degenerate and die' (1976 [1922]: 367). As a matter of fact, the colonial contact was thought to be the main trigger of such degenerative process. Lévy-Bruhl points out that 'the institutions of the primitive, as their languages, decompose quickly, as they have to endure the presence and action of the whites' (ibid.: 368).

In those days, this posture was certainly not a French exception. The economy of this text does not allow me to explore in depth a wide range of ethnographic traditions, but everyone recalls the last words of the Preface of *Argonauts* where Malinowski laments the fast disappearance of anthropologists' objects of study. Similarly, Evans-Pritchard insisted that 'another, and very cogent, reason for studying primitive societies at the present time is that they are rapidly being transformed and must be studied soon or never' (Evans-Pritchard 1951: 9), while Raymond Firth presented *The Work of the Gods in Tikopia* as a book that 'describes a vanished past, a set of institutions not known to many of the young Tikopia themselves' (quoted by Metcalf 2002: 118). On the American side, the theme of the vanishing savages was equally in vogue. Suffice it to read *Ishi*, narrated by Theodora Kroeber (1964) as an example of the last savage Indian of North America, the ultimate trace of a Neolithic society exterminated by the Whites. With the same tone, Edward Sapir describes the nostalgia of the last Indian man:

[He] finds himself in a state of bewildered vacuity. Even if he succeeds in making a fairly satisfactory compromise with his new environment, in making what his well wishers consider great progress towards enlightenment, he is apt to retain an uneasy sense of the loss of some vague and great good, some state of mind that he would be hard put to it to define, but which gave him a courage and joy that latter-day prosperity never quite seems to have regained for him. What has happened is that he has slipped out of the warm embrace of a culture into the cold air of fragmentary existence. (Sapir 1924: 414)

While Native Americans underwent terrible traumatisms from their contact with European colonizers, whether this is the Indian man's or Sapir's own nostalgia is hard to tell ...

In short, at the very foundation of our discipline lie these 'ghosts', as they are termed by Benoit de L'Estoile (2010: 399), these traditional societies who experienced traumatic encounters with Euro-American colonizers, but whose existence also reveals the complex relationship existing between the colonial moment and its 'imperialist nostalgia' (Rosaldo 1989), an exo-nostalgia for lost paradises. Interestingly, in most founding texts, one feels the persistence of an evolutionist thinking. Considerable were the efforts made by early social and cultural anthropologists to leave the racial swamps of social Darwinism.[9] However, an evolutionist temporality is still visible, underlying their writing. Their style is pre-apocalyptic, demonstrating the persistence of a line of thought that took for granted the irreparable loss affecting the fragile populations under study. Importantly, the anthropologist was mostly portrayed as an observer and a prophetic announcer of a cultural disaster soon to happen. If these populations were perceived as the latest survivors of a bygone era, the anthropologist was the last witness of these paradises moving irremediably from equilibrium to destruction. I like the formula forged by Ramon Sarró, 'ethnography as the art of being late' (2009), to describe the regret felt by various early anthropologists that they were conducting fieldwork at the very moment when traditional systems were thought to collapse. They were arriving 'too late' in the field. Such a catastrophist tone persists, particularly in France where the successors of Marcel Griaule adopted the same exo-nostalgia. For instance, among the Baga of Guinea in the 1950s, Denise Paulme writes: 'The anthropologist arrives here too late to take note of beliefs or rituals of which participants, when they perform them, no longer understand their meaning' (Paulme 1957: 7). And she adds: 'Pressed on all sides, Baga society will soon be gone. It is already too late to note the essential' (Paulme 1958: 407). Having conducted research among the Baga myself, fifty years after Denise Paulme, I realize how, whilst denouncing the ravages of colonialism and imported religions, she 'exo-nostalgized' their vanishing, which, as a matter of fact, has not occurred yet (Berliner 2005b, Berliner 2014).

All in all, this 'too-latism' reminds me of what Vladimir Jankélévitch wrote about as the 'complacency to the irreversible' (1974: 154), an 'impotency before the impossible' (ibid.: 177) characterized by the expression 'too late'. When one can no longer bend fate, when resisting the irreversible is impossible, these two words express 'the bitterness of regret' (ibid.: 187). Like a doctor facing someone in agony, the nostalgist feels powerless against the passage of time, as did many early anthropologists. Some of them were outraged and sensed in it a personal loss. Especially in the US, the 'disappearing native' trope constituted a political allegory told to gain some recognition for what indigenous people had been through. It was a critique of the present, a quality often recognized in nostalgia (Bissel 2005), and the basis of their political indignation. Others developed a discursive interest for an object they thought was waning, without expressing strong feelings towards it. However, militant or not, their exo-nostalgia constituted the ground for their scientific endeavour. As a better-than-nothing resistance to their feeling of temporal powerlessness, they started to urgently archive and collect ethnographic data (what has been called 'salvage ethnography'). A feeling for a disappearing Other, a theoretical perspective, such exo-nostalgia soon became a practice, institutionalized in university departments and materialized in museum object collections.[10]

*   *   *

Historically, anthropology lent its passion to pristine, cultural essences, seen as disappearing, and set itself against the modern colonial juggernaut. However, scholars began to realize the durability of cultures as well as the absence of a nostalgic bent among the people they studied. Little by little, anthropologists from the major traditions abandoned their exo-nostalgic posture, their primitivist fantasies, and they substituted them with a discourse on the 'extraordinary ability of societies to resist erosion' (Warnier 2007: 92). Such recognition also paved the way for serious studies of the ways in which local ordinary people manage their cultural environments as they wish, in a usually non-nostalgic way.

In the 1940s, Malinowski himself began to question his anti-historical perspective (Kuper 2000). With humour, Ralph Linton writes in 1945 that 'the old line ethnologist is in the seventh heaven if he can find a group which has never seen a white man before and he views the current opening up of the far corners of the earth with all the alarm of any craftsman whose livelihood is threatened. Ethnologists of the younger generation are less worried by the march of events' (Linton 1945: 10). Indeed, this younger generation started to question the old guard's notions of temporality and fragility and it adopted a strong position against nostalgia-based approaches. As early as Herskovits's acculturation and Balandier's social change theories, the acknowledgment that 'societies don't die, they change' or 'it's okay, they have appropriated it' consecrated anthropologists' interest in social change and cultural persistence, and people's own perceptions of history and change. For instance, Melville Herskovits, an American anthropologist based at Northwestern University and a student of Boas, had developed, since the early 1930s, an interest in cultural transmission, emphasizing the need to approach cultural stability and change together (Herskovits 1956 [1947]). Seeking the existence of continuities ('retentions') between Africa and the US, he founded a field of research on African survival in the Americas, the memory of African slaves and the transatlantic cultural heritage, a vein also explored later by Roger Bastide in France (Bastide 1970). In most major anthropological traditions, nostalgia for lost paradises was replaced by real-istic perspectives about acculturation, incorporation and reinterpretation of new cultural elements, but also about resistance to change and the persis-tence of native elements. The same anti-primitivist perspective was adopted by theorists of urbanization and modernization (à la Gluckmann) and later on in the 'enchantment of modernity' paradigm, by the Comaroffs and Peter Geschiere, among so many others.

Beyond regional traditions, most contemporary anthropologies are now the heirs of these historicist postures. Cultural change and persistence mani-fest themselves through a copious use of notions such as memory (Berliner 2005a), resurgence, revival, reinvention, resilience, syncretism, invented traditions, heritage, habitus and neo-traditionalism. All these notions imply continuity with the past and give scholars the opportunity to consider the persistence of their objects of study – that is, the reproduction of societies through time, the continuity of representations, practices, emotions and institutions, despite dramatic changes in context. Read, for example, the first subtitle of the introduction to Christian Hojbjerg's last book – 'Things Do Not Always Fall Apart' (Hojbjerg 2007). According to him, one should seriously reconsider our assumptions about traditions and local commu-nities that 'need not always fall apart in the encounter with hegemonic outside forces, even in cases involving planned, physical destruction of core cultural symbols' (ibid.: 4). In the same vein, Bruce Knaupf remarks that, in Melanesia, 'indigenous practices and indigenous beliefs are far from dead; indeed, they resurface with creative regularity' (Knaupf 1996: 133). Beyond social tensions arising from post-colonialism, the author was struck by 'the practical ways in which people find continuities and creative spaces as they engage the possibilities and constraints of change' (ibid.: 133). It is the same fascination with the persistence of a transformed past in the present that animates the beautiful *The Weight of the Past* by Michael Lambek (2002). In

Madagascar, Lambek explores how 'the ancestral past permeates present-day Mahajanga and its environs' (ibid.: 13). While Mahanjanga seems completely absorbed by modernity, 'behind gates and fences, in groves on the outskirts and in the distant countryside, at night, in cupboards, in tombs and under wraps, in embodied practices and in the moral imagination, lies the past – all the more powerful for remaining discretely concealed and protected; set apart but immanent' (ibid.: 13). Accordingly, beyond loss and fractures remains a cultural system, 'a set of practices that continue to produce a coherent, polyvalent and insightful way of comprehending and engaging social change' (ibid.: 161). At a closer look, so many contemporary ethnographies aim at demonstrating how indigenous practices and beliefs are still alive and how people create continuities in turbulent times. Think of the notion of 'structure of the conjuncture' invented by Sahlins (1985) to account for how people reproduce their culture while transforming it. Beyond historical traumatic events, the effects of colonialism, urbanization, industrialization, socialism and globalization, the past does not evaporate, but persists in multiple creative ways. Cultural transmission in fragmented worlds. Continuity in change.

* * *

Anthropologists' ideas of temporality and persistence have, indeed, considerably changed since the time of the founders. However, their discourses are still crafted within nostalgic narratives. In the next pages, I discuss which forms anthropologists' nostalgias take today. Obviously, there are many ways in which to be a 'nostalgist' (Faubion 1993: 36). I do not want to give the impression that all ethnologists are involved in this posture in the same way. Perhaps one must divide them into those who fall for nostalgia and those who do not, as in life where some regret more than others the passage of time. I remember the late Luc de Heusch, Professor of Anthropology at the Free University of Brussels, who until his death lamented the paradigmatic changes happening in our discipline. De Heusch considered that anthropology, with modernization, had lost its traditional object of study (mainly, the ethnic people without writing), very much like his mentor Lévi-Strauss. Not as extreme as the Belgian structuralist, there are still anthropologists to support an exo-nostalgic position. I think here of the admirable work of French anthropologist Philippe Descola that represents the legacy of Lévi-Straussian anthropology in France. His last book, *Par-delà nature et culture* (2005), offers a vast regional comparative work, mostly drawing on examples taken from so-called 'non-industrial' societies, and proposes an ambitious typological project, rooted in comparative erudition and empiricist rigour. Descola has discovered four regimes of identification (animist,

totemic, naturalist and analogical). Each conveys specific theories of identity
and otherness, regimes of knowledge, as well as local worldviews or cos-
mologies, within which divergent notions of physicality and interiority are
deployed. But what is obtained from his typological approach faces a range
of critiques. In particular, an almost exclusive focus on what Descola calls
'non-industrial societies' (sociology supposedly dealing with 'post-industrial
societies') seen as laboratories, smaller demographically, and with less
contacts with the 'outside world' (ibid.: 154), where the schemes of identification and relation are more visible. Although Descola rejects nostalgia for
authenticity, such preference for so-called 'non-industrial societies' cages his
work into an exploration of the exotic. Treating these societies as discrete
entities somehow preserved from global changes (urbanization, colonialism,
creolization and so forth), one is left wondering how such typologies do work
for Amazonian youngsters educated in large cities, Westerners schooled in
India and Aborigines living in shantytowns. Reading Descola's piece left
me pensive about historical traumas, ruptures and contingencies, as well as
the global dissemination of people, ideas and forms of life, and how these
could challenge his beautifully crafted typology. Yet such use of the classical 'waning savage' trope is rare among anthropologists today. In the West,
the traditional exo-nostalgia has lost much of its appeal.[11] I contend that, in
many instances, anthropologists' exo-nostalgia 'is not what it used to be'.[12]

   First, if nostalgia is not what it used to be, one finds expressions of
anthropologists' exo-nostalgia in the choice of their subjects of study. No
doubt that they still have their favourite Others. Empathic identification,
which lies at the very foundation of our discipline, does not work the
same way with all categories of actors encountered in the field. Although
Otherness is now broader in its definition than in the past (including Wall
Street traders, Chinese entrepreneurs, educated Aborigines and UNESCO
experts), many anthropologists long for the 'local'. 'Local' is a complex
emotionally loaded notion that replaces the no-longer-politically-correct
'indigenous', but where similar ideas of cultural/social particularism and
heterogeneity converge. I believe lots of us have nowadays nostalgized the
particular and the heterogeneous. Let me speak very honestly about my own
research in Northern Laos. For a number of years, I have conducted fieldwork in Luang Prabang, the former royal town of Lao People's Democratic
Republic. Luang Prabang was a neglected town after the Socialist Revolution
of 1975 owing to its association with the royal family. Since 1995, it has
been turned into a UNESCO listed heritage site and a tourist attraction,
where French Indochina is somehow glorified. My research has shown
that such transformation is rendered possible by the concatenation of
UNESCO projects, cosmopolitan gentrification, tourism development and

state programs (Berliner 2012). During my field study, I could not resist the magnetism of cultural particularity and heterogeneity. Concretely, I felt greater empathy for Luang Prabang residents troubled by the fact that they live under the heritage regulations and wanting to modify their dwellings as they please. I manifested less sympathy for the UNESCO bureaucrats, not to mention the backpackers, although I conducted interviews with all of them. I laid my sympathies with the 'local' Lao – the indigenous people flooded by tourists with their appetites to want to preserve past customs around the world so that they can consume it in their leisure. Again, I do not expect every anthropologist to identify with this description, but many are senti- mentally drawn to the *indigenousness* of their interlocutors, whether they are close or far away. This might seem obvious, but anthropologists still need their 'savages', their particular and heterogeneous locals against the idea of an undifferentiated modernity. And I would add this: participant observa- tion functions precisely as a nostalgic quest for intimacy and sincerity with locals (although actual fieldwork can be riddled with conflicts and lies). Most researchers long for the experience of the Malinowskian encounter, even with UNESCO experts and Wall Street traders. By treating participa- tion observation as the key method of anthropology, but also by constantly going back to the Preface of the *Argonauts,* alone and with our students, have we not nostalgized our methodology itself?

Exo-nostalgia exists for the local, but also for the weak and the power- less. I agree with Zsusza Gille when she writes that, as anthropologists, 'we only feel compassion towards the "little people"' (Gille 2010: 288). Although scholars have, for a while now, turned their attention to the people in power ('studying up'), I believe that, on many occasions, exo-nostalgia still manifests itself through compassion for a powerless Other. The threat of the vanishing and the positioning of the anthropologist as a pre-apocalyptical observer constitute the premises of many contemporary monographs. Kuklick argues that today the 'putative cause of cultural extinctions is not the extension of colonial power, but the steamroller of globalization' (Kuklick 2008: 5). To be more precise, in these times of crisis that never end, the effects of globalization, the development of neoliberalism, the growth of social and military insecurity, global warming and so forth, constitute new threats, sometimes deadly, for groups and individuals. Nowadays, the fragile and little Other is no longer the disappearing cultural savage, the powerless colonized (although it still can be in specific cases). No, it is rather the poor, the weak, the suffering, the powerless facing social instability, urban poverty, economic migration, war and political disempowerment. The list of contri- butions in this vein is too voluminous to even begin to report, but think of Esperanza, the Mexican street peddler described by Ruth Behar (2003), the

Parisian homeless by Patrick Declerck (2001) and the crack dealers in New
York by Philip Bourgeois (2003). Their tone is comparably pre-apocalyptic.
Similar in many ways to the 'too-latism' of the early anthropologists, the
indignation in front of loss and crisis is dominant in these texts.

Some, like Nancy Scheper-Hughes (1995), argue that anthropology has
always been committed to social issues and that it must be a militant
discipline useful to its powerless subjects of research. This is not the place
to discuss such moral issues. However, to explain why researchers tend to
identify, often unconsciously, with the powerless, many explanations can be
invoked. Don Kulick refers to the existence of a masochistic pleasure whose
'essence is the substitution with another self' (Kulick 2006: 936), a suffering
self. Such identification to the powerless, he says, provides pleasure to the
fortunate anthropologist who, usually, belongs to socially and economically
privileged environments and has interiorized a desire for power (colonial
and capitalist).[13] For my part, I am not surprised by anthropologists' long-
term attachment to 'little' fragile people in the face of crises. All in all, it is
deep-rooted in their disciplinary exo-nostalgia, an indignation and a theoretical stance in front of irreversible loss. Interestingly, it also reveals specific
forms of engagement with the future. Most literature emphasizes that nostalgia is crafted within 'horizons of expectations' in the present (Boyer 2012,
Koselleck 2004). Hope is never far away from nostalgia. Certainly, anthropologists' nostalgias are intertwined with their desire to imagine another
world: a world able to resist cultural homogenization and to preserve ethnic
diversity, a world where social and political recognition can be gained for
the powerless.

Notes

1. This is my translation from Zweig (2008 [1922]). Many thanks to Olivia Angé,
   Holly High, Laurent Legrain, Christoph Brumann, Chris Hann, Patrice
   Ladwig, Gonzalo Santos and Oliver Tappe for very insightful comments on
   earlier versions of this text.
2. See also Ivy 1995 on 'discourses of the vanishing' in contemporary Japan.
3. It is worth noting that, in Europe, the political use of cultural loss mostly concerns two categories of people: the descendants of immigrants and the rural
   world, both considered in a state of cultural disorientation.
4. All translations from French to English are mine.
5. I do not have the necessary space here to develop this question. However, while
   anthropologists in the West were building a science on a primitivist nostalgia
   for distant Otherness, a 'rusticophilia' (to use the word coined by Michel de
   Certeau), an ethnographic interest in the 'popular' and the 'rural' emerged

at the same time and led to the institutionalization of folklore studies in the second half of the nineteenth century in Western Europe.

6. By 'major traditions', I mean American, British, French and German anthropologies. Of course, such discussion should be expanded with regard to other national traditions, in China, Russia, India, Brazil or Japan, among others (see Kuklick 2008).

7. Take France, for example. From Marc Abélès' political anthropology to Jean-Pierre Olivier de Sardan's *Anthropologie du développement*, passing by Jeanne Favret-Saada, Christian Bromberger and Alban Bensa, there are multiple anthropologies in France today, many of them having ingeniously incorporated influences from British and American traditions. Yet the impact of Claude Lévi-Strauss is paradigmatically enormous and subsequent generations of anthropologists are still compelled to define themselves in relationship to him (Berliner 2010b).

8. Proust concludes *Swann's Way* with these words that reveal the nature of such lonely anguish: 'The memory of a certain image is but regret for a certain moment; and houses, roads, avenues are as fleeting, alas, as the years' (Proust 1992 [1913]: 476).

9. To Vacher de Lapouge and Gobineau, the ideologists of social evolutionism, it had become apparent that some societies were stronger than others, and the theory of natural selection was 'extended to the relationship of the colonizer and "inferior" colonized races' (Pichot 2000: 83). In their view, the so-called inferior races constituted 'evidence of a state of humanity overtaken by European races and [were] destined to disappear in the name of progress' (ibid.: 141). So was the extinction of races naturalized.

10. There are many texts discussing the historical relationship between anthropology and museology. I particularly like the book edited by Karp and Lavine (1990).

11. Except for some anthropologists working with UNESCO and other international preservation agencies who often exhibit a patrimonialist exo-nostalgia. More research needs to be conducted about these nostalgic experts.

12. '*La nostalgie n'est plus ce qu'elle était*' (1978) is the title of an autobiography by French actress Simone Signoret. Although the content of the book prosaically describes her life, its title, dubbed with irony (a lament for the changing nostalgia), is mind-boggling as it invites us to reflect upon the dynamism of nostalgic postures through time.

13. Although stimulating, Kulick's text poses many questions, including the use of psychoanalysis only to explain the essence of our discipline (Berliner 2013).

References

Appadurai, A. 1996. *Modernity at Large: Cultural Dimensions of Globalization*. Minneapolis: University of Minnesota Press.

Arendt, H. 1972. *La crise de la culture*. Paris: Editions Gallimard.

Barth, F., A. Gringrich, R. Parkin and S. Silverman. 2010. *One Discipline, Four Ways: British, German, French, and American Anthropology (Halle Lectures)*. Chicago: University of Chicago Press.

Bastide, R. 1970. 'Mémoire collective et sociologie du bricolage', *L'Année Sociologique* 21: 65–108.

Baudelaire, C. 1869. *Oeuvres Complètes. IV. Petits Poèmes en prose*. Paris: Michel Lévy Frères.

Behar, R. 2003. *Translated Woman: Crossing the Border with Esperanza's Story*. Boston: Beacon Press.

Bendix, R. 1997. *In Search of Authenticity: The Formation of Folklore Studies*. Madison: University of Wisconsin Press.

Berliner, D. 2005a. 'The Abuses of Memory: Reflections on the Memory Boom in Anthropology', *Anthropological Quarterly* 78 (1): 183–97.

———. 2005b. 'An "Impossible" Transmission: Youth Religious Memories in Guinea-Conakry', *American Ethnologist* 32 (4): 576–92.

———. 2010a. 'Anthropologie et transmission', *Terrain* 55: 4–19.

———. 2010b. 'Polyglot Perspectives', *Anthropological Quarterly* 83 (3): 679–90.

———. 2012. 'Multiple Nostalgias: The Fabric of Heritage in Luang Prabang (Lao PDR)', *Journal of the Royal Anthropological Institute* 18 (4): 769–86.

———. 2013. 'Le désir de participation ou comment jouer à être un autre', *L'Homme* 206: 151–70.

———. 2014. *Mémoires religieuses baga*. Paris: Somogy Editions.

Bissell, W. 2005. 'Engaging Colonial Nostalgia', *Cultural Anthropology* 20 (2): 215–48.

Bourgeois, P. 2003. *In Search of Respect: Selling Crack in El Barrio*. Cambridge: Cambridge University Press.

Boyer, D. 2012. 'From Algos to Autonomos: Nostalgic Eastern Europe as Postimperial Mania', in M. Todorova and Z. Gille (eds), *Post-Communist Nostalgia*. Oxford: Berghahn, pp. 17–28.

Clifford, J. 1986. 'On Ethnographic Allegory', in J. Clifford and G. Marcus (eds), *Writing Culture*. Berkeley: University of California Press, pp. 98–121.

Declerck, P. 2001. *Les naufragés. Avec les clochards de Paris*. Paris: Plon.

de L'Estoile, B. 2010. *Le goût des autres. De l'exposition coloniale aux arts premiers*. Paris: Flammarion.

Descola, P. 2005. *Par-delà nature et culture*. Paris: Flammarion.

Evans-Pritchard, E. 1951. *Social Anthropology*. London: Cohen and West Ltd.

Fabian, J. 1983. *Time and the Other: How Anthropology Makes its Objects*. New York: Columbia University Press.

Fabre, D. 2008. 'Chinoiserie des Lumières. Variations sur l'individu-monde', *L'Homme* 185–186: 269–300.

Faubion, J. 1993. 'History in Anthropology', *Annual Review of Anthropology* 22: 35–54.

Foessel, M. 2012. *Après la fin du monde. Critique de la raison apocalyptique*. Paris: Editions Le Seuil.

Gille, Z. 2010. 'Postscript', in M. Todorova and Z. Gille (eds), *Post-Communist Nostalgia*. Oxford: Berghahn, pp. 278–89.

Herskovits, M. 1956 [1947]. *Man and His Works: The Science of Cultural Anthropology*. New York: Alfred Knopf.

Herzfeld, M. 1997. *Cultural Intimacy: Social Poetics in the Nation-State*. London: Routledge.

High, H. 2011. 'Melancholia and Anthropology', *American Ethnologist* 38 (2): 217–33.

Hojbjerg, C. 2007. *Resisting State Iconoclasm among the Loma of Guinea*. Durham: Carolina Academic Press.

Ivy, M. 1995. *Discourses of the Vanishing: Modernity, Phantasm, Japan*. Chicago: University of Chicago Press.

Jankélévitch, V. 1983. *L'irréversible et la nostalgie*. Paris: Flammarion.

Jeudy, H.-P. 2010. *Le désir de catastrophe*. Belval: Circé.

Karp, I. and S. Lavine. 1990. *Exhibiting Cultures: The Poetics and Politics of Museum Display*. Washington, DC: Smithsonian Institution Press.

Knaupf, B. 1996. *Genealogies for the Present in Cultural Anthropology*. New York: Routledge.

Koselleck, R. 2004. *Futures Past: On the Semantics of Historical Time*. New York: Columbia University Press.

Kroeber, T. 1964. *Ishi in Two Worlds: A Biography of the Last Wild Indian in North America*. Berkeley: Jed Riffe and Associates.

Kuklick, H. 2008. *A New History of Anthropology*. Oxford: Blackwell.

Kulick, D. 2006. 'Theory in Furs: Masochist Anthropology', *Current Anthropology* 47 (6): 933–52.

Kuper, A. 2000. *Culture: The Anthropologists' Account*. Cambridge: Harvard University Press.

Lambek, M. 2002. *The Weight of the Past: Living with History in Mahajanga, Madagascar*. New York: Palgrave Macmillan.

Lapierre, N. 2001. *Le Silence de la Mémoire. A la recherche des Juifs de Plock*. Paris : Le Livre de Poche.

Lévi-Strauss, C. 1955. *Tristes Tropiques*. Paris: Plon.

———. 1975. 'Entretien avec Claude Lévi-Strauss', in *Les sociétés primitives*. Lausanne: Editions Robert Laffont-Grammont.

Lévy-Bruhl, L. 1976 [1922]. *La Mentalité Primitive*. Paris: Retz-C.E.L.P.

Linton, R. 1945. *The Science of Man in the World Crisis*. New York: Columbia University Press.

Lowenthal, D. 1998. *The Heritage Crusade and the Spoils of History*. Cambridge: Cambridge University Press.

Malinowski, B. 1922. *Argonauts of the Western Pacific: An Account of Native Enterprise and Adventure in the Archipelagos of Melanesian New Guinea*. London: Routledge and Kegan Paul.

Marcus, G. and M. Fischer. 1999. *Anthropology as a Cultural Critique: An Experimental Moment in the Human Sciences*. Chicago: University of Chicago Press.

Mauss, M. 1968. *Essais de sociologie*. Paris: Editions de Minuit.

Metcalf, P. 2002. *They Lie, We Lie: Getting on with Anthropology*. London: Routledge.

Paulme, D. 1957. 'Des riziculteurs africains', *Cahiers d'Outre-Mer* 10: 257–78.

——. 1958. 'La notion de sorcier chez les Baga', *Bulletin de l'IFAN* 20: 406–16.

Pichot, A. 2000. *La société pure. De Darwin à Hitler*. Paris: Flammarion.

Poulot, D. 2006. *Une histoire du patrimoine en Occident, XVIIIe-XXIᵉ siècle: du monument aux valeurs*. Paris: Presses universitaires de France.

Proust, M. 1992 [1913]. *Du côté de chez Swann*. Paris: Le Livre de Poche.

Renaut, A. 2009. *Un humanisme de la diversité. Essai sur la décolonisation des identités*. Paris: Editions Flammarion.

Revault d'Allonnes, M. 2012. *La Crise sans fin. Essai sur l'expérience moderne du temps*. Paris: Le Seuil.

Robbins, J. 2007. 'Continuity Thinking and the Problem of Christian Culture: Belief, Time, and the Anthropology of Christianity', *Current Anthropology* 48 (1): 5–38.

Rosaldo, R. 1989. 'Imperialist Nostalgia', *Representations* 26: 107–22.

Sahlins, M. 1985. *Islands of History*. Chicago: University of Chicago Press.

Sarró, R. 2009. *The Politics of Religious Change on the Upper Guinea Coast: Iconoclasm Done and Undone*. Edinburgh: Edinburgh University Press (International African Institute).

Sapir, E. 1924. 'Culture, Genuine or Spurious', *American Journal of Sociology* 29: 401–29.

Scheper-Hughes, N. 1995. 'The Primacy of the Ethical: Propositions for a Militant Anthropology', *Current Anthropology* 36 (3): 409–20.

Signoret, S. 1978. *La nostalgie n'est plus ce qu'elle était*. Paris: Le Seuil.

Spencer, H. 2002 [1898]. *Principles of Sociology in Three Volumes*. New Jersey: Transaction Publishers.

Tornatore, J. 2010. 'L'esprit de patrimoine', *Terrain* 55: 106–27.

Warnier, J. 2007. *La Mondialisation de la culture*. Paris: La Découverte.

Zweig, S. 2008 [1922]. *Le voyage dans le passé*. Paris: Grasset.

Chapter 2

Missing Socialism Again? The Malaise of Nostalgia in Post-Soviet Lithuania

Gediminas Lankauskas

'1984: The Survival Drama'

1   During the show '1984: The Survival Drama' taking place in the territory of and inside the Soviet bunker ... [later in this document referred to as the Show], Visitors, participants ... become citizens of the USSR.

2   Participants will receive instructions and orders which must be carried out without objection.

3   In case of disobedience participants may receive psychological or/and physical punishments and may be excluded from the Show.

Verbatim from the English translation of *Confirmation* (*Terms of Engagement*) provided to participants before entering the Bunker.

'Come on, come on! ... Move!', a burly guard, sporting the uniform of a Soviet military officer, boomed in Russian as we filed through a door opening onto a long flight of stairs of crumbling concrete. Comprised of some forty persons, our group hastily descended into the windowless Bunker. After the door slammed shut behind us with a creaky groan, we lined up for an inspection in the narrow underground hallway. A few light bulbs were glaring above our heads. Tugging on a leash wrapped around a door handle, a ferocious German shepherd called Amur was barking breathlessly. The subterranean air was heavy with the smell of cigarette smoke, mould and damp earth. When Amur calmed down, the guard began the inspection. After examining our appearance from head to toe, he began intoning in Russian a long list of rules of conduct to be observed in the Bunker (see the opening quotation). Clad in lumpy oversized jackets of grey, black and blue, we were transformed into citizens of the USSR. The calendar was reset to 1984.[1] Our 'survival drama' (*išgyvenimo drama*) in Soviet Lithuania was about to begin.

The present essay is about the 'survival drama' in the Bunker (*Bunkeris*), an experiential-immersive theme park located underground in the vicinity of Vilnius, the Lithuanian capital. Guided by professional actors, visitors participate in – and 'survive' – a string of interactive performances of mock KGB interrogations, torture sessions, medical examinations, Soviet-era shopping, civil defence training and so forth. These enactments of social-ism at the Bunker interest me as commemorative performances where the period of communist rule is represented using a rich repertoire of memo-rial media, ranging from visual imagery and discourse to acoustic and gustatory effects. While I pay close ethnographic attention to specific ways in which the Bunker performance as an embodied and sensuous act works to externalize memories of the Soviet era, my principal concern is with participants' response to this subterranean sideshow of socialism. These reminiscing subjects interest me as morally engaged social actors who, provoked by the 'survival drama', connect with and contest the socialist era as a biographical and historical past. Their recollections also speak to complexities and complications of forgetfulness, or amnesia, in Lithuania's post-socialist present.

I begin with a brief overview of the current landscape of remem-brance (I call it mnemoscape) in Lithuania – a landscape replete with multiple referents to the history of this Baltic nation, both distant and recent. The essay then moves on to discuss some of the conceptual trends prevalent in anthropological memory studies recently undertaken in post-socialist contexts. Central to this discussion is a critique of the dominant paradigm of 'nostalgification', which governs much of the research con-cerned with social remembrance in contemporary Eastern Europe. Simply put, this section argues that there is more to post-socialist memory than 'nostalgia'. Combining historical exposé, ethnographic description and theoretical commentary, the second part of the essay takes the reader back to the Bunker for more drama of socialist 'survival'. Presented in this part are also three scenes from the performance, along with the com-mentary of my interlocutors – the principal dramatis personae of this study. The closing section gathers together the key arguments of the essay into a conclusion.

Lithuania's Post-socialist Mnemoscape

Following the demise of the Soviet Union in 1991, in Lithuania, as in many other ex-socialist republics, erasing Marxist-Leninist history from memorial consciousness was among the most urgent tasks at hand. Vast panels portraying robust workers and peasants were promptly torn down, Lenin's voluminous writings vanished from library shelves and statues of distinguished comrades were removed from squares and parks of the newly independent country. By the mid-1990s, Lithuania's post-Soviet landscape was thoroughly cleansed of all referents to socialist history. After almost five decades of communist rule, this Baltic nation resolutely turned westward – to modern, capitalist 'Europe'. Although ideological insignia of the socialist past were decidedly out of public sight, socialism was not out of people's minds. Reordering immediate environments by erasing all referents to an undesirable past may aid forgetting, but it does not guarantee instant and complete amnesia. Letting go of the past is an inherently ambiguous and paradoxical process, one that hardly ever follows a straight trajectory towards a complete deletion of particular memories. Forgetting is often complicated by recurrent moments of recollection.

Far from forgotten, today socialism looms large in the memorial consciousness of many – certainly not all – Lithuanians. Visual arts exhibits, documentaries, scholarly researches, biographical writings, recuperated brands of Soviet-era consumer goods, as well as museum displays and experiential theme parks (the Bunker is one example) instantiate some of the public domains where socialism as a recollected past is made part of the present.[2] Persons representing different generations invoke socialism in their daily discourses and practices as they reminisce how 'good' or 'bad' it was. Meshing conflicting sentiments of yearning and desire, rupture and loss, disdain and contempt, recollections of Lithuanian history between 1940 and 1991 are at once nostalgic and traumatic, comforting and painful, reassuring and unsettling. I further elaborate on this argument below. Although prominently present, socialism of course is not the only past populating the mnemoscape of contemporary Lithuania whose neoliberal and 'European' future continuously folds itself back into multiple national pasts (cf. Huyssen 1995: 9). The years between 1918 and 1940, a time of geopolitical independence and the burgeoning capitalist economy, the era of colonial tsarist rule (1795–1918), the 'glorious' Commonwealth of

Poland-Lithuania (1569–1795), among other, even more distant pasts, are part of ongoing post-socialist remembrance.

Recently, many of these disparate pasts converged in a kind of competitive cacophony of memory at decade-long celebrations of the thousandth anniversary of the first mention of the name of Lithuania in an obscure Germanic manuscript in 1009. The numerous festivities organized to mark the momentous occasion included folk festivals, handicraft fairs and shows promoting 'traditional' cuisine. A significant component of the celebrations was an ambitious multimillion-dollar project to reconstruct a sixteenth-century palatial residence of royal rulers (*Valdovų rūmai*) in the centre of Vilnius, which is currently still incomplete. The recent proliferation of new monuments representing the nation's long-dead kings, martyrs and bards also attests to the restored significance of the nation's pre-socialist history.

In the broader context of the former Soviet bloc, Lithuania's heteroglossic or multi-voiced mnemoscape is neither exceptional nor particularly remarkable. The emergence of similar complexity and 'non-synchronicity' of social recall – its temporal hybridity we might say (cf. Huyssen 1995: 8) – has been documented by researchers working in other East European settings as well (Verdery 1999). Socialism, however, has been the most privileged past in memory studies conducted in the region. Nostalgia has become the dominant conceptual paradigm.

The Spectre of Nostalgia

In her recent commentary on the pervasiveness of the concept of nostalgia, Maria Todorova (2010: 1), paraphrasing Marx, has observed: 'A specter is haunting the world of academia: the study of post-communist nostalgia'. Various manifestations of the socialist past in the contemporary European East have been theorized as objectifications of a longing or yearning for the 'goodness' of socialist times now irretrievably gone (Bach 2002, Berdahl 2010, Klumbytė 2009, Todorova and Gille 2010; see also Sarkisova and Apor 2008). Interweaving the biographical and the historical, in contemporary Eastern Europe the nostalgic recall of socialism – as a kind of individual and collective knowledge of the past – has been explored as a rich resource providing those remembering with important cognitive means with which to anchor themselves in the unsettling and disorienting milieu of the ongoing socioeconomic and political transformations. Otherwise put, nostalgic reminiscences have been investigated as important vehicles helping social actors distance themselves from the present, vehicles that are existentially empowering and socially stabilizing – they take us back 'home'. As etymologists instruct us, the noun nostalgia (from *nostos,* 'returning home' plus *algos,* 'pain, ache, grief'), Greek in origin, refers to a melancholy desire, to return to the safety, comfort and predictability of metaphoric domicile, a trope that also conjures up an idyllic imagery of familial togetherness, well-being and coherence.[3] 'Home', as Mary Douglas (1991: 290) has argued, works as an important organizer of social space and time, and as such provides 'directions of existence'. Nostalgia, one can say, is a pre-eminently 'homey' or domestic concept.

To be sure, in today's European East nostalgia in its many manifestations looms large in memories of socialism – a historical and biographical period remembered wistfully by many as a vanished 'home'. This very metaphor was recently invoked by one of my interlocutors. During my research visit to Lithuania in 2010, a well-known intellectual in his seventies, who associated himself with political dissidence and 'the social alternative' (*socialinė alternatyva*) during the socialist era, to my great astonishment, launched into a lengthy diatribe describing how the Soviet state, while undeniably authoritarian and oppressive, managed to ensure that justice and equality prevailed among its citizens. 'The home then had a good master . . . and now?' he stated longingly (see also Lankauskas 2006).

But not all post-socialist memory is nostalgic, that is, about elegiac recuperation of, and escape to, a 'better' time past recalled through tropes of domesticity. Not all events and experiences are remembered because they are coveted. Unwanted or 'unmemorable' pasts are also integral to the commemoration of socialism. Nostalgia does not accompany every recollection and is not everywhere (cf. Nadkarni 2010, Pilbrow 2010). To claim that it does and is, as many theorists do, is to look for conceptual and analytical shortcuts. We seem to have forgotten that those remembering make socialism part of the present not only because they want it back but, paradoxically, because they do not. Representations of socialism for many East Europeans, especially those of older generations, serve as reminders of what ought to be erased from memorial consciousness. The presence of such memory works to negate that particular past as a time of profound disruption, destruction and trauma. This past in turn becomes an important temporal resource on which actors draw to make claims to 'suffering' and 'victimhood' in the post-socialist present (see below). Such dispositions towards relatively recent socialist history are not nostalgia – they are not about yearnings to return to and be at 'home'. They are counter-, or at the very least, non-nostalgic recollections. Such reminiscences externalize socialism as a time of existential homelessness, we might say; they are not about possessing but about losing 'home'. Seduced by the 'goodness' of nostalgia, we seem to have overlooked 'bad' and 'non-nostalgic' memories of socialism.

But where is nostalgia's persistent allure? Why has it acquired such conceptual dominance? How did post-socialist studies fall under its spell, becoming virtually 'nostomaniac', as Dominic Boyer (2010: 19) has aptly put it. Could it be that researchers – those of the 'native' kind who experienced socialism first-hand and those who learned about it from books in 'the West' – rush to equate most of the memory of socialism with nostalgia because *they* want to keep socialism remembered as a quaint, endearing and 'homey' past (cf. Gille 2010: 287)? Perhaps, the current supremacy of nostalgia in post-socialist studies can be attributed to the emergence of a kind of nostalgic scholarly industry that yearns for a well-defined temporal 'other' as an object of study. After all, the 'nostalgification' of Eastern Europe makes this part of the world appear more culturally 'exotic' and temporally out of sync with future-oriented visions of Western modernity. Nostalgia, thus, helps orientalize the European East (cf. Boyer 2010: 21–22).

There is at least one more reason, I think, for nostalgia's ascendancy. As an analytical tool, it is a catch-all, feel-good ('homey') concept that can be conveniently bent and stretched to describe a wide spectrum of memorial practices, including those that have little to do with nostalgia. Because of its conceptual expansiveness, nostalgia 'can be made to "happen" by (and to) anyone', as Linda Hutcheon (2000: 191) has observed. Nostalgia is certainly 'happening' in post-socialist studies and is becoming one of those totalizing blanket terms that mean everything and nothing.

Circulating in social science discourses since the 1970s, nostalgia has received its share of criticism. Despite being dismissed many times over as analytically inept and superficial, and being negatively characterized as 'affective, sentimental, ahistorical, conservative, consumerist, kitschy' and even 'morbid', nostalgia perdures remarkably (Lowenthal 1989, Ladino 2004). Attempts have been made to break it down into more nuanced types or subgenres. Some nostalgias have been identified as 'hegemonic', 'working class', 'mass' (Stewart 1988), others as 'imperialist', 'official' and 'colonial' (Ladino 2004, Rosaldo 1989, Todorova 2010), still others as 'structural' (Herzfeld 2005) and 'practical' (Battaglia 1995); the list goes on.

Yet despite such endeavours to refine it conceptually through taxonomic classification and specification, nostalgia as an analytical device remains unwieldy and cumbersome. The trouble with nostalgia, even when it is broken down into more sophisticated 'specialty' categories, is that it tends to gloss over complexities, contradictions and ambiguities of memorial practices in social life. Otherwise put, nostalgia totalizes and simplifies;

it often conceals more than it reveals. It may help us build neat models of 'positive' memory – Boym's (2001) oft-cited dualism of 'reflective versus restorative' nostalgia comes to mind – but it renders remembrance lifeless and provides us with an incomplete picture of the mnemoscape that we strive to understand and explain.

Furthermore, not unlike such much-maligned concepts as 'tradition', 'community', or 'culture', to mention a few, nostalgia unproblematically turns reminiscences into things. Otherwise put, it reifies social memory (cf. Berliner 2005). Yet as we know it is not a thing but a multi-voiced, or heteroglossic, process. Not unlike speech, to invoke Mikhail Bakhtin (1986), memorial discourses and practices are constituted through a multiplicity of competing genres. Nostalgia is just one of them. Genres and sub-genres of memory may be helpful heuristic devices, but they can (and do) quickly distract us from the complexity and complications of 'really existing' memory in social life. They tidy up or model memory into bounded units of analysis. It is not, however, the tidiness but messiness of memory that we need to describe and interrogate. It is therefore imperative that we push our theorizing beyond mere classificatory identification and description of genres (which is certainly important), and that we inquire more rigorously into their 'untidy', ambiguous coexistence – into how they overlap, blend and interlock, as well as how they complement and contest each other. As recent interdisciplinary memory research has shown, a particular past can be recalled in many ways – through a multiplicity of genres we might say – within the same collectivity and even by the same person. Laced with yearnings of return to a 'better' past, nostalgic reminiscences often compete with 'counter-nostalgic' remembrance of rupture, disjuncture, or loss in a complex polylogue (Scanlan 2004).

Besides, memories of all genres are fluid, so to speak – they do not stand still. This is especially true in contexts of volatile and unsettling change, such as the contemporary European East. Interrogating nostalgia in the broader context of other memory genres and making it concrete through the fine-grained detail of ethnographic description and analysis is one, and perhaps the only, way to gain a deeper grasp of how it works as a mode of commemoration. Kathleen Stewart (1988: 2) has written that nostalgia 'is a cultural practice, not a given content; its forms, meanings and effects shift with the context – it depends on where the speaker stands in the landscape of the present'. As ethnographers striving better to understand what nostalgia – and memory more broadly – is, we need to pay closer attention to the context and especially to the reminiscing speaker – or, as I will show below, the performer – engaged with the past.

Memory in Performance

Memory acquires social significance when it is externalized and is represented by those remembering, that is, when it is pushed out from the hidden realm of consciousness into public domains of social life. A past is not a past if it exists only as 'things inside our heads' (Fentress and Wickham 1992: 1). To matter socially and culturally, a past must be 'outside'. History books and biographies, films and photographs, retro songs and folk festivals, museums and memorials exemplify some of the sites of cultural recollection and representation of pastness. Rather than 'seeking where memories are preserved in [the] brain or in some nook of [the] mind' (Halbwachs 1992: 38), anthropologists look for their concrete cultural manifestations.

In ethnographic research, reminiscences become particularly interesting when they are represented in social interaction and are made accessible to the senses. Otherwise put, memory becomes socially alive and meaningful when actors can see, hear, or even touch, smell and taste it (see descriptions of the Bunker performance below). As a 'dramatizing' event (Myerhoff 1996: 397) that usually activates and engages many senses simultaneously, performance constitutes an effective site for animating the past and putting it on public display. According to Paul Connerton (1989: 5), recollection and performative acts are especially intimately interconnected: 'if there is such a thing as social memory . . . we are likely to find it in commemorative ceremonies; but commemorative ceremonies prove to be commemorative only in so far as they are performative'.

Distancing myself from theorists who see all social and cultural exchanges as constituted through expressive performative practice – Erving Goffman (1959) and other symbolic interactionists come to mind here – in this essay I take performance to be an intentionally enacted, purposeful social event unfolding in space and time that is marked off from habituated routines of daily social life (cf. Diamond 1996, McAllister 2006, Shieffelin 1985, 2005). I do not see all of social life as a theatre where actors wear masks and costumes and perform their selves as they interact with different others. To qualify as performance, a particular discourse or practice must be imbued with symbolism and charged with 'extraordinary intensity and heightened significance' (Fabian 1990: 16). Otherwise put, a performance must contain the betwixt and between (or liminal) dimension of 'time out of time' spent in a place located away from quotidian routes and routines. Besides, performative events usually are intended for others to see, that is, they address an audience (albeit the audience and performers sometimes coincide). A theatrical rendition of Shakespeare's *King Lear*, a Catholic mass, a Japanese tea-drinking ceremony, a gift-opening rite at a Christmas party and a hockey game are some of the instances of what I would recognize as performance. In Victor Turner's (1988) terms, among key identifying features of performance are 'anti-structure' and reflexivity. An efficacious performance disrupts the patterned flow of the everyday ('structure'), provoking a critical reflection on and re-examination of social reality, whether it be past or present. Particularly powerful performances engender not only reflection but also action – they move participants to question and even remake that reality (cf. Bell 1997: 73).[4]

Because commemorative performances usually dramatize the past by orchestrating at once several senses (through a kind of synaesthesia, we may say), they are well equipped for dislodging memory from the confines of the mind and making it socially present 'outside'. Because recall in performance is multi-sensed, so to speak, it is also always embodied. Any performance is both a sensuous and bodily or somatic act. One is hardly conceivable without the other. As Lassiter (2002: 140) has observed, performed memory is 'a process of consciousness enacted, felt, and made real in the body' (cf. Climo and Cattel 2002, Connerton 1989, Diamond 1996).

Commemorative performance and its constitutive components interest me not as a static text to be seen and 'read' through interpretive analysis but as a dynamic and dramatic memorial process cohering around 'the cultural sentience of the body' (Stoller 1995:7). Without wanting to dismiss the dominant visualist and textualist paradigms as being of little analytical use, I call for a more somatic, so to speak, and sensuous perspective in the study of commemorative performance. Otherwise put, my approach is largely phenomenological, one that seeks to emphasize bodily modes of re-collecting, re-presenting and knowing the past (cf. Howes 1991: 3). To gain a deeper understanding of how these modes work, we need to be mindful of the broader social and historical contexts in which they unfold. 'All performance . . . is situated, enacted, and rendered meaningful within socially [and historically] defined situational contexts' (Bauman 1992: 46).

For an ethnographer interested in memory, commemorative performance is a particularly rich and rewarding site of investigation not only because of the wealth of the expressive symbolic media it mobilizes, but also because of its temporal reference to the past. Performances of this genre are about re-membering, re-making, re-constructing and re-presenting, where the prefix 're-', meaning 'back, again, anew', acknowledges previously existing visual forms, discourse and practices (Diamond 1996: 2). To be sure, the lexicon of 're-' may be important in discussion of commemorative performances. But that is not the whole story. These social events can also dis-member, un-make, de-construct and mis-represent the past, as we shall see below. They are not merely about 're-'.

As mentioned, commemorative performances (as any other performance for that matter) are sensuous and somatic acts that implicate participants' senses and their bodies, enabling them actively to engage with the past as social agents. Writing about cultural performance more generally, Turner (1988: 24) has observed that it 'represent[s] the eye through which culture sees itself and the drawing board on which creative actors sketch out what they believe to be more apt or interesting "designs for living"'. In performances that take commemoration as their principal organizing theme, such 'sketching' concerns life's 'designs' both in the past and in the present. It is therefore essential that in our investigations of social recall we pay close attention to ways in which memory comments on times gone by and current. We should not forget to interrogate remembrance as a kind of social knowledge about life lived then and now. Memory makes sense when studied in and as history.

Performances are usually scripted social events but they never reproduce the script to the letter. Reproduction does not equal mere replication. No performance is enacted the same way twice. These events always leave room for interpretation, invention and improvisational 'sketching'. They may be about embodied representation but they are also about contestation.

Performances can be structured and circumscribed within the parameters of space and time but they are never completely 'fixed' (cf. Myerhoff 1996). They are emergent and contingent social occasions that often run the risk of slipping, tripping and even failing – 'there is always something aesthetically and/or practically at stake' (Schieffelin 2005: 129). Performances that explicitly engage with the past constitute especially fruitful settings in which to examine how memory slips, trips, or fails altogether, as well as how it reconstitutes and reasserts itself.

The underground space of the Bunker, or The House of Creativity as it was known during the Soviet era, and its 'survival drama' afford a productive ethnographic locus in which to explore such features of memory work in performance. The 'drama' enacted at this *lieu de mémoire* (Nora 1989) along with the commentary of its participants provide valuable material for a critical discussion of nostalgia and remembrance more generally after socialism.

'The House of Creativity': Dead and Alive

Constructed on the orders of Leonid Brezhnev's apparatchiks during the Cold War, the Bunker was a top-secret strategic object known by its code name the House of Creativity.[5] Hiding behind the ironic misnomer – the austere, clandestine House was anything but creative – was an underground structure of steel and concrete comprised of an intricate maze of windowless hallways and chambers, two levels deep and 8,200 square feet in size. The Bunker was built as a back-up radio and television station, engineered to withstand the blast of a nuclear bomb whose launch by capitalist America, the Kremlin's ideological arch rival, was seen as highly possible. Completed in 1985, shortly before Mikhail Gorbachev's policies of glastnost and perestroika came into effect, the Bunker was equipped with Soviet state-of-the-art communication technology, had a direct line to the Central Committee of the Communist Party, contained autonomous systems of electrical power and heating, and permanently employed a dozen or so maintenance and security personnel, most of whom lived in an apartment block located within the Bunker's perimeter.

During the military crackdown on Lithuania's independence movement, *Sąjūdis*, in January 1991, Moscow sent its elite troops to the House of Creativity, believing that the leaders of the movement had used the broadcast centre to mobilize the nation against the communist authorities. In fact, the 'official' radio and television centre located in downtown Vilnius was used for this purpose. The troops stayed in the Bunker for several weeks, until the supplies of food and cigarettes ran out. Gone with the elite troops was also most of the communication equipment – dismantled, looted, damaged. According to Raimundas Dabužinskas, who was employed as a caretaker at the Bunker at the time, the same troops took part in the bloody confrontation with unarmed protestors on the streets of Vilnius on 13 January 1991, a violent event that left fourteen civilians dead and 164 injured.[6]

The Bunker was abandoned in the autumn of 1991, and two years later the Red Army withdrew from Lithuania, by then an independent ex-Soviet nation. Empty and desolate, the House of Creativity languished submerged in the ground until the Prison Department, in 1996, attempted to convert it into a high-security jail. The endeavour was unsuccessful, and the Bunker was forgotten for an entire decade. It began to stir again in 2007 when its underground spaces were transformed into a museum of socialism – a project conceived by Rūta Vanagaitė, an independent curator and producer, and financially supported by the Cultural Commission of the European Union.[7]

As 'European money' flowed, the defunct House of Creativity filled with countless Soviet-era artefacts collected in Lithuania, Russia and Belarus, which were used to reconstruct 'typical' interiors of a doctor's office, polyclinic, high-school classroom, general store, dining room of communist nomenklatura, canteen for 'ordinary' people, detoxification cell, KGB interrogation chamber, Lenin's Room and so forth. Some of the artefacts on display at the museum were purchased in flea markets, others were donated by individuals looking to rid their private spaces of Soviet 'junk'. The Bunker truly came to life after its displays became sites for interactive three-hour performances known as 'survival drama', intended to give visitors a taste of the 'harsh' daily life in the USSR.[8] Today, for 75 litas (approximately $31 US) the Bunker offers scheduled interactive performances throughout the year and accommodates special requests from groups and individuals interested in visiting the museum on their time. The Bunker's cavernous underground space can also be rented for birthday celebrations, prenuptial stag parties, anniversaries and *cementovkės*.[9]

Layered with temporal referents to Lithuania's recent Soviet history – the Cold War, the perestroika years, the time of surging mobilization for national independence – the Bunker is a place that both commemorates and condemns socialism. It is a metaphoric grave where Marxist-Leninist legacy, along with its terror, squalor and despair, lies dead and buried. This grim grave – paradoxically – is also a locus where socialism lives on as a setting of post-socialist consumption, entertainment and leisurely exploration. A betwixt-and-between place par excellence, today the Bunker deals in fun and fear, pleasure and pain, creativity and control – 'a stock in trade of amusement parks' (Wallace 1989: 163). A memorial locus of 'pseudo menaces' expressed through contrasting yet complementary extremes, it is a liminal zone of 'dark tourism', a zone out of ordinary time and place.[10]

I now return to the former House of Creativity for a more ethnographic and phenomenological exploration of the 'survival drama' – a performance of socialist remembrance and forgetting.

'Dreadful Socialism' as Our History

'Next!' the KGB interrogator exclaimed and took a long drag on his smouldering cigarette. Then he turned the dusty shade of the table lamp towards us, fully exposing its glaring light bulb. Dovilė cautiously stepped forward, approached his desk and sat down on the metal chair riveted to the cement floor. We stood motionless behind her in a straight line. His sagging face covered in grey stubble, cigarette ashes strewn on his well-worn jacket, the interrogator blurted out the first question:

'Name?'
'Dovilė Mockutė.'
'Where do you work?'
'At a bank.'
'Do you know where you are?'

'In the Bunker.'
'What bunker?'
'Soviet bunker . . .'
'Any relatives abroad?'
'Yes.'
'What?'

The exchange of choppy questions and answers continued in rapid succession for several more minutes, until Dovilė shifted uneasily in her chair, and cracked a smile. 'I'll show you smiling; I'll show you joking! . . .' the KGB apparatchik, visibly irritated, yelled at Dovilė, 'suspected' of being a 'people's enemy' involved in anti-state activities. 'Sing the Soviet anthem, sing it, can't you hear me!' he shouted, handing Dovilė a piece of paper with hand-scribbled lyrics of the anthem. Then he turned on the tape recorder placed on his desk, and the interrogation room filled with voices of a male choir solemnly singing in Russian: '*Soyuz nerushimyi respublik svobodnykh splotila navyeki Velikaya Rus'! . . .*'.[11] 'Everyone sing, don't just stand there . . . Aren't you Soviet citizens?' the agitated interrogator now screamed at the top of his lungs, banging his fist on the desk. Startled by the singing and commotion in the interrogation room, Amur, the guard dog, began to bark again. The Bunker was reverberating with a deafening cacophony.

At lunch, Dovilė, her friend Marija and I sat together. Above us, a banner extending the length of the wall proclaimed in Russian: 'Proletarians of all countries, unite!' On the long table covered in red cloth, there sat our Soviet lunch: a watery wiener, a slice of bread and a cookie; lukewarm tea was served in a crudely manufactured standard-issue glass, popularly known as *granyonnyi*, or 'the edgy one'. After I introduced myself to Dovilė and her friend, we began to chat about our experience in the Bunker.

Both born in the mid-1980s and with childhood memories of daily life in Gorbachev's 'late socialism', my interlocutors found the 'survival drama' instructive and illuminating, if unnerving. 'The noise, the [KGB] interrogation, the ordering around, the icky food, the smell, the lights . . . Socialism! Dreadful!' Dovilė concluded. 'But it's our history . . . We need to know it . . .' 'It's important to remember it. Paganism, the battle of Žalgiris, tsarism, gulags, and KGB are all our past', Marija concurred.[12] 'Shut up!' the guard exclaimed, overhearing our brazen conversation that broke the Bunker rules of conduct. Abruptly silenced, we turned back to our lunch.

I approached Dovilė and Marija again after we resurfaced from the Bunker – disoriented, delighted to see the blue sky above us. Dovilė pulled out a mobile phone from her purse and called her father to let him know that the 'drama' was over and that she had 'survived' it. An hour or so

later, Dovilė's father, Šarūnas, parked his shiny Mazda outside the fenced
perimeter of the Bunker grounds and came to greet us. Clad in tight-fitting
blue Levis and a Lacoste tee-shirt, a high-ranking executive at an insurance
company in his fifties, Šarūnas did not approve of his daughter's visit to the
museum of socialism and was quite incredulous when I told him about my
research interests. 'You study how people remember socialism? Really?' he
asked in disbelief. 'We need to move away from all this . . . I will never go to
see this [Bunker]. History this, history that . . . Enough already! Let's think
about the present, so much to do *now*.'

    Dovilė's story might seem 'atypical'. In studies of post-socialist memory
it is usually the older generations, persons who lived most of their adult
lives under communist rule, who invoke it as a biographical and historical
past worthy of remembering, in negative or positive terms (see, for instance,
Klumbytė 2009, Skultans 1998). Young people are commonly discussed as
actors who see little or no value in recollecting Marxist-Leninist history. In
the case at hand, however, it is someone born during the 'late socialism' of
the 1980s who insists on commemorating it as a significant component of
'our history'. For Dovilė and her friend Marija, to know this history well,
and to display that knowledge to others, is to make claims of belonging to
the imagined community of the nation (Anderson 1995) and to assert one's
patriotic allegiance to it. Such claims also speak to the moral imperative
to remember; they concern an obligation and responsibility to recall the
national past (Blustein 2008: 15).

    Both in their twenties, the two women represent a growing cohort of
young Lithuanians who, in response to encroaching transnationalism and
globalization, look for ways to reproduce and reinforce their national identities and loyalties (see Mantas's story below).[13] Always containing many
pasts, history is an invaluable symbolic resource in this endeavour. Dovilė's
and Marija's remembrance of socialism, I suggest, is nationalist. They recall
and discursively appropriate the socialist past – as the possessive pronoun
'our' suggests – as a significant constituent component in the nation's historical narrative. Their memorial engagement with the Soviet era is hardly
suggestive of nostalgia.

The Dentist's Drill and Mnemonic Search

'When was your last check-up?' a Russian-speaking female actor impersonating a dentist clad in a white coat and oversize cylindrical hat asked
Mantas, a shy, lanky young man. 'Six months ago . . . My teeth are fine,
healthy', he responded promptly in Lithuanian. 'I'll determine how fine

they are, not you . . . Sit in the chair! The chair, I said!' As Mantas slowly lowered himself into the wobbly reclining chair, the dentist powered up the drill and shone the overhead light into his mouth. Clutching the arm-rests tightly, Mantas was shaking. 'Open wide!', the doctor shrieked as she tried to poke the drill into his mouth, feigning a dental procedure. Several of Mantas's fellow participants stood in the doorway of the dental office, watching anxiously. Suddenly Mantas pushed the zealous Soviet dentist aside and jumped out of the reclining chair. 'Enough, little woman!' (*Užteks, moteriške!*), he protested, heading towards the door, visibly upset: 'What are you doing, citizen?', the appalled medic exclaimed in Russian. 'You signed the Confirmation [see the opening lines above] . . . Do what you are told, not what you please – or face the consequences!', she threatened, the drill still abuzz in her right hand.

I met with Mantas in a stylish café in the Old Town of Vilnius several days after our visit to the Bunker. 'How are your teeth?' I asked. 'All of them fell out, not surprisingly . . .', he replied and laughed. A law student in his early twenties, born in 1989, Mantas found the Bunker 'interesting', albeit the performance, in his view, was somewhat over the top. Despite his run-in with the dentist, he appreciated the interactive component of the underground 'drama', although he noted that the boundaries between the performance and the audience could have been better respected. Because Mantas – unlike Dovilė who 'had relatives abroad' and was not 'serious' – answered the KGB interrogator's questions to his satisfaction, he was almost 'recruited' to the Soviet secret police.

With virtually no experience of the 'actually existing socialism' and with only vague recollections of the fall of the USSR, Mantas had a keen inter-est in the years of communist rule, an interest fuelled by the many stories told and retold by his maternal grandmother. Identified as a socially perni-cious 'bourgeois element' by the Soviet Lithuanian state in 1949, she and her husband, well-to-do farmers from northern Lithuania, were exiled to a village in the Irkutsk region.[14] Mantas's mother was born in Siberia shortly after her father died in a logging accident. In 1958, his grandmother and mother, still an infant at the time, returned to Lithuania from the forced exile. As we sipped coffee, Lady Gaga's latest hit blasting in the background, Mantas recounted:

> My grandmother still talks and talks about Siberia . . . about how much they suffered there: about the food-ration cards, medicinal herbs, folk songs, backbreaking work in the snow-bound forests, Arctic cold during the long winter, pesky mosquitoes in the summer, clandestine Catholic bap-tisms, weddings, and funerals . . . She shows us photos, illegal hand-written

newsletters . . . At times it feels that I myself have gone through Siberia (*per Sibirą perėjau*). When my granny saw the Bunker on TV, she said that I should go and get a taste of Soviet life for myself . . . She was growing tired of telling stories about the exile.

For Mantas, the Bunker offered a glimpse of the 'harsh' life in Soviet Lithuania and generated a slew of new questions about socialism. He wanted better to comprehend how the state could be so violent towards its own citizens, why they did not rebel against its injustice and brutality, why his grandparents were deported but other farmers were not. He emphasized several times that it was his responsibility to understand this as a Lithuanian (cf. Dovilė's and Marija's remarks above). At the time of our interview, Mantas was planning to join a 'patriotic' study tour, known as 'Mission Siberia', offering young Lithuanians a more hands-on, in situ experience of the history of Stalin's gulags. He did not expect ever to find his grandfather's grave but hoped to get 'at least a bit closer to him'.

Mantas's story instantiates one of the paradoxical features of social memory: one need not experience a particular past to remember it. Inherently intersubjective and dialogical, social memory works well vicariously, so to speak, via other persons' recollections and through public representations of history (performative enactments of pastness are especially effective in this regard). One can remember past events without ever being part of them. His grandmother's narratives depicting daily life in Siberian labour camps, complemented by the Bunker performance, makes the socialist past a vivid 'memory' in his consciousness. Indeed so vivid that at times it seems to Mantas that he had 'gone through Siberia' himself. His remembrance is both biographical and historical, meshing reminiscences of personal daily experiences in Siberia with memories of national trauma and suffering. Motivating him in this memorial pursuit is not nostalgia but a desire to piece together a familial past that was shaped by socialism in profound existential ways. Mantas's vicarious memories of the Soviet past is a kind of quest, pursuit, or search of pastness – a Proustian *recherche* of a lost time – rather than a restoration of, or nostalgic reconnection with it. Placing himself in the narrative of the nation's destiny, Mantas seeks to transform remembrance of catastrophic rupture into reproductive continuity and in doing so makes a 'cosmological argument' linking the familial, intergenerational and national, and more expansively, connecting the dead and the living. To paraphrase Bruce Kapferer (2012: 69), remembrance of state-inflicted 'evil', paradoxically, becomes a possibility for imagining ontological coherence and order as a person and member of the nation (Casey 2000: 15, Huyssen 1995: 3).[15]

Mantas's recollection can also be seen as 'pragmatic' in that it is purposefully mobilized to accomplish specific tasks (Lambek 1996: 240). He strives to 'remember' socialism in order to know his family's life history and, through it, himself. Such knowing in turn defines him as a Lithuanian. Not unlike in the case of Dovilė and Marija, Mantas's memories of the Soviet past link up with issues of national identification and belonging. They point to 'the ... reciprocal relations between the social and the intimate, and the centrality of memory ... to creative refashioning of the self' (Antze and Lambek 1996: xx).

Shopping Soviet Style and the Memory of 'Bygones'

'Available today are shampoo from the GDR, condensed milk, Vietnamese lip balm; sardines, women's underwear, dry fish, instant Indian coffee are also available ... We might get toilet paper next week. Sausage can be purchased, but only 300 grams per customer ...' a grouchy clerk at the variety store (he was also the guard who conducted the inspection at the beginning of the show) was informing a crowd of restless shoppers matter-of-factly. When they surged forward in an attempt to take a closer look at the half-empty shelves, the clerk intoned: 'Citizens, back up ... Don't lean on the counter, we'll call the militia ... you're breaking social order.' Holding onto his wife's arm, one frustrated shopper, Pranas, a stocky, balding man in his early seventies, exclaimed in heavily accented Russian: '*Stolichnaya* [vodka]? ... Available?' 'Let's see ... Man, come round to the back door [of the store]. We'll discuss it there,' the clerk urged Pranas, and rubbed his thumb against his index finger energetically, hinting that vodka was available, provided the customer was willing to pay for it more than its set retail price.

The clever clerk was asking for a bribe. Pranas, taken aback, exclaimed: 'That's not how it was! No one asked for bribes so openly back then. You guys, don't remember or what?' he challenged the actor impersonating the clerk. A nervous laughter swept through the store. The 'drama' was momentarily suspended, its authenticity in question. The performance 'slipped' from the past into the present; the past became the present. Its script disrupted in a brief moment of contestation, the show transformed into a showdown. In an attempt to repair the stalled performance, an elderly woman at the back of the store exclaimed: 'They showed it right ... It was sometimes even that open. Perhaps you never took or gave bribes?', she now challenged Pranas. His wife, Genutė, weighed in with an objection: 'This is not an accurate enactment!' (*netiksliai suvaidinta*). In no time the escalating dispute was silenced by the self-important store clerk. We moved on to Lenin's Room, back to the USSR.

On that hot July day, I did not have a chance to interview my fellow 'Soviet shoppers' – Pranas and Genutė – after the show, as they rushed back to their summer cottage (*sodas*), just several kilometres down the road from the Bunker, where a wilting kitchen garden was awaiting a good watering. 'Call us!' Genutė urged me, writing down her mobile phone number in my day book.

Two weeks later, Genutė, Pranas and I sat under a sprawling apple tree at their *sodas*. In the kitchen garden, a water sprinkler was stuttering, squeezed in between lush lettuce, dill, potatoes and beets – staples of their suburban subsistence economy. Pranas was pouring beer into plastic tumblers lined up on a folding table. 'To help memory flow better . . . it's a serious matter', he explained. Pranas and Genutė were pensioners. In the 1960s they met at a state-run footwear factory in Vilnius, where they worked for over thirty years. Their only son, a recent economic émigré, lived with his family in Ireland.

My hosts told me that they were reluctant to spend a whole afternoon away from their peaceful cottage, enduring 'some survival drama'. But the July day was oppressively hot and the Bunker, a short ride away through the forest, beckoned with its cool, underground spaces. It surely provided some respite from the heat, but the 'drama' was a disappointment, as they told me repeatedly. The couple was critical of the Bunker performance, finding its dramatized representations of daily socialist life inaccurate and exaggerated. Genutė stated:

> What kind of spectacle is this? An affectation of a show . . . [*išsidirbinėjimas*]. We spent a heap of money [150 lt; approx $62 US] to see this! And they didn't even get it right . . . Ridiculous! [*Juokinga!*][16] Those who did not go against the authorities under the Russians did not see such scary, spooky stuff . . . Life then was hard but we lived it, raised our son . . . managed with what we had. We had family, friends, the workers' collective . . . we knew how to 'spin' [*suktis*].[17] If you knew how to work the system, if you were strong, you did OK. They [authorities] pulled the wool over our eyes [*mulkino*], we knew that . . . It was not easy, I don't want it back. Let bygones be bygones . . . [*kaip buvo, taip buvo*].

Pranas lamented that as retirees on meagre pensions that added up to 1200 litas per month (approximately $490 US) between them, they struggled, but they now lived in 'a free Lithuania, without the Russians . . . Better'. 'Perhaps too much freedom! Look how many of us have emigrated to the West. We lost our son, grandson. They are now "Irish", imagine! But it's better for them there I think . . . The son works as a roofer, sends us some money occasionally . . . We constantly think about how it is for them there, how it will be,' Pranas stated, his fourth beer glass already empty. He also added that grocery stores were now full, unlike 'back then'. Although he and his wife could afford only basic necessities for daily use, he felt 'good' seeing that it was no longer as in the Bunker variety store. For him, the perceived consumer abundance, albeit much of it off limits, was an indication of Lithuania's new-found prosperity and positive post-socialist change.

Pranas and Genutė remembered socialism as a biographical past shaped by the invasive Soviet state. In their retrospection this past is recalled not as a good life but as a life lived well – with dignity, pride, a sense of purpose, with social savvy and skill. Both regarded themselves as successful citizens of socialism because they knew how to 'spin' their way through it, seeing all the while its fakeness or 'inauthenticity' as a sociopolitical and economic order. Effective 'spinning' required a great deal of cultural knowledge, as well as substantial investment in social networks and their constitutive informal contracts (family, friends, the workers' collective), as sites for storing and reproducing valued social capital. It is this knowledge of how socialism worked, or more precisely, how people positioned themselves in, and how *they* worked, socialism that Pranas questions at the Bunker store: 'No one asked for bribes so openly back then,' he critiqued the standoffish clerk. It was not so 'scary, spooky', Genutė stated, throwing the authenticity of the performance into question. Both critique the performance not as a *re-* but as *mis*-representation and, drawing on their knowledge of socialism, rewrite its script. Pranas and Genutė's narrative is both memorial and moral – one that recounts a story about a struggle in, and competent mastering of, a system.

Again, I am reluctant to conceptualize my interlocutors' memorial commentary as nostalgia. Provoked by the Bunker performance, and subsequently prodded by my interview questions, my informants recall the Soviet-era vividly but express no yearning for it. Although for both socialism was once a metaphoric 'home' where they strove (and succeeded) to live well in the face of pervasive economic and social constraints imposed by the state, they conveyed no desire to return to it. Instead of unproblematically 'nostalgifying' such reminiscences, I propose to think of them as memory of 'bygones' (cf. Genutė's phrase cited above: *kaip buvo, taip buvo*). Such memory is not about going back and metaphorically reinhabiting a particular idealized past, but about a past once inhabited and now gone. This past is retrieved without the affective entailments of 'homecoming' that inform nostalgic recollections. The memorial relationship with this past is one of temporal distancing rather than approaching, of rupture rather than continuity. Recall Šarūnas's stance towards the Soviet era as 'forgettable' or 'unmemorable' biography and history, and his insistence on the need to focus on the present. While for Pranas and Genutė that present is about their pitiful pensions, for Šarūnas, a successful insurance company executive, it is about promise of profits.

Pranas and Genutė's principal concern is the neoliberal and increasingly transnational present they inhabit and negotiate in 'free' Lithuania today, some two decades after socialism's demise: making ends meet as impoverished pensioners, tending to their kitchen garden as an important seasonal source of home-grown nourishment, thinking about 'how it is and how it will be' with their son and his family who emigrated to Ireland in search of employment. For these retirees, socialism is more of an afterthought, or 'after-memory', so to speak – a life once lived and decidedly gone, if not entirely forgotten.

By Way of Conclusion

Taking the sensuous performance of the *1984: Survival Drama* at the Bunker as its principal ethnographic site, this essay has examined one of many representations of Lithuania's Soviet past at the current moment of post-socialist change – a moment in the nation's history informed by futuristic visions of 'Europe' and neoliberal modernity. Made present in different cultural forms, socialist recollections represent only one memory in the multi-voiced (or heteroglossic) mnemoscape of contemporary Lithuania. In the public domain, socialist remembrance coexists and competes with reminiscences of other, more distant pasts: 'paganism, Žalgiris, tsarism, gulags . . .', to cite Marija again.

I have attempted to show that commemorative performance as an embodied and sensuous act constitutes a productive 'dramatizing' event for examining how memory is externalized, displayed, disputed and reconfigured by its participants. Although scripted and locked in space and time, commemorative performance – as a dynamic, processual and interactive social occasion – can engender rupture and 'slippage'. Such moments of malfunction are especially conducive to examining how recollections of a given past are negotiated and contested (recall Pranas and Genutė's questioning of the representation of bribing practices in the Soviet command economy of shortage).

In an effort to argue for a more thoughtful and nuanced theorizing of remembrance of the socialist past, throughout this essay I have been disinclined to conceptualize my interlocutors' engagements with that past in terms of nostalgia. I have referred to their recollections as *recherche*, proposed to think of them as pragmatic recollection (Dovilė, Marija, Mantas), and tentatively termed them as memory of 'bygones' (Pranas and Genutė), all the while remaining reluctant to 'nostalgify' them. It has not been my intent to consign nostalgia to the dustbin of analytically useless concepts – much socialist remembering can certainly be identified and insightfully investigated as nostalgic. Rather I have suggested that nostalgia is in need of a good refinement, sharpening and deconstructing, procedures that would help us move away from totalizing arguments, neat dualisms and tidy typologies.

As Pranas stated, remembering socialism is 'a serious matter', but it is also a complicated one – selective, strategic, multi-directional and oftentimes messy. To be sure, not everyone is engaging with this past. Some of my interlocutors position themselves firmly in the present (recall Šarūnas's dismissive remarks regarding history; cf. Pranas's and Genutė's comments) and see little or no social value in recollecting socialism or indeed any other period in the nation's history. *Now,* not *then,* is the principal referent in their temporal anchoring. Others, however, view socialist recall as a significant cognitive and moral resource for biographical and national self constitution (notably Mantas's story).

I have used the Bunker as a *lieu de mémoire* through which to inquire into remembering and forgetting of socialism in contemporary Lithuania. Yet this *lieu* is not merely about memory, amnesia and their associated complications. A popular destination of 'dark tourism', the former House of Creativity and its sensuous show are also about what can be called memorial entertainment, or perhaps more pithily, mnemotainment. The Bunker experience is 'mnemotaining' not only because of its dramatic performance of socialism as packaged and commercialized history, but also because of the setting in which the drama unfolds. In other words, the Bunker is intriguing as a performing place eliciting a wide range of responses from those who experience it (Coleman and Crang 2007: 10).

Finally, reinvigorated remembrance of the era of communist rule in Lithuania, as in many other locales of the former Soviet bloc, suggests that the category 'post-socialist' continues to make sense (Humphrey 2002). Temporally we may conceptualize Eastern Europe in terms of *post-* or *after* socialism, but the Marxist-Leninist era is not exactly *past* because it is still (or again) very present in different domains of social life. Socialism is at once in and out, going and gone, dead and alive – persisting in an ambiguous interplay of remembrance and amnesia.

Notes

1. The reference is, of course, to *1984*, George Orwell's science-fiction novel of dark satire, published in 1949, in which he describes how an authoritarian, invasive state comes to dominate and control the daily lives of its citizens.

2. For a more detailed treatment of such sites of socialist memory, see Lankauskas 2006. The Bunker has been recently discussed in Klumbytė 2009: 92–96. Yet another interactive site commemorating Soviet history, a defunct 1960s military base known today as 'Soviet Spirit: An Exposition of Militarism', located in northwestern Lithuania, still awaits ethnographic scrutiny; for a video with English subtitles, see <http://www.zemaitijosnp.lt/en/> (accessed 14 April 2011).

3. For a helpful discussion of the etymology of the word nostalgia and its different uses through history, see Davis 1979: 1–7.

4. For a thorough and lucid discussion of performance theory in anthropology, as an offshoot of the larger body of the social theory of practice (or praxis), see McAllister 2006: 43–49, 67–80.

5. The phrase refers to a kind of communal retreat intended for seasonal use by Soviet aesthetic elites, such as actors, writers, and visual artists (*kūrybos namai* or *дом творчества* in Russian).

6. *See* Delfi TV: *Nepapasakota istorija: kas vyko slaptame bunkeryje 1991 m. sausį?* [An Untold Story: What Happened in the Secret Bunker in January 1991?]; http://tv.delfi.lt/video/nVEEcjiC/ (accessed 17 April 2011); on the January events, see also Smith et al. 2002: 111–126.

7. A member of the European Union (EU) since 2004, Lithuania has been a beneficiary of Brussels' generous funding set aside to promote innovative 'cultural projects' (*kultūriniai projektai*) among the Union's junior members. The establishment of the Bunker museum was part of the broader pan-European initiative of 'Culture Live' and 'Vilnius, the Cultural Capital of Europe, 2009'.

8. The 'drama' was directed by Jonas Vaitkus, produced by Rūta Vanagaitė. For video footage of the museum and excerpts of the 'drama', see Delfi TV: *Atgal į praeitį: socializmo muziejus po žeme* (I and II) [Back to the Past: An Underground Museum of Socialism, Parts I and II]: <http://tv.delfi.lt/video/y6714FAQ/> and http://tv.delfi.lt/video/5E7kgqOJ/ (accessed 17 April 2011).

9. Borrowed from Russian (*цементовка*), this colloquial word refers to social events that usually entail copious consumption of food and alcohol, and are meant to improve sociability and bonding ('cementing') among friends, classmates, colleagues, or co-workers.

10. On significance of liminality in tourist experience, see Tucker 2002.

11. The first lines of the Soviet anthem: 'The indestructible Union of free republics, joined forever by the Great Rus!'

12. In today's Lithuania, 'the pagan times' are recalled by some – in primordialist, essentializing terms – as a timeless era of harmonious and prosperous social life. Lithuania was among the last in Europe to convert to Christianity, in 1386. The battle of Žalgiris, or Grünewald, is remembered today with considerable national pride as a military event where the joint army of the Lithuanian-Polish state defeated the Christianizing Teutonic order in 1410. The tsarist period (1795–1918) is usually recollected as a time of Russia's colonial domination and oppression.

13. For a more detailed discussion of the emergence of Lithuanian 'neo-national-ism' among younger generations, see Lankauskas 2010.

14. Located in south-central Siberia, north of the Mongolian-Russian border, the Irkutsk region was notorious for its political prisons and camps of punitive hard labour, or gulags. Between 1944 and 1953, some 118,000 Lithuanians were deported to Siberia as political or ideological 'enemies' of the Moscow regime (Rudienė and Juozevičiūtė 2009).

15. For a collection of essays examining the intersection of historical events, memory and kinship, see Carsten 2007 and Skultans 1998.

16. Marx's famous dictum – history repeats itself as farce – comes to mind here.

17. *Suktis*, or 'spinning', refers to one's resourcefulness to make do with limited material means in the command economy of shortage. Extensive use of social networks of family members, friends, and co-workers was key for successful 'spinning' – a kind of habitus, in Pierre Bourdieu's terms, combining structure and action in mutually reinforcing ways. This practice was grounded in a system of dispositions, which 'designate[d] a way of being, . . . a habitual state . . ., a predisposition, tendency, propensity, or inclination' (1989: 214).

References

Anderson, B. 1995. *Imagined Communities: Reflections on the Origin and Spread of Nationalism*. London: Verso.

Antze, P. and M. Lambek (eds). 1996. *Tense Past: Cultural Essays in Trauma and Memory*. New York: Routledge.

Bach, J. 2002. '"The Taste Remains": Consumption, (N)ostalgia, and the Production of East Germany', *Public Culture* 14 (3): 545–56.

Bakhtin, M. 1986. *Speech Genres and Other Late Essays*. Austin: University of Texas Press.

Battaglia, D. 1995. 'On Practical Nostalgia: Self-Prospecting among Urban Trobrianders', in D. Battaglia (ed.), *Rhetoric of Self-Making*. Berkeley: University of California Press, pp. 77–96.

Bauman, R. 1992. 'Performance', in R. Bauman (ed.), *Folklore, Cultural Performances, and Popular Entertainments*. Oxford: Oxford University Press, pp. 41–49.

Bell, C. 1997. *Ritual: Perspectives and Dimensions*. Oxford: Oxford University Press.

Berdahl, D. 2010. *On the Social Life of Postsocialism: Memory, Consumption, Germany*. Bloomington: Indiana University Press.

Berliner, D. 2005. 'The Abuses of Memory: Reflections on the Memory Boom in Anthropology', *Anthropological Quarterly* 78 (1): 197–211.

Blustein, J. 2008. *The Moral Demands of Memory*. Cambridge: Cambridge University Press.

Boyer, D. 2010. 'From Algos to Autonomos: Nostalgic Eastern Europe as Postimperial Mania', in M. Todorova and Z. Gille (eds), *Post-Communist Nostalgia*. New York: Berghahn, pp. 17–28.

Bourdieu, P. 1989. *Outline of a Theory of Practice*. Cambridge: Cambridge University Press.

Boym, S. 2001. *The Future of Nostalgia*. New York: Basic Books.

Casey, E. 2000. *Remembering: A Phenomenological Study*. Bloomington: Indiana University Press.

Carsten, J. (ed.). 2007. *Ghosts of Memory: Essays on Remembrance and Relatedness*. Malden, UK: Blackwell.

Climo, J. and M. Cattell (eds). 2002. *Social Memory and History: Anthropological Perspectives*. Walnut Creek, CA: Altamira Press.

Coleman, S. and M. Crang. 2002. *Tourism: Between Place and Performance*. New York: Berghahn.

Connerton, P. 1989. *How Societies Remember*. Cambridge: Cambridge University Press.

Diamond, E. 1996. 'Introduction', in E. Diamond (ed.), *Performance and Cultural Politics*. New York: Routledge, pp. 1–12.

Davis, F. 1979. *Yearning for Yesterday: A Sociology of Nostalgia*. New York: Free Press.

Douglas, M. 1991. 'The Idea of Home: A Kind of Space', *Social Research* 58 (1): 287–307.

Fabian, J. 1990. *Power and Performance*. Madison: University of Wisconsin Press.

Fentress, J. and C. Wickham. 1992. *Social Memory: New Perspectives on the Past*. Malden, UK: Blackwell.

Gille, Z. 2010. 'Postscript', in M. Todorova and Z. Gille (eds), *Post-Communist Nostalgia*. New York: Berghahn, pp. 278–89.

Goffman, E. 1959. *The Presentation of Self in Everyday Life*. Garden City, NJ: Doubleday.

Halbwachs, M. 1992. *On Collective Memory*. Chicago: University of Chicago Press.

Herzfeld, M. 2005. *Cultural Intimacy: Social Poetics in the Nation-State*. New York: Routledge.

Howes, D. 1991. *The Varieties of Sensory Experience: A Sourcebook in the Anthropology of the Senses*. Toronto: University of Toronto Press.

Humphrey, C. 2002. 'Introduction: Does the Category of "Post-socialism" Still Make Sense?', in C. Hann (ed.), *Post-socialism: Ideals, Ideologies, and Practices in Eurasia*. London: Routledge, pp. 12–15.

Hutcheon, L. 2000. 'Irony, Nostalgia, and the Postmodern', in R. Vervliet and A. Estor (eds), *Methods for the Study of Literature as Cultural Memory*. Atlanta, GA: Rodopi, pp. 189–207.

Huyssen, A. 1995. *Twilight Memories: Marking Time in a Cultural Amnesia*. New York: Routledge.

Kapferer, B. 2012. *Legends of People, Myths of States: Violence, Intolerance, and Political Culture in Sri Lanka and Australia*. New York: Berghahn.

Klumbytė, N. 2009. 'Post-Socialist Sensations: Nostalgia, the Self, and Alterity in Lithuania', *Lietuvos etnologija* [*Lithuanian Ethnology*] 9 (18): 93–116.

———. 2010. 'The Soviet Sausage Renaissance', *American Anthropologist* 112 (1): 22–37.

Ladino, J. 2004. 'Longing for Wonderland: Nostalgia for Nature in Post-Frontier America', *Iowa Journal of Cultural Studies* 4. Retrieved from <www.uiowa.edu/~ijcs/nostalgia/nostint.htm> (accessed 7 April 2011).

Lambek, M. 1996. 'The Past Imperfect: Remembering as Moral Practice', in P. Antze and M. Lambek (eds), *Tense Past: Cultural Essays in Trauma and Memory*. New York: Routledge, pp. 215–33.

Lankauskas, G. 2006. 'Sensuous (Re)Collections: The Sight and Taste of Socialism at Grūtas Park, Lithuania', *The Senses and Society* 1 (1): 27–52.

———. 2010. 'Others, the Nation, and its (Dis)integration in "European" Lithuania', *Journal of Contemporary European Studies* 18 (2): 193–208.

Lassiter, L. 2002. 'Kiowa: On Song and Memory', in J. Climo and M. Cattell (eds), *Social Memory and History: Anthropological Perspectives*. Walnut Creek, CA: Altamira Press, pp. 131–42.

Lowenthal, D. 1989. 'Nostalgia Tells It Like It Wasn't', in C. Shaw and M. Chase (eds), *The Imagined Past: History and Nostalgia*. New York: Manchester University Press, pp. 18–32.

McAllister, P. 2006. *Xhosa Beer Drinking Rituals: Power, Practice and Performance in the South African Rural Periphery*. Durham: Carolina Academic Press.

Myerhoff, B. 1996. 'Death in Due Time: Construction of Self and Culture in Ritual Drama', in R. Grimes (ed.), *Readings in Ritual Studies*. Upper Saddle River, NJ: Prentice Hall, pp. 393–412.

Nadkarni, M. 2010. '"But It's Ours": Nostalgia and the Politics of Authenticity in Post-Socialist Hungary', in M. Todorova and Z. Gille (eds), *Post-Communist Nostalgia*. New York: Berghahn, pp. 190–214.

Nora, P. 1989. 'Between Memory and History: Les Lieux de Mémoire', *Representations* 26: 7–25.

Pilbrow, T. 2010. 'Dignity in Transition: History, Teachers, and the Nation-State in Post-1989 Bulgaria', in M. Todorova and Z. Gille (eds), *Post-Communist Nostalgia*. New York: Berghahn, pp. 82–95.

Rosaldo, R. 1989. *Culture and Truth: The Remaking of Social Analysis*. Boston: Beacon Press.

Rudienė, V. and V. Juozevičiūtė. 2009. *Genocido Aukų Muziejus: Ekspozijų Gidas [The Museum of Genocide Victims: An Exposition Guide]*. Vilnius: Centre for Research of Genocide and Resistance.

Sarkisova, O. and P. Apor. 2008. *Past for the Eyes: East European Representations of Communism in Cinema and Museums after 1989*. Budapest: Central European University Press.

Scanlan, S. 2004. 'Introduction', *Iowa Journal of Cultural Studies* 4. Retrieved from <www.uiowa.edu/~ijcs/nostalgia/nostint.htm> (accessed 7 April 2011).

Schieffelin, E. 1985. 'Performance and the Cultural Construction of Reality', *American Ethnologist* 12 (4): 707–24.

———. 2005. 'Problematizing Performance', in G. Harvey (ed.), *Ritual and Religious Belief: A Reader*. New York: Routledge, pp. 124–138.

Skultans, V. 1998. *The Testimony of Lives*. New York: Routledge.

Smith, D., A. Pabriks, A. Purs and T. Lane. 2002. *The Baltic States: Estonia, Latvia, Lithuania*. New York: Routledge.

Stewart, K. 1988. 'Nostalgia – A Polemic', *Cultural Anthropology* 3 (3): 227–41.

Stoller, P. 1995. *Embodying Colonial Memories: Spirit Possession, Power, and the Hauka in West Africa*. New York: Routledge.

Ten Dyke, E. 2000. 'Memory, History, and Remembrance Work in Dresden', in D. Berdahl, M. Bunzl and M. Lampland (eds), *Altering States: Ethnographies of Transition in Eastern Europe and the Former Soviet Union*. Ann Arbor: University of Michigan Press, pp. 139–57.

Todorova, M. 2010. 'Introduction: From Utopia to Propaganda and Back', in M. Todorova and Z. Gille (eds), *Post-Communist Nostalgia*. New York: Berghahn, pp. 1–13.

Todorova, M. and Z. Gille (eds). 2010. *Post-Communist Nostalgia*. New York: Berghahn.

Tucker, H. 2002. 'Welcome to Flintstones-Land: Contesting Place and Identity in Goreme, Central Turkey', in S. Coleman and M. Crang (eds), *Tourism: Between Place and Performance*. New York: Berghahn, pp. 143–59.

Turner, V. 1988. *The Anthropology of Performance*. New York: PAJ Publications.

Verdery, K. 1999. *The Political Lives of Dead Bodies: Reburial and Postsocialist Change*. New York: Columbia University Press.

Wallace, M. 1989. 'Mickey Mouse History: Portraying the Past at a Disney World', in W. Leon and R. Rosenzweig (eds), *History Museums in the United States: A Critical Assessment*. Chicago: University of Illinois Press, pp. 158–80.

Chapter 3

The Politics of Nostalgia in the Aftermath of Socialism's Collapse

A Case for Comparative Analysis

Maya Nadkarni and Olga Shevchenko

A spectre is haunting Europe – the spectre of Communism.

Marx and Engels, *The Communist Manifesto*

Introduction

It is good to be young in any system, even in one that falls within an inglorious and lustreless era of our history. . . . [T]hat's when we chased girls, that's when we were drunk, that's when we were young. . . . [T]here was shit in the Kádár-era pancake, but there was pudding on top.

Barta Balázs, *Index* website (www.index.hu), 19 October 2000

I fear that, after listening to these [reminiscences], the former KGB informants and disciplinarians will rejoice . . . And will infect today's youth with their longing for the past.

G. Il'in, *Obschaya Gazeta*, no. 23, 6 November 1998

I know that I will never feel as carefree and as blissful as I did back then. Although if I found myself back there, I would howl from all the idiocy of that life. I guess I didn't make my share of mud pies in that sandbox . . .

> And now the fun is gone, and my little scoop and pail are lost somewhere
> . . . But the best ice-cream is still the waffle cone for twenty kopecks.
>> One of over 400 Russian responses to an Internet list (posted on www.
>> livejournal.com) *'You come from the [19]70s/[19]80s if . . .',* 6 April 2003

Just months after the political transformations of 1989 and 1991, when
nothing seemed more impossible than the return of state socialism to the
former Soviet bloc, communist symbols and iconography suddenly acquired
new visibility, rather than fading into obsolescence. Over the next decades,
communism would enjoy a healthy afterlife as a cultural and political commodity, from hammer-and-sickle tee-shirts in Bulgaria, to popular collections of socialist-era songs in Russia, to trendy 'workers' canteen'-themed
restaurants in Budapest – all falling under label 'nostalgia'.

It is thus no surprise that the spectre of communism would also
re-emerge to haunt the former Soviet-bloc states, this time in the form of
public debates about the attractions and dangers posed by these cultural
practices. Indeed, nostalgia would become such a central term for analysing
how post-socialist societies relate to the recent past that it raises the question
of why it became so widespread in the first place – both as a phenomenon
and as a conceptual category through which to unify disparate cultural phenomena across the region. What did these nostalgias have in common, and
what made them different from nostalgias elsewhere?

What makes the similarity of these memory practices so remarkable
is that the experiences of socialism in Eastern Europe were so dissimilar
compared to that of the Soviet Union. Communist rule lasted longer in the
USSR than it did in Eastern Europe and was fuelled primarily by internal
political dynamics, not by constant negotiation between local party elites
and the external imperial power. The ideology of socialism, by extension,
was somewhat less orthodox in Eastern Europe, where elites of different
countries explored different ways to 'nationalise' communist doctrine as
a way to respond to the crises of the post-Stalinist system of the Soviet
bloc. Unsurprisingly, these differences did not cease with the fall of communism, but only became more apparent. Because the socialist system was
not viewed as indigenous but was rather associated with the external power
of the Soviet Union's imperialism, its break-up in 1989–1991 was juridi-
cially and politically more complete in Eastern Europe than in the former
Soviet Union countries. Communism's legacies, therefore, both in terms of
Communist ideology and the lasting institutional forms and practices of late
socialism, are more observable today in post-Soviet Russia than in Hungary
or the Czech Republic. This is evidenced, for example, by the fact that the
Communist party survived in post-Soviet Russia as a major political agent,

whereas in Eastern Europe there was a conscious attempt to remodel the left along the lines of social democracy: an attempt that – as shall be discussed later – made the political uses of nostalgia more problematic.

These differences raise a number of questions, which we answer in this chapter drawing examples from both Hungary and Russia. Did the popularity of similar cultural/historical symbols (socialist-era consumer products, iconic images, cultural products of late socialism) have the same significance in national contexts that followed very different trajectories after 1989? That is, when do apparently identical memory practices in the two countries reflect similar memory work, and when are these mere superficial resemblances? Indeed, when do these resemblances facilitate key misrecognitions of nostalgic practices both within and across national borders? And, ultimately, what is it that shapes the cultural and political implications of these apparently similar nostalgic practices in each given case – or, in fact, makes them politically effective or able to be incorporated into politics at all?

To make such distinctions, we argue, requires not only ethnographic attention to local cultural contexts, but also to internal variation within these contexts. Whom do specific forms of nostalgia address, and how is this audience defined (age group, economic class, etc.)? And who is terming these practices nostalgic in the first place – those who define themselves as participants or observers, 'locals' or 'exiles', in support of these practices or in opposition?

As these questions about location suggest, the power of nostalgia is precisely its susceptibility to being co-opted into various political agendas, which nostalgia then cloaks with an aura of inevitability. This in turn has produced innumerable critical discourses devoted to deciphering these agendas – discourses that tend to assume that the very structure of nostalgia endows it with a particular political meaning. Such essentialism seeks to define the inherent properties of nostalgia, rather than view these properties in their social embeddedness as products of the different subject positions of those who encode and decode these nostalgic practices. That is, these critics look for the substance of the phenomenon – whether that be phrased in terms of a 'return to communism' or the equally rose-tinted version of the past purported by right-wing reactionary politics – and not the social relations that produce it (institutional breaks, generational change, international network alliances, etc.). Thus, domestic cultural commentators attempt to distinguish 'good' from 'bad' nostalgias, scanning each manifestation for signs of its cultural 'health', while foreign mass media similarly divide nostalgia into either the thoroughgoing commodification of communist symbols (and hence, the triumph of capitalism) or, in contrast, the proof of dangerous atavistic cultural attachments. Meanwhile, scholars at home and abroad have attempted to pose correctives to these mainstream arguments by viewing these very same nostalgic practices as critical and subversive, and thus an endorsement of neither the socialist past nor the capitalist present.

Rather than participate in these discourses – which we also view as part of the larger 'nostalgia industry' – in this chapter we examine the different logics that undergird the nostalgic cultural practices these commentators attempt to describe: political kitsch, 'Proustiana', postmodern, etc. Can political intention – and the ability to mobilize this intention for politics – be divined from the different structures of post-socialist nostalgia? Using comparative examples from Hungary and Russia, we argue to the contrary that both the meaning and significance of nostalgic practices only emerge from within a larger field of political possibility. Similar practices, inspired by similar sets of longings, can thus follow very different political trajectories in terms of their political interpretation ('reactionary' versus 'reflective', in Boym's terms [2001]) as well as their political impact. Any analysis of post-socialist nostalgia must thus guard against two temptations: reading politics into nostalgia (that is, assuming inherent political meaning or implications to specific nostalgic practices) and reading nostalgia into politics (assuming that every reference to the past is indeed a nostalgic one).

Background

For a cultural practice so fundamentally concerned with the past, nostalgia is firmly rooted in modernity. Coined in the late seventeenth century as a term to describe the physical sufferings endured by Swiss soldiers stationed abroad, nostalgia initially signified a melancholic state associated with geographical rather than temporal displacement. What later made the term so fit to describe the peculiar discontents caused by the flow of history was, as Peter Fritzsche suggests, the modern Europeans' deepening awareness of the accelerating pace of social change that engendered not only unsettlement, but also 'a compelling historical understanding that appeared to deny the possibility of resettlement' (2002: 77). In other words, in the aftermath of the French Revolution and increasingly since, remaining in one's native place could no longer prevent the experience of displacement. The new generations of Swiss soldiers were bound to face disappointment upon their return home, since their sites of origin, transformed in the time of their absence, no longer seemed familiar.

Nostalgia, then, is a product of a particular temporality and way of approaching history (a 'regime of seeing', as Fritzsche would have it): one that views individuals and societies as caught up in a destructive and irreversible flow of time.[1] It emphasizes the irretrievability of the past as the very condition of desire. Indeed, longing in nostalgia is never longing for a specific past as much as it is longing for longing itself, as writers from Susan Stewart (1993) to Svetlana Boym (2001) have pointed out (drawing from Lacan). Such longing is made all the safer by the fact that the object of that desire is deemed irrevocably lost. Nowhere is this 'longing for longing' more visible than in instances of material or sensory nostalgia, where the physical object deployed as emotional mnemonic, be it a re-run of an old film or a madeleine dipped in tea, is structurally incapable of satisfying the desire that it stirs, for the simple reason that this desire is self-referential. What is at stake in each case is not the film or pastry, nor even the historical period each signifies, but rather the individual's memory of past desire (whether an alternative present or a particular version of the future), and the awareness of the impossibility of experiencing this desire again.

This is not to say that the referential content of nostalgia is irrelevant; rather, that it is opportunistic and changeable. What persists despite nostalgia's historical promiscuity is its peculiarly modern optics and the effect it creates of simultaneous connection with and dissociation from the imagined past. To think productively about nostalgia, then, is to treat it as a 'cultural practice, not a given content' (K. Stewart 1988); that is, to attend to how the meaning of nostalgic practices, far from being predetermined by their historical referents, is shaped situationally in the process of their creation and re-enactment.

Turning to the manifestations of post-socialist nostalgia, one is struck by how closely the themes of spatial and temporal displacement intertwine. Communist ideology, of course, was deliberately and emphatically anti-nostalgic. But given the insularity of the Soviet bloc (within which Paris and Prague, as Lidia Libedinskaia (2000) has remarked, were experienced as being as inaccessible as the moon and Mars), spatial displacement through emigration or exile was experienced as having the same finality as the flow of history. While this is no longer the case, a different kind of spatial displacement – this time following economic, rather than political logic – makes geographical distances *within* the country feel insurmountable to the many Russian families who are unable to afford long-distance travel. More significantly, the very historical transformation that the socialist countries have undergone during the past twenty-odd years has been experienced by many of their subjects, as well as observers, in geographical terms. 'We experienced ten years earlier what all of Russia experienced after *perestroika*', says Rita D., one of Svetlana Boym's respondents who immigrated to the US years before 1991. 'Now . . . it seems that the whole of the former Soviet Union went into immigration, without leaving the country' (Boym 2001: 328).

This substitution of spatial for temporal imagery, however, tells only part of the story. While space can, at least theoretically, be traversed, the flow of time is utterly irreversible. It is this irreversibility that gives nostalgia its modern meaning of incurable affliction. The years of post-socialism, therefore, saw not only a shift from a spatial to temporal logic of nostalgic desire (a shift that paralleled the historical evolution of the term), but also a realization, uncomfortable for some and welcome to others, that the rupture nostalgic desire attempts to breach could only deepen with the passage of time.

The very existence of the nostalgic practices of the past decades has thus helped to create rather than overcome the sense of dislocation from the socialist past. In other words, a sense of break from the past is necessary for nostalgia to exist in the first place; the perception of loss is the precondition for discourses of return and recovery. In this, nostalgic practices differ from reactionary politics whose agenda is precisely to reconstruct the past in the present, thus denying that anything of value can be irrevocably lost. This analytical separation, however, does not prevent reactionary politics from attempts to appropriate nostalgic sentiments in its own interests (attempts that, as we will show below, can occasionally succeed). In these attempts, images and associations that gain power through nostalgia are used as symbolic currency to attract support for projects whose agendas may be motivated entirely by contemporary interests. The American Right's appropriation of broad societal nostalgia for the 1950s in order to advance conservative family policies, for example, has been written and remarked upon (Coontz 1992). Closer to home, nostalgia for the socialist past was used with similar success to gain public acceptance of the Russian youth organization *Iduschie Vmeste* [Moving Together] organized in 2000 by a former Presidential administration bureaucrat Vasilii Yakemenko.[2] The rationalizations put forth by the supporters of the movement lay bare nostalgia's fundamental preoccupation not with the past, but with the fantasies that structured that past, since the most common defence of the movement one of us heard from her Russian respondents went along the lines of 'at least under socialism, young people believed in something'.[3] Nostalgic rhetoric notwithstanding, however, the organization's neoconservative ideology had little to do with cherishing the memories of the past, and in fact targeted communism, alongside fascism, as an example of ideology 'built on hatred and murder, on deceit and betrayal, on blood and suffering of nations'.[4]

The Logic of Nostalgic Desire

What is the longing that set into motion the wheels of post-socialist nostalgic desire? As the example of *Iduschie Vmeste* suggests, in so far as a general answer to this question is possible, it has to start from an examination of the fantasies that socialism spurred into being. Perhaps the most central of these fantasies, and one shared throughout the socialist camp, was the fantasy of the capitalist Other, a fantasy to which the developed capitalist countries responded in kind, by generating an image of an equally stereotyped socialist doppelganger. It is difficult to establish which of these fantasies, having disappeared after 1989–1991, left a greater gap in the symbolic order. But the ease with which both Western onlookers and their East European counterparts have embraced many post-socialist nostalgic discourses suggests that the fantasy of moral and political certainties of the Cold War might be missed on both sides of the vanished Berlin Wall.[5]

This political fantasy of the West had a number of different dimensions. For the millions of those who drew their knowledge about life outside the Iron Curtain from official sources, Western countries represented the ultimate dystopia that rendered the socialist reality enviable by comparison. This depiction could be employed to justify 'temporary hardships' and mobilize public acceptance of unpopular political and economic measures, if not actual support. The loss of such a stable referent made it much more difficult to normalize the relative deprivations of post-socialism through external comparison.[6]

At the same time, other socialist subjects, including many members of the liberal intelligentsia, drew upon the notion of the Western 'Other' during the Cold War as the repository of Western ideals of democracy, and thus as the ultimate political reference to model 'ideal' and 'proper' political behaviour. This fantasy, however, also did not outlive its dystopian counterpart. As post-socialist countries entered into the stage of international realpolitik, their citizens were forced to confront the less glamorous reality that Western countries primarily seek to defend their own national interests, rather than to maintain the political principles upon which they were founded. Political disappointment with the West's 'betrayal of its own principles' is thus inseparable from the symbolic role the West played for the political imaginary under socialism. Post-socialist nostalgia gives shape to the mourning over this loss of the moral and political certainty of pre-1989 idealism.

But, as the residents of the former Eastern bloc would be quick to point out, the fantasies of the capitalist Other entailed not only political divisions, but more importantly, projections of consumer desire and fantasies

of material abundance and 'normality' more generally (Fehérváry 2002).
While post-war socialist regimes strove to measure up to the consumer standards attained by advanced capitalist countries,[7] the pace and rules of the
competition were not of socialism's own making, and the outcome of the
competition was largely not in its favour (Crowley and Reid 2000, see also
Buck-Morss 2000). As a result, Western goods were endowed with a magical
and transformative capacity based on their perceived higher quality,
unavailability and prestige; consumer utopia appeared to be located just
outside socialism's borders, in a Western culture characterized by Coca-
Cola, bananas and unlimited consumer choice. The characteristics of this
utopia, however, were markedly socialist in that this abundance was fantasized as available to everyone; today's frequent indictments of the social
injustices of the 'abundance of the few' recall the allure of this fantasy and
the disappointment associated with its failure. As a result, formerly disparaged items of socialist mass production have acquired the authenticity that
Western products are now perceived to lack. They are now embraced as
vehicles of the once-utopian dreams and desires for the idealized West, and
as silent witnesses of an era in which consumer abundance was imagined
as universally available.[8]

    This reversal reveals nostalgia as a practice centred on the unattainable
structure of past desire – the impossibility of re-experiencing the fantasy of
the West as it was once construed. Regardless of whether this disappointment is mild or acute, such nostalgia also represents a way to mourn one's
'lost childhood innocence' in not only personal but sociopolitical terms.
Coming to terms with the harsh realities of the market economy is narrated
as a collective entrance into adult life: a theme made visible in a number of
German and Hungarian coming-of-age films that take place at the time of
the political transition.[9] In the Russian context, this generational narrative
has been complicated by the fact that the same period is associated with a
loss of yet another fantasy, this one peculiar to the Soviet cultural imaginary.
This fantasy is the one of international prestige and geopolitical power,
buttressed by the very real military presence of the USSR throughout the
Eastern bloc, but interpreted on the level of daily consciousness in the mis-
leadingly benign terms of assistance to and cooperation with the 'brotherly
nations' of the Warsaw pact. The experience of witnessing this fantasy
recast by its former subjects in the substantially less flattering terms of
imperial aggression added more than a touch of bitterness to the Russians'
experience of 1989–1991, so that in the Russian case, the loss of innocence
(with its connotations of inevitability and natural progression) became
inextricably – and problematically – tied to a less palatable fall from grace.
Clearly, not all nostalgic practices in post-Soviet Russia draw on the two

fantasies to an equal extent, but there always remains a possibility that nostalgia for the lost innocence of socialism can get misrecognized or phrased in terms of nostalgia for former glory (as well as vice versa). As we shall argue, this contradictory nature of nostalgic desire in the Russian context lies at the very heart of the ambivalence nostalgic practices evoke among Russia's liberally inclined cultural commentators, and it undergirds their reluctance to endorse practices that, in the East European setting, may appear politically less problematic.

Because post-socialist nostalgic practices do not concern the past itself, but rather the subjects' memory of their own past investments and fantasies, what is also at stake in this loss is not only one's former innocence or grandeur but the imagined futures these fantasies projected. As Walter Benjamin argues, this loss of a projected future is what gives the out-of-date detritus of consumer culture in particular such poignancy, and endows socialist consumer products once reviled as cheap and inauthentic with the auratic appeal once invested in difficult-to-attain Western goods (Buck-Morss 1991). Too recent to possess age value as relics, these objects in their obsolescence nonetheless have the potential to reveal the diverse utopian fantasies once embedded within them, by making palpable the disjuncture between these former dreams of the future and the present reality. Thus, the seemingly trivial and impersonal consumer products of socialist mass production ironically offer a powerful idiom through which to mourn the personal and societal naïveté they are perceived to represent.

The forms and practices of post-socialist nostalgia have mesmerized not only the countries of the former Soviet bloc, but also their Cold War counterparts. One reason for the Western media fascination with this topic undoubtedly stems from the loss of its Cold War political 'Other', a logic by which the end of state socialism in Eurasia and Eastern Europe proved the triumph of democratic ideals, and the commodification of political icons into kitsch demonstrates the success of capitalism. In addition, however, post-socialist nostalgia also appeals to the desire to see oneself through the Other's desiring gaze (the lost structure of fantasy that both East and West mourn). That is, nostalgia also mourns the loss of the flattering fantasy – also thoroughly disenchanted by the East's experience of a market economy – by which the West perceived even the most banal elements of its everyday life to be an envied and unattainable luxury in the eyes of its ideological enemy. For example, a scene in *Moscow on the Hudson*, a Columbia Pictures film from (not inconsequentially) 1984, portrays the abundance of an average American grocery store as so overwhelming to new Russian émigré Vladimir that he keels over in a faint. In contrast, today's Western popular mythologies do not offer any such equivalent;

the 'Other' of the contemporary West, Islamic fundamentalism, exhibits no comparable fascination with the consumer paradise of modern capitalism.[10]

For other observers, on the other hand, post-socialist nostalgia offers a vision of popular resistance to capitalism that more traditional forms of political mobilization have failed to ensure. It gives voice not only to the loss of the fantasy of the West as imagined utopia, but also to the dissolution of socialism's own utopian aspirations (both the grandiose ones expressed by ideology and the more prosaic ones embodied in its consumer goods). This vision interprets post-socialist nostalgia as a critique of the present, as well as of the capitalist triumphalism that would discard the legacies of socialism wholesale without stopping to ask what might remain of value from the past, in terms of both politics and personal memory. As a result, it often collapses into a politics by which every nostalgic gesture towards the past is read as subversive, even though these same nostalgic gestures may be used with equal effectiveness to maintain the status quo. Thus, for these (predominantly Western) nostalgia enthusiasts, the value of nostalgic practices stems from the critical distance these practices are hoped to provide post-socialist individuals otherwise immersed into the culture of late capitalism.

While many local cultural commentators would tend to agree concerning the inherently political nature of nostalgic practices, for them the political meaning that nostalgia holds is typically the opposite: inherently conservative and politically dangerous. To use a distinction proposed by Gasan Gusejnov (2003), while in the case of nostalgia enthusiasts, the political meaning of nostalgic memory is shaped in a rhetorical field created by the opposition Soviet communism – American capitalism, the local critics usually see the field as defined by the parallel between communism and social nationalism. Given the shift of interpretative context, it is hardly surprising, then, that the ideological value of nostalgic practices shifts correspondingly. Instead of summoning hopes of resistance against the hegemony of neoliberalism, nostalgic practices signify a dangerous denial of socialism's totalitarian legacy, and a willingness to forget (and thus, risk repeating) the mistakes of the past. Although this viewpoint cannot be considered properly nostalgic (unless one introduces a category of nostalgic repulsion to counter the more self-explanatory nostalgic attraction), it does adhere to the logic of nostalgia in that it exhibits a similar preoccupation with the past, this time centred around the desire *not* to desire it, and it is thus equally fascinated by past fantasies as dangerous allurement or temptation to others.

Types of Nostalgic Practices

What has been the relationship of these various fantasies to the actual cultural practices of post-socialist nostalgia? Nostalgia may make visible the desire for a structure of fantasy now perceived as lost, but it does not seek to recreate these fantasies. Rather, it has taken on forms defined by structures of intention that fully inhabit the present-day realities of post-socialism.[11]

Thus, the first form of nostalgia to emerge after the transition was the commodification of the official symbols of communist ideology, such as busts of Lenin and Soviet medals. In Budapest, for example, young entrepreneurs opened a pizzeria called 'Marxim'; decorated with red banners and barbed wire, it is still in operation today. In Russia, entrepreneurial artists enriched the standard variety of painted wooden *matryoshka* dolls popular with the tourists by including satirical portrayals of stackable communist founders, Marx, Engels and Lenin, with Stalin, Khruschev and Gorbachev also making occasional appearance. But as the very speed with which these phenomena emerged makes clear, these cultural practices were not concerned with nostalgia itself, but rather with *making nostalgia possible* by establishing the necessary break between past and present. Mocking and ridiculing the ideological symbols associated with the socialist past, these practices self-consciously deprived previously potent images of their prior meaning. While the agenda to which this symbolic practice contributed was new, the practice itself was not. In fact, it drew directly on the tradition of subversive political humour under late socialism, when icons sacred for communist ideology were subverted through their incorporation into everyday profane contexts (as in jokes and anecdotes, or in the underground artistic trend of Sotsart started by Moscow painters Vitalii Komar and Alexander Melamid, who humorously used iconographic clichés of socialist realism in paintings with titles like 'Stalin and the Muses' or 'Stalin in front of a Mirror').[12] In a sense, late socialist subversion anticipated the post-socialist use of images in that it commercialized ideological icons before such commercialization became an actual possibility. The very name of Sotsart obviously evoked the more internationally recognized trend of Pop Art, which in its own way exposed the close connections between ideology and commercialism.[13]

Converting political icons into kitsch was thus part of the necessary symbolic work of that time. It rendered former icons powerless and enabled post-socialist subjects to look back at the past with no fear of its return. Although such a threat no longer remains, this type of nostalgia is nonetheless still much in evidence today (e.g., Budapest's Statue Park Museum of socialist-era statues; the socialist relics still widely available for sale on Arbat street in Moscow; and the Communism Tours widely available in many East European Cities).

The materials of such nostalgia (hammers and sickles, shades of 'communist' red) are familiar and its logic (mocking what once was presumably feared) is simple, unlike the more ambivalent pleasures discussed below. In contrast to the subversive and risky nature of these practices under socialism, the post-socialist production of Soviet-themed kitsch has been fuelled by market logic and is targeted primarily at the outsiders to

3.1 A stand advertising a communism-themed hostel and tours in Krakow train station. Photo by Olga Shevchenko

3.2 A leaflet for communism-themed tours in Krakow. Image courtesy of Crazy Guides®

whom it provides reassuring evidence that socialism is comfortably (and profitably) dead, and that capitalist logic reigns supreme, regulating the circulation of socialist relics as commodities. This nostalgia of political kitsch has thus been popular with foreign tourists and media, since it is the one most legible – and hence performed most emphatically – to non-locals.

Beginning in the mid 1990s, however, two other forms of nostalgic practices appeared, both characterized not by a concern with historical disjuncture but rather with establishing continuity between past and present selves. The first form of nostalgia, which might be glossed as 'Proustiana', is similar to political kitsch in that it is also expressed through the marketing, consumption and display of material culture. (Like kitsch, it is also very easily commodified, although the only place where it appears to be genuinely profitable so far is Germany.) Here, however, the objects of memory are not relics of the former regime's ideology, but rather the detritus of the previous era's everyday life, and they conjure up a humour based not on mockery, but rather ironic affection. They thus serve as what Winnicott (1953) terms 'transitional objects' in that they provide a convenient combination of materiality (the ability to be manipulated in the present) with their signification of the past state of the subject (much like the teddy bears in his classic example). Moreover, since many of these objects were products of socialist-era consumer culture, their sudden transformation in social value also enables commentary on the post-socialist East's disenchantment with the once-idealized West. The density of meaning and memory sedimented onto such objects has made them fashionable as commodities (the renewed popularity of East German brands in Germany; the temporary revival of the soda 'Bambi' in Hungary and of 'Baikal' and 'Buratino' in Russia, see figure 3.3); in curatorial practice (the exhibit *Our Happy Childhood* in the Historical Museum in Moscow; the exhibits *Kitsch and Cult* and *Fingerprint of the Twentieth Century* in Budapest), as well as popular and academic studies of nostalgia at home and abroad (such as the book *Szivárvány Áruház* (Rainbow Department Store, 2002), a collection of photographs and personal memories of socialist-era toys and products, which went through several editions). The popularity of documentaries as well as re-televised socialist-era films and television programs similarly demonstrate the success of 'Proustiana' in that these visual texts are often read as cultural artefacts of Soviet life.

But these films need not merely serve as objects of memory; the extra-diegetic sights and sounds they index also conjure up the settings and atmospheres that structured the socialist era. This next form of nostalgia similarly refers to everyday life under state socialism, yet while it intersects with nostalgia for socialist-era material culture, it is primarily concerned

3.3 Supermarket shelves lined with Soviet-era brands: *Baikal* and *Limonad* on the bottom, and 1980s-stylized *Pepsi-Kola* on the top. Photo by Olga Shevchenko.

with embodied knowledges and practices that composed everyday life. It seeks to evoke past embeddedness in both actual and metaphorical spaces of socialist-era sociality: the habitus (in the sense of ingrained dispositions) of late socialism. Here, a discourse of loss predominates over that of recovery, because while the materiality of objects gives the perception of greater access to and continuity with past selves, the cultural emotions and sensibilities of a lost age are less easily retrieved. Indeed, the 'sociality' these nostalgic practices attempt to evoke (nostalgia parties, group singing activities, theme cafes and restaurants like *Zhiguli* in Moscow and *Menza* in Budapest) could only come into existence as a coherent entity once the era was perceived to have irrevocably passed, and thus could be fantasized as desirable in the first place.

The attempt, however partial, to conjure up this mode of being in the world is central to the success of such programs as *Starye Pesni o Glavnom* (Old Songs about the Most Important), which, between 1995 and 2000, relied on the physical re-enactment of the communal singing rituals of the past[14] in the hope of reconnecting with lost sociability through the reproduction of the same bodily motions. Mimicking the practices of informal kitchen gatherings of the 1960s and 1970s, this show offered its studio audience the opportunity to join voices with celebrities of the same era in singing songs of their youth. These re-enactments of socialist-era rituals of communality, however, entailed a crucial slippage of meaning. Originally valued for their disconnection from the world of socialist officialdom, these practices were now misrecognized as representative of the entire socialist experience, thus allowing participants to overlook their initial political function (cf. Faibisovich 1998).

As these appeals to communality make clear, what both nostalgia for material culture and nostalgia for the habitus of socialism share is a discourse on cultural belonging that stands in stark opposition to the international language of political kitsch described in the first type of nostalgia above. Both nostalgias depend upon acts of reading and recognition that demonstrate competence at deciphering a cultural inheritance (however grudgingly embraced) that outsiders are assumed incapable of comprehending. For example, a collection of socialist songs called 'The Best of Communism' was number one in Hungary for several weeks in 1998, but while the foreign media interpreted this popularity in terms of political kitsch, Hungarian informants explained that they valued these songs neither despite nor because of their political content. Instead, their nostalgia was based upon the personal and communal experiences associated with these songs (singing around the campfire, stealing one's first kiss, etc.), rather than the ideology they represented. Similarly, in the case of socialist-era consumer goods, both Russians and Hungarians explain their nostalgic attachment not as 'proof' of the superiority of the former regime and its economic system, but rather as an expression of national loyalty. In other words, the relevant axis of comparison for them is not capitalism versus socialism, but rather the West versus Hungary/Russia. (The irony here is that many of these products were bought by Western-owned multinationals during the 1990s and thus remain 'Hungarian' or 'Russian' only in the memories of their consumers.)

Another type of nostalgia similarly defined in terms of its interpretative practice is the fashionability of socialist historicity itself with the generation too young to have concrete memories of state socialism. This is not a difference in the *object* of nostalgia (as in the first three types listed above), but rather in the subject's *relationship* to it: one of abstraction rather than materiality; historical citation rather than a metonymic slide into personal memory; ironic distance rather than longing. Those who practice such nostalgia are not interested in consuming a specific historical image or object, but rather the aura of 'pastness' to be found, for example, at the popular socialist-era-themed *Cha-Cha-Cha* coffee shop located in the early 2000s in a Metro underpass in Budapest. Evoking a hip, generalized sense of retro without being anchored by a specific local history, these sites exemplify what Fritzsche calls 'nostalgia without melancholy', and Marilyn Ivy (1995: 56) has termed 'nostalgia of style' – a postmodern nostalgia without a referent and hence without pain, as opposed to 'modernist nostalgia', which still longs for an origin.

Finally, if 'nostalgia without melancholy' adheres to nostalgic forms while emptying them of their emotional content, another form of historical politics retains the longing for origins but foregrounds the historical promiscuity inherent to nostalgia, with practices that aim to preserve national identity through a non-discriminatory embrace of all events and periods of national history. It is accomplished through practices of state institutions, from minor ones, such as the issue of historical postal stamps, to large-scale, such as the notorious return of the Soviet national anthem passed by the Russian Duma with Putin's approval in 2000. While these moves are often thought and spoken of in terms of nostalgia, nostalgic language does not seem adequate for describing the mechanism of these practices' effectiveness, since they draw their power not from exploiting popular attachment to a particular historical era, but rather from lumping all historical referents – socialist and earlier – together in an effort to achieve an unproblematic historical continuity and legitimacy.[15] The debate around Russian state symbols demonstrates the importance of this distinction: along with the Soviet-era national anthem, the Duma also approved the pre-revolutionary Russian tri-coloured flag and the two-headed eagle as symbols of the Russian Federation, thus suggesting that the task of integrating diverse historical periods trumped the nostalgic task of pledging allegiance to any particular one.[16] It is this all-too-wide historical embrace that is increasingly becoming the go-to strategy of working through the past in Putin's Russia.

Ironically, what necessitates this strategy in the first place is arguably the fact that *all* periods of Russian history are experienced as potentially discreditable. In other words, it is the recognition of *impossibility* of nostalgia for a specific historical period that enables these practices to hold broad rhetorical sway.

Nostalgia beyond Good and Evil

The multiplicity of nostalgic types discussed above points to the danger associated with naturalizing the distinction that is often drawn both by local cultural observers (Ivanova 1997) and in academic discussions (Boym 2001) between 'good' (ironic, self-reflexive, elegiac) nostalgias and their 'bad' (aggressive, political, reactionary) doppelgangers. 'Good' ('reflective') forms of nostalgia are either interpreted as apolitical, or are associated with subversive, critical, progressive politics (although what the exact take on this politics may be differs among commentators). Correspondingly, 'bad' ('restorative') nostalgia is seen as explicitly reactionary and regressive, and is typically interpreted as evidence of the inability to part with the past. Evidence of this type of nostalgia embraces phenomena as diverse as the revival of the old TV programs, the popular attachment to the Brezhnev era (in Russia) and Kádár era (in Hungary) that emerged in polls in the early 2000s, and the Russian hardliner V. Anpilov's opposition to the removal of Lenin's corpse from the Mausoleum.

As we have been pointing out throughout this chapter, not every wistful reference to the past can productively fit under the heading of nostalgia. For the category of nostalgia to retain analytical rigour, it has to be distinguished from other types of investment in the past, such as images of the Golden Age, nationalist mythologies and reactionary politics more broadly. Peter Fritzsche (2002) makes the case for such separation by pointing out that while a reactionary insists on the necessity of reinvigorating lost traditions and installing them in the present, nostalgic longing – which reinforces the very distance between past and present by attempting to breach it – acknowledges the impossibility of doing so, preferring instead to contemplate and lament the bygone moments from afar.[17] Once such qualifications are made, however, the task of distinguishing between 'bad' and 'good' cases of post-socialist nostalgia has to be reformulated into the task of exploring the distinction between the nostalgic practices themselves and the political programs to which these practices may or may not contribute. In other words, the ideal types of 'reflective' and 'restorative' are most productive not when they refer to the ethnographic types of nostalgic practices discussed in the previous section (and which, via Fritzsche, cannot be restorative by definition), but to the political projects into which they can be incorporated in each particular context.

Ethnographically, the problem with applying the categories of 'restorative' and 'reflective' nostalgia to actual behaviours is that most nostalgic practices tend to fall in between, or (more frequently) function as both. Thus, as Natalia Ivanova (1997) points out, while the Russian TV Show *Starye Pesni o Glavnom* was envisioned by its creators as an exercise in irony and self-estrangement, the bulk of its audience whole-heartedly embraced and celebrated the opportunity to join their voices in tunes of their past without a trace of sarcasm. Nonetheless, sincere as the audience's involvement may be in this case, one would be hard-pressed to argue that the longing for the lost home (i.e., 'restorative' longing) trumped the longing for longing itself (i.e., the 'reflective' one) in their enjoyment of the program. The distinction seems particularly muddled since many of the Soviet-era songs featured in the program contained elements of longing for far-off lands and times in their original lyrics. These tourist ballads and urban adventure songs spoke of the Soviet youth's desires for travel and action, and extolled the virtues of exploration and displacement. It would be a simplification, therefore, to argue that these songs, as now reproduced in the program, attest to the audience's longing for the 'home' of socialist sociality, since the home itself is imagined here in terms of homelessness and longing.[18]

To state this more broadly, the same practice may be used to signify a number of different things: a discomfort with the new expressed in a wistful longing for the old sociality; or, on the contrary, skilfulness at consuming the past with 'proper' ironic distance by spinning socialist retro in new capitalist ways; or even the spirit of *stiob*, the sarcastic political humour under the previous regime. Indeed, the same emotions may coexist within the same individual. After all, material success and fluency with the new transnational 'rules of the game' does not preclude a resistance to fitting seamlessly within the new global order. In Hungary, for example, a popular ad campaign in 2001 for the beer Dreher played upon its audience's perceived ambivalence by presenting a dazzling selection of slang, images and icons from the socialist 1980s with the slogan 'We speak one language' (*Egy nyelvet beszélünk*). This assertion of solidarity (and, to outsiders, cultural intranslatability) ended with a group of successful, yuppie Hungarian thirty-somethings, enjoying their Dreher beers at a fashionable bar. It thus used post-socialist nostalgia not to mourn the past, but to support the status quo by suggesting that one can 'have it all': be culturally distinctive and, at the same time, produce oneself as European by consuming and achieving at 'Western' levels (Nadkarni 2010).

Apart from the polysemy of nostalgic practices, there is another factor that complicates the task of making an assessment of a given practice's inherent political significance: in order to retain an aura of authenticity, nostalgia has a stake in insisting on its political neutrality: its apolitical if not anti-political quality. This tendency holds even (or, rather, especially) in nostalgic expressions that explicitly or implicitly critique today's state of affairs, since the legitimacy of the challenge that nostalgia advances against the post-socialist political order is premised precisely on the non-partisan quality of memory that alone can lend it an aura of objectivity. Thus, in our fieldwork experience, even explicitly critical statements of older Russians were often preceded by qualifications that denied the speaker's investment in a particular political agenda. For example, denouncing the corruption of the 1990s, Vera, a Muscovite cleaning lady in her forties, told one of the authors, 'I am not going to claim that the communists were not stealing. Yes, they stole. But we did not know, did not have to see it. Yes, there were many negative aspects. And yet, I would say . . . that I lived decently. Perhaps not in luxury, no, but there was some kind of soulfulness among people. Everyone had more or less the same way of life'. If political criticism is concealed here as nostalgia, nostalgia itself is concealed as a non-partisan account.

Considering Vera's political convictions (she consistently voted Communist throughout the 1990s), one would be tempted to question the political neutrality of her nostalgia. Yet it may be instructive to compare her recollections of bygone soulfulness with the expressions of nostalgia articulated by young Russians and Hungarians in their memories of material culture and private lives of the socialist era. The recurrent refrain that accompanies memories of one's childhood possessions, pioneer camp adventures or school encounters sounds not unlike Vera's (and is also frequently couched in terms of soulfulness): the era was, in the words of one Hungarian informant, 'stupid, but nice: a part of my life'. Why do such statements sound less ideologically objectionable to liberal readers than Vera's musings? Why do they comfortably fall into the category of reflective nostalgia, while Vera's memories of socialism belong to the far less attractive and more politically dangerous restorative kind?

One possibility is that the rhetoric of Proustiana is simply more credible in its purported political neutrality. As its very name suggests, it has respectable foreign ancestry, and its manifestations are not confined to the former socialist countries. After all, as many of our informants pointed out, 'isn't everyone nostalgic for their childhood?' Moreover, this understanding of Proustiana as being a more global and hence more neutral practice has another implication, given that it is practiced primarily by a younger, urban/cosmopolitan yuppie class with the careers and disposable income to purchase these objects and to frequent trendy socialist-themed bars (as well as to write editorials and cultural commentary denouncing the older generation's nostalgia). By asserting the difference between their own forms of nostalgia and that of their older and, typically, less well-travelled compatriots, this ascending elite can 'have it all' in yet another way: to be nostalgic and yet progressive, to indulge in pleasurable melancholy for the past as they enjoy the fruits of the present. And while there is no reason to doubt that nostalgic desire can, indeed, combine all these things, it appears that in this particular case, their modernity comes at the expense of projecting political backwardness onto nostalgic practices elsewhere.

Does all of the above mean that nostalgic practices cannot be assessed in terms of their political and ethical implications, and that any value judgment should remain beyond the reach of social and cultural analysis? This need not be the case. The principles for such an assessment, however, should focus not on creating taxonomies of inherently reactionary and progressive practices or intentions, but rather on the ways in which these practices fit into the larger field of political possibilities in every given case. In other words, the kernel of political significance of nostalgic practices is determined by the larger sociohistorical logic of national post-socialist development, so that identical practices, or even identical intentions animating these practices, fulfil radically different social functions depending on the context in which they unfold.

Nostalgia between Innocence and Responsibility

As the examples above make clear, the nostalgias we have described and the moral evaluations assigned to them tend to fall along generational lines, and indeed they function as important signposts of group belonging. Message boards on the internet in the early 2000s, for example, featured topics that refer specifically to a child's experience of late socialism; responses to the questions 'You come from the [19]70s/[19]80s if . . .' include 'Your parents were summoned to school because you were trading [foreign] gum wrappers right in front of the teachers' room', or 'You remember that you shouldn't take candy or chewing gum from foreigners; they say one boy was poisoned that way'. The slower pace of obsolescence of socialist goods, however, also meant that a greater range of ages shared similar experiences and objects, so that consumer 'generations' under socialism did not change at the same pace as today, where the difference of a few years can mean mutual unintelligibility in terms of popular culture. Thus, the appeal to socialist memory in itself can function as an appeal to collective experience (or more precisely, an experience fantasized as collective the moment it vanished). Socialist nostalgia both reinforces generational boundaries and provides the fantasy of uniting across them, as when members of different generations join their voices in singing the 'yard songs' of the past.

What enables this fantasy of cross-generational belonging, however, is that the younger generation's nostalgia is often misrecognized as following the same logic as that of the older generation, both by the individuals themselves and by cultural critics and observers. To some extent this perception is accurate: all generations are subject to Proustiana, although the physical objects that trigger it may differ across generational lines.[19] But the older generation of both Russians and Hungarians does not always partake in the more consumption-oriented nostalgic practices of those who came of age as communism ended, and nor does this younger generation intend for practices constructed as both nostalgic and fashionable to be open to all. Indeed, those who spent much of their adult lives under socialism have had their own reasons for voicing nostalgic sentiment. These reasons usually reflect this older generation's economic deprivation and sense of alienation from post-socialist reality, although this rhetoric of alienation (which presupposes a preceding stage of authenticity) should not be taken at face value, since in itself it can be thought of as part and parcel of the nostalgia industry. A more adequate way to conceptualize this experience of post-socialist transition is as an experience of radical disjunction between one's habitus and the 'field' of cultural and economic practice – a condition that generates what Bourdieu (1977) calls 'hysteresis of habitus': the unsettling lack of fit between one's internalized dispositions and the new 'rules of the game' that constantly reminds individuals of their lack of agency and control. Understandably subject to hysteresis of habitus to a greater extent than their younger counterparts, the generations that came of age prior to the mid 1980s may voice nostalgic sentiment not as a way to express their allegiance to the socialist field of practice, but rather to articulate their frustration over the current state of disjuncture.

For the younger generation who came of age during the political upheavals of the late 1980s and early 1990s, what has been at stake is not the assertion of past agency and present-day alienation, but rather recuperating the experiences of an era now remembered as innocent and apolitical. A number of films have thus attempted to appeal to this demographic by chronicling their adolescent turmoil against a backdrop of political transition. In these films, personal rites of passage invariably take priority over national ones, such as the teenaged indifference to the defining landmarks of Hungary's peaceful political transformations in the film *Moscow Square* (2001), a gentle comedy that follows a group of graduating high school students in the final days of socialism. Indeed, this emphasis upon adolescence is metaphorical as well as literal, given the widespread perception that these societies were collectively forced into adulthood by the political transition.

Projecting nostalgia into childhood makes it possible to evade its political implications by tying it to the period when perception is by definition pre-political. Those who came of age at the time of the political transition are old enough to have concrete memories of the previous regime, yet young enough to discard possible questions of responsibility and petty compromise altogether. Yet the very fact that these subjects explicitly dismiss their nostalgia as mere longing for the universal experience of childhood suggests the opposite: the persistent suspicion that the politics of these practices are something that needs to be justified. Each new film or fad has thus been accompanied by articles and reviews that make a point of arguing that the objects and practices themselves had little to do with politics, and even when they did – i.e., the Young Pioneer songs mentioned earlier – they were not actually perceived as such at the time. In other words, these subjects claim, nostalgia for the relics of an era does not mean nostalgia for its political ideology as well, any more than nostalgia for the 1980s in thirty-something Americans represents an endorsement of the policies of the Reagan administration. The difference is simply that the material culture of this generation's youth is an artefact of a now-discredited regime, and so any manifestation of nostalgia tends to be placed within a political frame, by locals and foreigners alike.

But just as childhood is a time when one is not even aware of political considerations, the objects now targeted by nostalgic desire are associated with the practices and material culture of everyday life, a sphere that many people choose to remember as similarly depoliticized. That is, not only are people nostalgic for the dreams of their youth, and for a certain level of material comfort and security provided by the paternalist state, but they are also nostalgic for the very distinction between public political involvement and private material concerns encouraged in post-1956 Hungary and in stagnation-era USSR. Unlike the nostalgia for one's understandably limited perception of childhood, however, this nostalgia is based upon a misrecognition, since the material sphere *was* political: Kádár's and Brezhnev's regimes drew their legitimacy from the unwritten social contract through which the populace retreated from public involvement into their own private affairs and material concerns, receiving in exchange relative security and freedom from political harassment. This political nature of the material sphere accounts for the emphasis post-socialist discourses have placed upon consumption and consumer culture.

It also underlies the frequent adage that 'in Brezhnev times, everyone had enough to eat'.

Nostalgic memory, then, is purposefully constructed as non-political in both the object of its longing and in its contemporary implications. But this is where the Russian and Hungarian cases differ, since the political context in which such remembering takes place plays a crucial role in how politically (in)consequential nostalgic memory can claim to be. In 2001, for example, the head of the socialist Hungarian Workers' Party proposed that the state permit the erection of a statue to János Kádár, who had led Hungary through three decades of relative economic security under socialism. One of Hungary's recently established commercial television stations, TV2, devoted its weekly news roundup *Diary* (*Napló*), to examining this campaign and to collecting viewer opinions via its weekly phone-in poll. To the presenters' apparent surprise, 80 per cent of those who phoned in agreed that Kádár deserved a statue of his own, and the question for the following week's poll ('Is it better now to be young?') also received an emphatic response in favour of the past.

This catchphrase later found its way back into public currency as the Workers' Party campaign slogan for the national elections in 2002, but the party was unable to leverage the emotional capital of Kádárism into political gain. Instead, in the first round of elections, the Workers' Party once again failed to win the 5 per cent necessary to gain parliamentary representation. Why did this nostalgia fail when imported into the political arena? As the interviews *Diary* conducted during their polls made clear, nostalgia for Kádárism could only have political force insofar as it was constructed as explicitly non-political. That is, as long as politicians, celebrities and average Hungarians alike could justify their fond memories solely in terms of material comfort and security, the emotions summoned by nostalgia were effective across the political spectrum, which at that time was split fairly evenly between right and left. The Hungarian Socialist Party (HSP), impatient to reinvent itself as a European socialist party with no links to the past, could make vague reference to protecting the concerns of the 'simple people' without taking responsibility for the injustices of socialism; while the right-wing could dismiss nostalgic practices as merely the expression of dissatisfaction with post-socialism on the whole rather than an endorsement of communism and hence a specific rejection of right-wing anti-communist discourse. In contrast, bringing nostalgia explicitly into the political sphere would invalidate its usefulness and emotional legitimacy. It would subject the left to a critique of the Kádárist regime's lack of democratic values, and it would be read as an overwhelming rejection of right-wing ideology.

Indeed, nostalgia would prove to be effective politically only when it was invoked as a dangerous threat. In the months preceding the 2002 elections, the right-wing coalition government then in power argued that its main opponent, the HSP, was not a new European party but merely the inheritor of the sins and corruption of the past era. Warning that an HSP victory would mean the 'return of communism' to Hungary, these right-wing opponents thus targeted nostalgia as the sinister whitewashing of the socialist past. This war against nostalgia was exemplified in the government's opening of a 'House of Terror' museum, dedicated to the victims of fascism and communism, just months before the elections took place. The museum's exhibition included not only relics of authoritarian rule, such as tanks and torture chambers, but the same everyday consumer objects and socialist artefacts that had already been recuperated as nostalgia. In so doing, the House of Terror sought to delegitimize post-socialist nostalgia and its self-definition as apolitical, by implying that such Proustiana should be regarded as instruments of political terror, rather than objects of nostalgic affection. Ultimately, the HSP would win a narrow victory over its right-wing opponents, but the continued popularity of the House of Terror over the past decade suggests that such attempts to discredit – or at least introduce ambivalence into – nostalgic memory have nonetheless found a receptive audience.

Going back to the *Diary* poll, a similarly nostalgic breakdown of public sentiment is not at all unthinkable in the Russian context: a 2004 poll by Yuri Levada Centre reports that 46 per cent of the poll sample prefer the pre-perestroika state of affairs, although only 5 per cent see return of this era as possible (Press-vypusk 2004). However, the (mis)memories of socialist-era political disengagement appear more problematic here because they embody not only recollections of the past, but blueprints for the present. In other words, if the return of socialism at this point in history is widely recognized as impossible, the return of the familiar social contract of the stagnation era and the promise of stability in exchange for political disengagement represent the very essence of Putin's domestic politics. The non-political nature of nostalgic memory thus becomes incorporated into the profoundly political project of deepening the gap between the 'authorities' and the populace, and the material memory of socialism turns into a stake in this game.

This trend towards employing nostalgia politically can be read, for example, in the electoral materials of the businessman Aleksandr Pleshakov, founder of the Transaero airline and a member of pro-Putin party United Russia who ran for Duma elections in 2003. Pleshakov's strategy of attracting voters included repeated appeals to the shared experiences of socialism, from the memories of the 'holiday feasts', which 'smelled of laurel leaf and vanilla' and were preceded by 'store rush, queues for chicken, canned green peas *Globus* and *Ptich'e Moloko* candy boxes' to the experience of *subbotnik* (supposedly 'voluntary' weekend labours – OS) preceded by 'a ritual drink chased by cheese spreads and sausage for 2 roubles 20 kopecks a kilo'.[20] Innocuous by themselves, memories of everyday realities of socialism were invoked here as a type of political mandate. They were expected not only to position Pleshakov as 'one of our own', an individual sharing the readers' experiences and memories, but also to implicitly point to holiday feasts and collective drinking rituals as the ultimate stuff of life, thus sidelining political involvement and public participation as something inconsequential and unnecessary. The non-political promise of nostalgia, already witnessed in the Hungarian case, here turns into a tool of political alienation, uncontested by rivalling political parties.

Furthermore, because the longing for the lost fantasy of the West can coexist in the Russian case with the longing for the fantasy of one's own imperial presence, nostalgic recollections retain a possibility of yet another slippage: the very same practices/images that signify a lost body of cultural knowledge for some may be read as longing for the lost imperial grandeur by others. The leaflet for a karaoke cruise on board the Alexander Blok cruise ship illustrates this duality well. In the Hungarian context, a poster like this would most likely be read along the lines of the Dreher beer commercial discussed above, and it is not impossible that the actual clients of the karaoke cruise ship would partake in this reading as well. But given the images used in the leaflet, another reading is possible, one that accentuates imperial pride and the mourning for the lost edge in the global competition of the superpowers (in which the conquest of space was, of course, one of the privileged arenas).

Practices of nostalgia, as a result, retain in Russia a specific open-endedness that permits not only multiple readings, but also a possibility of misrecognition by those who enact them of their own motives. Disaffection and longing caused by the loss of a utopian fantasy can easily be misread as a longing for the Empire's lost greatness. For an example of such a mechanism of misrecognition, consider the much-discussed intelligentsia's drift towards populist and traditionalist politics (see Dubin 2001). Originally fuelled by the loss of the intelligentsia's utopian fantasy of the democratic capitalist West (a fantasy in which the intelligentsia as a social group was particularly invested), this disaffection is now interpreted (often by members of the intelligentsia themselves) as a mourning for the Soviet imperial presence, which is now phrased in terms of a 'strong state that is respected in the international arena'. On the surface, nothing could be further apart than these two fantasies. But the effect produced by the loss of one is so similar to the effect triggered by the loss of the other that two formerly opposite groups

3.4 Karaoke cruise flyer

(the democratically minded intelligentsia of 1989 and 'etatist' nationalists) often find themselves on the same side of the barricades.

The similarities in the nostalgic sentiments visible in Hungary and Russia, therefore, should not detract from an appreciation of the very real differences in how these similar practices function in each particular case. A number of other contextual factors contribute to this difference as well.

To note the most obvious one, since the socialist project was very much an import into Hungary, appeals for its political rehabilitation are all but impossible for parties across the political spectrum.[21] In addition, Hungary's membership in the EU gave the term 'irretrievability' an entirely different meaning from the one it has in the Russian context. In the former case, nostalgia's fixation on irretrievability has the meaning of being caught in the irreversible flow of European integration, while in the latter, it has more to do with the point of origin (and thus the irrevocable drift of a former superpower) than with the point of a (yet uncertain) destination.[22] Irreversible as both of these transformations may be, they thus generated different possibilities for collecting political dividends from avowedly non-political nostalgia. Hungarians, as it were, could 'afford' to be nostalgic as long as they saw no actual possibility of return to the Kádár era, whereas Russian nostalgic practices continuously face the danger of generating political capital for populist and imperialist projects. Thus, when individuals indulge in nostalgia, the important difference lies not with the inherently different structure of nostalgic desire itself in the Russian case, but rather with the wider space of political possibilities within which this desire can (or cannot, as in the Hungarian case) generate political capital.

There is, however, a sense in which, even in the Hungarian context, nostalgia has played an implicitly, if not explicitly, political role. Post-socialist nostalgia has enabled Hungarians 'to not talk about the past while talking about it': to retain childhood memories while refusing to pass definitive judgment upon the larger political and historical context within which they took place.[23] For some, this has provided a way to maintain personal continuity in the face of historical disjuncture and irresolution; that is, nostalgia enables its subjects to integrate their memories into personal narrative without either endorsing or condemning an era not yet perceived to have fully resolved into 'history'. For others, particularly the younger generation, the value of nostalgia has resided in its function as a communicative practice. It has offered a common idiom for discussing the past with others, regardless of how these memories fit into larger family or social histories during the socialist era, and independent of how positively or negatively Hungarians choose to evaluate the former system as a whole. From this standpoint, nostalgia for the everyday life of Kádár's Hungary appears to have provided one of the few safe discourses available for talking about the past. Indeed, given the often-polarized political and cultural climate of post-socialist Hungary,[24] such nostalgia has offered perhaps the *only* idiom through which to find common ground in discussions of the socialist era.

But as the fantasy of 'having it all' promised by the Dreher beer commercial suggests, such common ground may be only possible as long as the present appears to have triumphed over the past. That is, the condition for such nostalgia seems to be not only the irretrievability of state socialism, but the superiority of what emerged to replace it. With the recent years of economic and political crisis in Hungary, as well as the disenchantment with the failed promises of transition more generally, nostalgic practices have thus faded in popularity. In some cases, the waning of nostalgia has merely signalled the success of the commodification of specific relics of the socialist past and their integration into the present day, such that these former symbols of the past have become almost entirely detached from their referent. In other instances, the concept of nostalgia has itself become stigmatized, as when it is invoked to characterize the older generation's reactionary longing for the security and stability of the previous era. Now read as a socially divisive idiom of entitlement, such 'nostalgia' has become the target of broad resentment and political critique. The triumphalist nostalgia once pervasive in the early 2000s, however, has disappeared, along with the fantasy of mastering both the present and past that it then made visible. Thus, while we might expect that the experience of economic and political upheaval would only fuel nostalgic longing, it has instead overturned the very conditions for its possibility.

Conclusion

In May 1999, the Sakharov Museum in Moscow opened an exhibit entitled *The Idea of the Museum of the USSR*. The idea behind this exhibit was to generate responses and create a blueprint for a permanent exposition of the same name that would, as formulated by the Museum's director and human rights activist Yuri Samodurov, help the new democratic Russia 'to comprehend and experience the epoch of the USSR's existence as an epoch of a different civilization which sank into Lethe like Atlantis' (Samodurov n.d.). The response that the exhibit generated was highly controversial. Some visitors were happy to partake in a collective project of defining the nature of the Soviet era; many of the themes they proposed for display in the future museum would be already familiar to a reader of this chapter: artefacts of socialist period, elements of material culture, 'official' and 'unofficial' art and so on. 'I would like [for the museum] to show everyday life, with hopes, love, wishes for the better', wrote one visitor in the exhibit's Guest Book, 'lace curtains and children's beds. And how my Mom had to toil to procure even the bare necessities for her children'. Yet the idea of such a museum also elicited protests that came not only from communist hard liners, but also from those who saw Samodurov's project as a dangerous attempt to cater to the public's nostalgic sentiment. For them, the initiative meant that 'the rumours of the Empire's death were greatly exaggerated', as one liberal critic put it, and the Sakharov Museum was in the process of creating 'a living corpse' (Molok 1999).

The controversy surrounding the project of the museum illustrates the complexities and tensions inherent to the study of nostalgia. In light of the political leverage held in Russia by the Communist Party, the reservations of the museum's opponents were not hard to comprehend. Yet, given the idea's authorship, it is clear that imperial nostalgia was not the only – and, indeed, not the main – sensibility underlying this project. And if that is the case, one has to wonder whether, in resisting the sentiment that kept much of East European socialist-themed projects going, the museum's opponents were not, in fact, refusing their compatriots the humanity of their memory of the past and whether by their vocal protests against 'museumifying the Empire' they did not, in fact, keep it more alive.[25]

Whether due to the criticisms it had faced, or because of causes external to the project, the Museum of the USSR failed to materialize in the years following this announcement. However, in recent years, three more initiatives have been unveiled, each promoting what the authors considered 'the first Museum of the USSR'.[26] This time around, the rationale for the creation of such a museum was strikingly different. 'Museum of the USSR will bring in billions' was the headline of an article reporting on the discussion surrounding a proposal unveiled in 2012 at a cultural forum in Ulianovsk (Chernysheva 2012). In keeping with this logic of commodification, the architectural critic Georgii Revzin, too, justified his own proposal of a Museum of the USSR in Moscow by the need to build up 'the brand of the city' (*brend goroda*) by exploiting the aspects that make Moscow uniquely attractive to foreign tourists (Zubova 2011). But while the socialist past as an object of nostalgic desire may become increasingly instrumentalized, a parallel process of enchantment seems to be taking place among precisely the liberal circles of the Russian intelligentsia who eschewed the pleasures of nostalgia for socialism but who continue to mourn the opportunities lost during the early years after 1989. It may thus be time to think about post-socialist nostalgia in yet another sense: as nostalgia for the promised future of post-socialism itself and for the optimism that its early moments seemed to herald.

Acknowledgements

This is a revised version of the text that first appeared in *Ab Imperio* as 'The Politics of Nostalgia: A Case for Comparative Analysis of Postsocialist

Practices' (Maya Nadkarni and Olga Shevchenko, *Ab Imperio* 2004 [2]: 487–519).

Notes

1. Cf. the work of American sociologist Fred Davis who interprets nostalgia as a by-product of massive identity dislocations associated with social change without, however, historicizing the notion of social change itself (Davis 1979).

2. *Iduschie Vmeste* were later reorganized into *Nashi* in 2005 and Yakemenko himself was appointed Head of the Federal Youth Agency. In 2012 he announced that the *Nashi* youth movement, too, would be reorganized and shortly thereafter he was removed from his post with the Federal Youth Agency, so the future fate of the movement is unclear.

3. Admittedly, the factual accuracy of this statement, particularly when pertaining to the period of late socialism, is contestable at best (Yurchak 1997).

4. The quotation comes from the Moral Codex of Membership published on the now-defunct organization's website. Retrieved from <http://www.idushie.ru/rus/about/kodeks/index.php> (accessed 5 May 2004).

5. In this context, it is notable that Germany, which is the space where East and West came to look each other in the face, is the country most marked by the 'nostalgia industry' (Berdahl 1999).

6. The only remaining – and much utilized – option is the internal comparison through which many post-socialist subjects continue to normalize their condition in reference to 'others' who are doing worse. The 'others' of such comparisons, of course, are now almost exclusively the speakers' compatriots.

7. Indeed, there is evidence that even during the pre-war years, consumption was shaping up in the USSR to become an important arena of ideological competition with the capitalist West (Gronow 2003).

8. In fact, as a result of conflation between the two, objects that were originally produced in the course of a (failing) competition with, and often direct borrowing from, the West, may now be misrecognized as emblematic of the socialist 'abundance for all'.

9. Such as *Moscow Square* (*Moszkva tér*, 2001), *Sunshine Alley* (*Sonnenallee*, 1999) and *Good Bye Lenin!* (2003).

10. Some reactions to the bin-Laden-orchestrated attacks of 9/11, however, suggested that Western thinking was still caught in a mental warp of assuming the desiring gaze of its political Others. Thus, in the days following the attacks, the US media heroized everyday acts of leisure and consumption, such as attending baseball games and shopping at the mall. These activities were not only viewed as a demonstration of national indomitability and economic patriotism, but as a way to taunt bin Laden, who presumably envied such recreation while he 'hid in his cave'.

11. In other words, we argue that, in contrast to the two Gusejnov's models mentioned above, the actual practices of today's nostalgia exist in a different rhetorical field – one defined by tension between socialism and post-socialism.

12. See an article by Masha Lipman for a fascinating discussion of other ways in which late-socialist political humour remains unexpectedly relevant for the circulation of today's political images (Lipman 2004).

13. But while Pop Art approached commercial brands as ideology, Sotsart was rather concerned with exposing ideology as a brand.

14. See Paul Connerton for a discussion of the power that corporeal rituals have to create symbolic solidarities and to link individuals with the past (Connerton 1989).

15. Ilya Kalinin makes this point compellingly in Kalinin 2011.

16. The same historical omnivorousness was revealed in the electoral propaganda posters of United Russia in 2003, which featured images of Stalin and Budennyi alongside with those of Andrei Sakharov and Alexander Solzhenitsyn. A testimony to the fact that these posters are animated by a logic different from nostalgia is that a portrait of the recently deceased post-Soviet film star Sergei Bodrov graced the posters as well.

17. Renata Salecl points out that it is this disengaged sensibility that gives a nostalgic some degree of mental and psychological stability: since the desired period is irrevocably gone, the mourning individual need not take any responsibility for the present (Salecl 2000).

18. Cf. our earlier discussion of nostalgia as desire for the past structure of desire. Given this definition, the longing for home constitutes the longing for the fantasies and desires that structure this presumed site of origin. The very distinction between home and longing in the context of nostalgic desire thus becomes suspect.

19. Journalist Yulia Kalinina notes a peculiar role reversal that took place at the exhibition *Our Happy Childhood*: 'It is the adults that run the show. They rush from one display to another in enormous agitation, exclaiming "I had this one! And you? And me too! And this one, too!" The juniors follow them in quiet disbelief' (Kalinina 2002: 6).

20. Gennadii Krasukhin, who discussed Pleshakov's electoral materials in a liberal web-based journal (Krasukhin 2003), noted that his soliloquy entailed a telling slippage: unlike the cake of the same name, candy sets *Ptich'e Moloko* were never available for open sale; they could be purchased only in closed nomenklatura stores. Attempting to build solidarity by tapping into shared practical knowledge, Pleshakov thus unwittingly reveals his privileged background (and indeed, the bio blurb on the news portal Lenta.ru identifies him as the son of Petr Pleshakov, the Soviet minister of Radio Industry).

21. A testimony to this crucial difference in the political landscapes onto which nostalgic practices are projected is the fact that these practices threatened different political factions in the two countries in question. While nostalgic desire for socialism appeared most dangerous to the liberal and cosmopolitan

Russians, in Hungary it tended to evoke protest predominantly from right-wing nationalists.

22. Both ascension to the EU and the loss of the superpower status can, of course, be evaluated negatively as well as positively depending on the ideological position of the actor.

23. The same 'pacifying' effect of nostalgia could be observed during Paul McCartney's *Back in the USSR* concert in Moscow in 2003, when individuals from Vladimir Putin to the former dissidents could nostalgically recollect the days of their socialist-era 'Beatle-mania' without dwelling for too long on the fact that at the time, they had belonged to diametrically opposed ideological camps. Indeed, much of the event's success could be thought of in terms of the opportunities it allowed to a wide range of individuals to partake in the same collective identity framed in the now obsolete terms of the Cold War.

24. Historical politics in the first decade of post-socialist Hungary focused upon the failed revolution against the Soviets in 1956 as a way of distancing the more recent experience of Kádár's 'soft dictatorship' and evading the negotiated and bureaucratic nature of Hungary's political transition itself. While this emphasis was initially effective in excising Hungary's decades of post-1956 normalization, the memory of 1956 later became so politicized that its interpretations divided rather than united Hungarian post-socialist national identity.

25. Indeed, as James Young has argued aphoristically in his study of Holocaust memorialization, 'the surest engagement with memory lies in its perpetual irresolution' (Young 1993: 21).

26. One museum was purportedly opened in Cheliabinsk, the other two were proposed in Ulianovsk and in Moscow.

References

Berdahl, D. 1999. '"(N)Ostalgie" for the Present: Memory, Longing, and East German Things', *Ethnos* 64(2): 192–211.

Bourdieu, P. 1977. *Outline of a Theory of Practice*. Cambridge: Cambridge University Press.

Boym, S. 2001. *The Future of Nostalgia*. New York: Perseus Books.

Buck-Morss, S. 1991. *The Dialectics of Seeing: Walter Benjamin and the Arcades Project*. Cambridge: MIT Press.

——. 2000. *Dreamworld and Catastrophe: The Passing of Mass Utopia in East and West*. Cambridge: MIT Press.

Chernysheva, V. 2012. 'Muzei SSSR Prineset Milliardy', 1 October 2012. Retrieved from <www.rg.ru/2012/10/01/reg-pfo/muzey.html> (accessed 14 November 2012).

Connerton, P. 1989. *How Societies Remember*. Cambridge: Cambridge University Press.

Coontz, S. 1992. *The Way We Never Were: American Families and the Nostalgia Trap*. New York: Basic Books.

Crowley, D. and S. Reid. 2000. 'Style and Socialism: Modernity and Material Culture in Post-War Eastern Europe', in S. Reid and D. Crowley (eds), *Style and Socialism: Modernity and Material Culture in Post-War Eastern Europe*. Oxford: Berg, pp. 1–24.

Davis, F. 1979. *The Yearning for Yesterday: A Sociology of Nostalgia*. New York: The Free Press.

Dubin, B. 2001. *Slovo-Pis'mo-Literatura: Ocherki po Istorii Sovremennoi Kul'tury*. Moscow: Novoe Literaturnoe Obozrenie.

Faibisovich, S. 1998. 'Pesni o glavnom', *Neprikosnovennyi Zapas* 2: 4–7.

Fehérváry, K. 2002. 'American Kitchens, Luxury Bathrooms, and the Search for a "Normal" Life in Postsocialist Hungary', *Ethnos* 67 (3): 369–400.

Fritzsche, P. 2002. 'How Nostalgia Narrates Modernity', in A. Confino and P. Fritzsche (eds), *The Work of Memory: New Directions in the Study of German Society and Culture*. Urbana: University of Illinois Press, pp. 62–85.

Gronow, J. 2003. *Caviar with Champagne: Common Luxury and the Ideals of Good Life in Stalin's Russia*. Oxford: Berg.

Gusejnov, G. 2003. 'Revoliutsionnyi Simvol i Kommertsia', *Novoe Literaturnoe Obozrenie* (64). Retrieved from <http://magazines.russ.ru/nlo/2003/64/gus13. html> (accessed 29 January 2013).

Ivanova, N. 1997. 'Nostaliaschee', *Znamia* 9: 204–11.

Ivy, M. 1995. *Discourses of the Vanishing: Modernity, Phantasm, Japan*. Chicago: University of Chicago Press.

Kalinin, I. 2011. 'Nostalgic Modernization: The Soviet Past as "Historical Horizon"', *Slavonica* 17 (2): 156–66.

Kalinina, Y. 2002. 'Babushka s Peryshkami', *Moskovskii Komsomolets*, 12 March, p. 6.

Krasukhin, G. 2003. 'Na Zerkalo Necha Peniat', *Russkii Zhurnal*, 10 November 2003. Retrieved from <www.russ.ru/ist_sovr/20031110_kras.html> (accessed 5 May 2004).

Libedinskaia, L. 2000. 'Takaia Vot Istoria', *Voprosy Literatury* 3: 253–77.

Lipman, M. 2004. 'The Putin Toothpick', *The New Yorker*, 8 March 2004. Retrieved from <http://www.newyorker.com/archive/2004/03/08/040308ta_talk lipman> (accessed 28 January 2013).

Molok, N. 1999. 'Nashe Nasledie', *Itogi* 29.

Nadkarni, M. 2010. '"But It's Ours": Nostalgia and the Politics of Authenticity in Post-Socialist Hungary', in M. Todorova and Z. Gille (eds), *Post-Communist Nostalgia*. New York: Berghahn, pp. 190–214.

Press-vypusk 2004. 'Press-vypusk No. 30: Nostal'giia po Proshlomu', 19 March, 2004. Retrieved from <http://www.levada.ru/press/2004031901.html> (accessed 14 November 2012).

Salecl, R. 2000. 'Where is the Center?'. Retrieved from <www.westfaelischer-kunst verein.de/archiv/2000/ausstellungen/whereis/vortraege/salecl.pdf> (accessed 25 January 2013).

Samodurov, Y. n.d. 'The Idea of the Museum of the USSR: An Exhibition-Laboratory'. Retrieved from http://old.sakharov-center.ru/projects/ussr-museum/exhibit. htm (accessed 5 March 2014).

Stewart, K. 1988. 'Nostalgia – A Polemic', *Cultural Anthropology* 3 (3): 227–41.

Stewart, S. 1993. *On Longing: Narratives of the Miniature, the Gigantic, the Souvenir, the Collection.* Durham: Duke University Press.

Winnicott, D.W. 1953. 'Transitional Objects and Transitional Phenomena: A Study of the First Not-Me Possession', *International Journal of Psycho-Analysis* 34: 89–97.

Young, J. 1993. *The Texture of Memory: Holocaust Memorials and Meaning.* New Haven, CT: Yale University Press.

Yurchak, A. 1997. 'The Cynical Reason of Late Socialism: Power, Pretense, and the *Anekdot*', *Public Culture* 9(2): 161–88.

Zubova, E. 2011. 'Grigorii Revzin: Moskve Nuzhen Muzei SSSR', 12 December 2011. Retrieved from <http://slon.ru/russia/grigoriy_revzin_moskve_nuzhen_muzey_sssr-723783.xhtml> (accessed 14 November 2012).

Chapter 4

Why Post-imperial Trumps Post-socialist

Crying Back the National Past in Hungary

Chris Hann

I hate the entire twentieth century!
– Feró Nagy, song lyric

Jostling alongside such ubiquitous phenomena as heritagization and roots seeking, nostalgia for the recent socialist past is a well-documented feature of the politics of the past in most countries of the former Soviet bloc. Thanks to popular films such as *Good Bye Lenin* as well as numerous academic studies, the best-known case is that of the former German Democratic Republic. According to the late Daphne Berdahl (2010), *Ostalgie* never reflected a wish that socialists had remained in power, but rather gathered momentum as a means for East Germans to protest against the domination of their society by West Germans after 1990, and the devaluation of everything accomplished under socialism in the preceding decades. Others have gone further and cast this 'nostomania' as an imperialist construction of elites, the prominence of which in the Western media functions to emphasize the continuing backwardness and inferiority of the east in a nominally united Germany (Boyer 2010).

The GDR is a very special case. No other state of the former Soviet bloc was swallowed up by a powerful neighbour, and no other people in modern Europe has a historical burden comparable to that carried by the Germans, complicating and inhibiting recourse to long-term historical memory. In an earlier work (Hann 2012) I suggested that we might expect to find less nostalgia for the decades of socialism in places where the former polity fragments. As in the GDR, altered boundaries mean that there is new work to be done in cultivating collective identity. The emergence of nation states out of socialist federations (USSR, Yugoslavia, and even Czechoslovakia) was accompanied by much future-oriented rhetoric, not a Western colonization. Even where transformations were marked by violence, nostalgia for a more peaceful socialist past was muted in the new public spheres.

This chapter extends the comparative analysis to the more common post-socialist scenario, in which the boundaries of the state are unchanged. As in the former federal states, new elites have an interest in denigrating all that has gone before, i.e., socialism. But these elites are not colonizing co-ethnics from the West, and they do not need to fight – literally or metaphorically – to establish their nation state. Because this exists as a given since the pre-socialist era, the constellation of collective identity and temporal subjectivities is quite different. Closer inspection reveals that the currents and counter-currents of post-socialist nostalgia vary greatly. It is not surprising that, in the most comprehensive survey to date, Maria Todorova and Zsuzsa Gille (2010) approach this diversity on a country-by-country basis. In this chapter, I shall follow their example by outlining my own interpretation of the Hungarian case. I argue that to understand the temporalities pertaining to recent decades it is essential to look at history and collective memory over a much longer period. The first section therefore outlines the macro contours of Hungarian history since the mass dissemination of a new national consciousness in the course of the nineteenth century. Elite constructions of Magyar origin myths in this era were repeatedly invoked in later generations, with a short-lived hiatus in the early socialist decades. In the following section, I show how contemporary politicians manipulate the national *mythomoteur* in their efforts to direct all positive sentiments towards a pre-socialist past to which the present population has no direct connection. This past has multiple forms, from exotic tribal origins in Asia to the quasi-feudal regime of Admiral Miklós Horthy in the interwar decades. I emphasize the Habsburg Monarchy because Hungarian nationalism has a complex symbiotic relation with the last generations of imperial splendour. This is the era in which the key ethno-national myths were established. In the concluding sections I move to the micro level, namely the village of Tázlár on the western Great Plain, which I have known since 1976. I suggest that a strong ideology of private property inhibits villagers from public recognition of the accomplishments of the later socialist decades. However, a close-up look at two individuals suggests the persistence of nostalgia for socialism in the private sphere, and even an appreciation of its underlying ethics.

'History Stuffed Us into Its Pocket'[1]

One common way to express at least some aspects of the English word nostalgia in Hungarian is the verb *visszasírni*, literally to 'cry back'. Thus a person who cries back socialism is someone who, whether or not she was critical of socialism at the time, now yearns for its restoration, because conditions then seem preferable to conditions today. As in the former GDR, such utterances are better understood as a critical commentary on the present than as a desire to return to the era of one-party rule. On the face of it, the Hungarian case could hardly be more different from that of East Germany. In the last decades of socialism, under the regime of János Kádár (1912–89), Hungarian citizens enjoyed more freedom and better economic conditions than any other state in the Soviet bloc. Yet there appears to be relatively little nostalgia for this era two decades later. The Hungarian Socialist Party (prior to 1989 the Communist Party, officially known as the Hungarian Socialist Workers' Party) was trounced at the general election of 2010 and again in 2014. Even members of this party, and former cadres who left it in the convulsions of 1989–90, hesitate to 'cry back' the *ancien régime*.

Temporal subjectivities today cannot be grasped without exploring the peculiar mythomoteur of the Hungarians as shaped in pre-socialist generations. I borrow the concept of mythomoteur from John Armstrong, who elaborated it in his seminal exploration of *Nations before Nationalism* (1982).[2] Armstrong himself pinpoints the unusual duality of the Hungarian case. At the end of the nineteenth century the Hungarians celebrated the Millennium of the arrival of the nomadic Magyar tribes in the Carpathian basin. A century later, under King Stephen (967–1038), they converted to Christianity and began to take their place in (Western) European civilization. This decision to opt for the consolidation of a European state could be rationalized as essential for the survival of the group, but many Magyars did not find it emotionally easy to give up their traditions. With their non-Indo-European tongue and plentiful symbolic resources, they never lost the means to distinguish themselves from their new agrarian neighbors (Armstrong 1982: 47–50).

Political and cultural nationalism reached an early peak in the revolutions of 1848, when the nation's demands were presented on 15 March in Pest by the poet Sándor Petőfi. The revolution failed, and decades of Austrian repression followed. However, Hungarian aspirations were partially assuaged by the *Ausgleich* ('compromise') negotiated with Vienna in 1867, which effectively promoted the Hungarians from the status of subject people by awarding them a share in the empire. It was obvious to all that, while Budapest now exercised control over the Hungarian kingdom (where ethnic Hungarians were a minority of the population in many regions), real power remained concentrated in Vienna. The German language was more prestigious than the Hungarian. Whereas the Austrian territories of the *Vielvölkerstaat* (literally 'state of many peoples') were governed pragmatically through policies of 'divide and rule', the Hungarians endeavoured to assimilate their minorities through the education system. The results were paradoxical. In Budapest, many Germans and Jews opted voluntarily for a Magyar identity, yet the capital remained a cosmopolitan city of Mitteleuropa, with secessionist architecture and coffee houses comparable to those of Vienna. Processes of embourgeoisement were generally less advanced in the Hungarian half of the empire, and nationalism continued unabated. In the decades when statues of Bismarck were erected throughout the German empire, the Hungarians commemorated not the Emperor/King Franz Josef but their own romantic poets and rebellious noblemen. They also erected many monuments (some of them extremely large) to the *turul*, an exotic bird with a distant resemblance to a falcon, which, according to an anonymous twelfth-century chronicle (Rady 2009), figured prominently in the origin myth of the Magyars; these origins had nothing to do with European civilization.

Military defeat in 1918 brought the curtain down on this curiously dual Habsburg theatre state. In Budapest, the war was followed by the short-lived Republic of Councils in 1919, led by Béla Kun. The communist revolution was followed by the 'white terror' of Admiral Miklós Horthy, who eventually assumed power as Regent. The territory of the Hungarian state shrank dramatically following the Treaty of Trianon in 1920. Major cities of the historic Hungarian kingdom, not to mention a high proportion of its natural resources, its industry and the ethnically Hungarian population, were henceforth located outside the state. Trianon was rejected by all political groupings in Hungary, including those on the now emasculated left. The new Hungary, as dictated by the victorious powers, was universally considered to be 'mutilated' (*csonka*).

Under Horthy, a series of conservative governments ruled Hungary in the interwar decades. He and his ministers had the support of the overwhelming majority of Hungarians when they collaborated with Hitler to restore parts of Slovakia and Transylvania to Hungarian rule during the Second World War. Hungarians ended up fighting on the side of the Nazis against the Soviet army. They participated in the Holocaust, which eliminated the majority of the country's Jews. Towards the end of the war, power passed from Horthy to the Arrow Cross party led by Ferenc Szálasi, which was even more attached than other nationalist groupings to a sword-carrying turul in its symbolism. However, following the victory of the Red Army, within a few years the Communist Party was able to seize total control. With the state again confined to its Trianon boundaries, behind what Churchill dubbed the 'iron curtain', Hungary's second national humil-iation of the century was complete.

Things went from bad to worse in the 1950s. Following Stalinist terror and mass protests that took a strongly national form, hopes of reform were quashed by Soviet military intervention in November 1956. Some leaders of the uprising were executed. Mass collectivization was completed by 1961. However, the regime of János Kádár tried to avoid the errors of the preced-ing years. Political reconciliation ('he who is not against us is with us') was followed by radical economic decentralization in 1968. In the 1970s and 1980s the Hungarian variant of 'market socialism' gave most citizens oppor-tunities to earn supplementary income in the 'second economy', outside the formal institutions of the plan. Rural families were able to market the produce of their household plots and form a symbiosis with collective farms in the most successful variant of collectivized agriculture anywhere in the Soviet bloc (Swain 1985). Private paths of accumulation were tolerated, even stimulated. Millions of citizens were able to raise their living standards significantly. Travel to Western countries was liberalized, and controls over the media and popular culture greatly relaxed, to the extent that cabaret artists could satirize power holders on prime-time television. Despite all this, however, Kádár's regime was unable to rewrite history in a credible way, powerless to transcend the ignominious circumstances that had brought it to power. It was obliged to retain 4 April (Liberation Day – by the Red Army in 1945) as a national holiday. It had little choice but to endure the scuffles and small-scale protests of 'dissident' intellectuals on 15 March, the day of the 1848 revolution, strongly associated with the national poet Sándor Petőfi, which had been a national holiday in the pre-socialist era. Kádár's regime was obliged to classify 1956 as a 'counter revolution'. In short, this socialist 'compromise' or 'social contract' was limited in scope. The triumph of reformist factions within the Communist Party enabled economistic modernization but this was hardly the stuff with which to embellish national mythology. Although the Party made concessions to national sentiment (e.g., by tolerating and even supporting public criticism of the increasingly repressive policies of Nicolae Ceauşescu in neighbouring Romania), Kádár and his comrades remained pawns in an alliance dominated by Moscow; they could not aspire to don the mantle of national historical legitimacy.

In the 1980s, with János Kádár's health declining, international indebt-
edness rising and economic reforms no longer so successful or so novel, a
crisis set in. In the countryside, accumulation continued at a furious pace
(Lampland 1995). In the cities, however, intellectuals were questioning the
legitimacy gap and the consumerist orientation of the builders of market
socialism. The dissidents called for a re-evaluation of Hungary's moral
geography between East and West, and especially of the uprising in 1956;
they campaigned successfully for the reburials of its victims, along with the
repatriation of other deceased national heroes (Gal 1991, Zempléni 2002).
Historical memories were revitalized by increasingly public concern over
the fate of co-ethnics in Transylvania (Kürti 2001).

These efforts to alter temporal subjectivities and revive national agendas
gradually found resonance outside elite groups. The popular music scene,
which in the 1960s had largely mimicked that of the West, opened up in the
1970s to embrace Hungarian folk music, which had survived most vigorously
in Transylvania. The 'dancehouse' (*táncház*) movement flourished in the last
decades of socialism, supported by the government and yet in an uneasy
tension with it (Striker 1984). Another indication of a renewed concern with
the national past was the extraordinarily successful open-air production in
1983 of a rock opera by some of the country's best known pop musicians
(Hann 1990). While poking impudent fun at the devious machinations of
contemporary power holders, *Stephen, the King* looked all the way back to
the country's first King, who broke with pagan traditions by converting to
Christianity and committed his people to a future alongside Germans, within
Europe. Yet the hallowed symbolism of the papal crown was complemented
in the opera by the more exotic symbolism of earlier shamanic rituals, including representations of the turul. Eastern and Western elements of the mythomoteur share the opera's best tunes. Stephen's pledge of allegiance to Rome,
following the brutal execution of the virile rebel Koppány, is celebrated with
missionaries' prayers in Latin, taken from the Catholic mass. The subtleties
of János Bródy's libretto are lost in an anthemic conclusion, an escapist antidote to the economism of market socialism:

> The sun has risen, Stephen is our lord,
> The light of mercy floods over us,
> Our heart is grateful, our joy resounds,
> Beautiful Hungary, our sweet home.

Less than ten years later, in the best-selling album of 1991, Feró Nagy,
front man of *Beatrice*, sang more abrasively about the horrors of the twentieth century, including the 'red terror' as well as the white, and 1956. The
counter-revolution was now officially proclaimed to have been a revolution

and a new national holiday was introduced to mark it (23 October). The
national holiday on 20 August once again became the holiday of King
Stephen, with prominent religious colouring, rather than the secular commemoration of the socialist constitution introduced in 1949. Instead of
celebrating the arrival of the Red Army on 4 April, Hungarians could once
again celebrate their national poet Sándor Petőfi on 15 March, as they had
prior to socialism. The lyrics of 'I hate the entire twentieth century' were
devoid of religious symbolism, but Christianity rapidly became very visible
in the Hungarian public sphere; many schools, colleges and universities are
nowadays again under ecclesiastical control.

In the 1983 premiere of *Stephen, the King*, Feró Nagy had played Laborc,
an ally of Koppány, who screams out patriotic anti-Christian lines: 'We
don't want a God who doesn't speak Hungarian. Free Hungarians do not
need such a Lord'. The free Hungarian public of the 1990s was fascinated
by the paths followed by their pop stars. Levente Szörényi, responsible for
most of the music of *Stephen, the King*, favoured the Hungarian Democratic
Forum (conservative, with nationalist leanings), but his collaborator János
Bródy supported the Free Democrats. (The latter party was supported
primarily by intellectuals, including those associated with 'dissidents' and
'cosmopolitans'; it was increasingly marginalized in the second post-socialist
decade.) As for Feró Nagy, after enjoying his greatest commercial success
with his punk lament for the horrors of the twentieth century, he joined the
Hungarian Justice and Life Party founded by István Csurka. This party was
openly anti-Semitic and revelled in the extreme nationalist symbolism that
the socialists had suppressed during their four decades in power.[3]

If, as I have argued, Kádár's regime turned out to be rather benign
(almost 'socialism with a human face'), the question arises: why did none
of these popular entertainers endorse the Communist Party (now renamed
the Hungarian Socialist Party) in the first free election of 1990? This was
won decisively by the Hungarian Democratic Forum, which emphasized
the values of independence and of Christianity. The victory of the socialist party under Gyula Horn four years later surely did owe a great deal to
positive memories of the stability and prosperity of the 1970s and 1980s, as
evaluated in the context of the dislocation of the immediate post-socialist
years. However, the socialist-led governments of 1994–98, and especially
those in power between 2002 and 2010, beset by new economic challenges,
frittered away the socioeconomic credit built up by the long reformist regime
of János Kádár. When Viktor Orbán came to form his second government
in 2010, he enjoyed an unprecedented two-thirds majority in parliament.[4]
Two decades after the *rendszerváltás* ('system change'), the socialists now
polled only 17 per cent. In the public sphere at least, there is no room for any

positive representations of socialism. With hopes of a better future rendered even more illusory by the global financial crisis, other strands of nostalgia dominate. Some Hungarians are keen to explore their non-European roots and any link to the east (e.g., in the 1990s a reputable scholar reported, to enormous public interest, that he had located the grave of the national poet Sándor Petőfi in Central Asia). Others prefer to celebrate the imperial era of Mitteleuropa, which had ended in the aftermath of the First World War (with brief aftershocks in the course of the Second). Closer to the present, Orbán's FIDESZ party has acquiesced in (and sometimes encouraged) nostalgia for the era of Miklós Horthy, suggesting that his achievements on behalf of the nation have been falsely represented in the decades of communism. These yearnings for different phases of the pre-socialist past reflect the inability of socialist power holders to displace, or even significantly to modify, the symbols and myths established by the nationalists of the nineteenth century.

Nurturing Nostalgia

So far I have argued that the inglorious history of the twentieth century leaves Hungarians with little choice but to reach back to earlier fusions of religion and national identity, and especially to the years of imperial power, when their country was significantly larger than it is today, and at least a partner in running a remarkable empire. Of course, these temporal subjectivities do not persist naturally or emerge spontaneously, 'from below'. On the contrary, they are constantly manipulated by those in power. In Hungary, as elsewhere in Eastern Europe, socialist history textbooks have long been replaced by books that foreground the national narrative and place even greater emphasis on the injustice of Trianon. Extremist accounts of the past, including the most sensitive issues of the 1940s, have not found their way into textbooks but are readily available in bookstores throughout the country. Many villages nowadays mark their boundary with an inscription of the name of the settlement in the ancient runic script (*rovás írás*). Turul monuments are common, as are monuments commemorating the revolution of 1956.

In discussing the case of the former German Democratic Republic at the beginning of this chapter, I noted the role of the mass media (largely controlled by West German companies) in promoting while simultaneously mocking the phenomenon of *Ostalgie*. By contrast, Budapest does not offer tourists accommodation in the authentic surrounds of a prefabricated socialist apartment block, or guided tours by Trabant, or a museum of socialist everyday life as it was under Kádár. It does, however, boast a 'House of

Terror' in a downtown building used both by the socialist secret services and their fascist predecessors, thereby establishing an equivalence that is still problematic in Germany.[5] There is also a popular 'Memento Park' outside the city, which displays massive sculptures commemorating Soviet leaders, the Red Army and Soviet–Hungarian friendship. Here it is possible to have one's photo taken beside a Trabant, but this open-air museum invites one to gape in awe and horror, rather than indulge in wistful nostalgia.

Much more popular than these sites among Hungarians and prominent in the national imagination is the National Historical Memorial Park (*Nemzeti Történelmi Emlékpark*) at the village of Ópusztaszer, close to highway E75, between the cities of Kecskemét and Szeged. The flat landscape in this part of the Great Plain lends itself to the myth making that took root in the nineteenth century.[6] Most of the medieval settlements of this region vanished following the Ottoman conquest. In Ópusztaszer, the suggestive ruins of a large medieval monastery gave rise to the unlikely idea that this might be the site where, according to the anonymous medieval chronicle mentioned above, Árpád and his fellow tribal chieftains had conferred, following their arrival in the Carpathian Basin in 896. An elaborate monument to Árpád was erected following patriotic subscription by the citizens of the city of Szeged and unveiled in the course of the millennial celebrations of 1896.[7] To complicate matters, the citizens of Kecskemét proposed Pusztaszer as an alternative, equally plausible location nearer to their own city as the site of Árpád's epochal gathering. They celebrated in 1896 with somewhat different monuments, paying homage to all seven chiefs and placing a large turul atop a massive column.

Plans to develop these sites in succeeding generations foundered repeatedly due to lack of funds. In 1970, the socialist power holders decided to invest in the more southerly settlement, which in 1974 was renamed accordingly.[8] Ethnographers from the University of Szeged helped to construct a large *skanzen* (open-air museum) to celebrate the authentic folk culture (most exhibits date from the late nineteenth and early twentieth century). Environmentalists gave their advice concerning the associated nature reserve. The most important step in establishing this new park in the national imagination was the decision to make Ópusztaszer the permanent home of the *Feszti körkép*, a panoramic representation of Árpád's arrival in the Carpathian basin. This 'cyclorama' by the artist Árpád Feszti (conforming to an established genre of European nationalism) was a sensation at the Millennium in 1896 and a prominent carrier of the national mythomoteur in the Horthy years. After wartime damage, it was not accessible to the public. By the time a new rotunda had been constructed to accommodate the renovated canvas (the circumference was over hundred metres) at Ópusztaszer, one-party rule

4.1 Fragment of the Feszti panorama at Ópusztaszer

was over.[9] Feszti's romantic glorification of the nation was in any case better suited to the needs of post-socialist power holders. It is nowadays a popular destination for schoolchildren, who come in organized excursions to absorb nostalgia at an early age through the mediation of their teachers, but also for elderly visitors, some of whom can reminisce about when they last saw the panorama in the Városliget park in Budapest in the 1930s.

There is no shortage of other attractions at Ópusztaszer, other ways to 'step into the national past', as the glossy brochures put it. Cultural associations and commercial enterprises enhance the recreational and pedagogical experience, e.g., with the smells and tastes of traditional food and drink. Alongside traditional peasant costumes, visitors can admire cavalry officers in Habsburg era uniforms, or gendarmes of the Horthy era. In addition to temporary exhibitions, tourists can also enjoy a 'nomad park' and camp in an eco-friendly yurt. There is a daily display of horsemanship by local young men who flaunt shamanic paraphernalia as they invite spectators to 'celebrate our collective memory'. Socialism finds no mention here, even though the idea for this national memorial park originally came from socialist politicians desperate to deepen their legitimacy. Only in the main history exhibition is there a cursory tribute to the 'kids of 1956' who dared to oppose the Soviet military invaders. Another conspicuous absence for many years was an appropriately monumental turul, but this gap was filled on 29 September 2012 when Prime Minister Viktor Orbán unveiled a bronze over two metres high (it had to be larger, of course, than the nineteenth century bird in rival Pusztaszer) perched on an elaborate carved limestone pillar.

As usual, this new turul, the work of Péter Mátl, an ethnic Hungarian from Carpathian Ukraine, carried a large sword between its claws. The

4.2 Péter Mátl's *turul*, Ópusztaszer. Photo by Chris Hann

Prime Minister's speech celebrated the ethnic unity of all Hungarians by mixing Christian with pre-Christian mythology:[10]

> We are born into the turul just as we are born into our language and our history ... The turul is an archetype that belongs to the blood and the soil of the fatherland. The seven tribes who took the Carpathian basin a thousand years ago, the founder of the state St. Stephen and the turul are the national identity symbols of those who live today, those who have already died, and those not yet born ... This statue which we are inaugurating today on the feast day of St Michael is a monument to national unity. It reminds us that every Hungarian is responsible for every other Hungarian. The Hungarian nation is a world nation (*világnemzet*), for the boundaries of the country and the boundaries of the nation do not coincide ... This statue tells us that there is only one country, namely, one which is capable of uniting all Hungarians on both sides of the Trianon border into a single community.

Ungrateful Peasants

In the remainder of this chapter I want to develop the analysis with reference to my own ethnographic materials. Those of us with fieldwork experience dating back to socialist days tend to assume that this gives us a significant advantage over younger colleagues fresh to the field. Especially if we return repeatedly to the same community, we may claim privileged insights into the production of collective nostalgia and its modification in individual biographies, a claim that may not hold up to scrutiny.[11] I am all too aware of the pitfalls as I recall Hungary in the 1970s – definitely an exciting place to be an apprentice anthropologist. Generously funded through an official exchange programme with Britain, I had the luxury of a preliminary year in Budapest before moving 120 km south-east to the village of Tázlár for a second year of 'fieldwork proper'. The first year was indispensable for learning the language, which I accomplished primarily through sports and other recreational networks. Few of my new friends had good things to say about the regime. However, equally few abused it, either openly or in private. János Kádár's power was secure. Critical voices were as likely to stress the dangers of widening social inequalities through expanding market relations as they were to condemn the illegitimacy of a regime that owed its power to Soviet intervention. I was surprised to discover that Kádár himself was generally respected, even by people strongly opposed to communism. Even friends with unpleasant memories of their military service and strong objections to the restrictions on their foreign travel were upbeat the country's prospects. And many thought that the quality of the Western pop music of the 1960s was better sustained in Hungary than anywhere in the West!

The countryside was different. It was more difficult to obtain pop records and few families had any experience of travel abroad. Tázlár was little more than two hours away but the gulf between the sophisticated capital and the location of my economic anthropology project seemed vast. This should not have surprised me, since Hungary was still a largely agrarian country when the socialists came to power. Rapid industrialization in the early socialist decades had not been accompanied by an equally rapid rate of urbanization. Throughout the country, many workers commuted from villages and worked on household plots in their spare time, along with other family members. Tázlár was exceptional in a number of respects, notably in the degree to which its farmers had been able to continue family farming on their previous acreage even after formally joining a cooperative farm in 1960–61. I chose to work in a region characterized by 'specialist cooperatives' because this type seemed to exemplify the flexibility of Hungary's experimental willingness to depart from the orthodox principles of collective farming (Hann 1980).

This region of the Great Plain, mid-way between the rivers Danube and Tisza, only about an hour's drive from the memorial park at Ópusztaszer, had been abandoned following the Ottoman conquest. The resulting *puszta* (empty, uninhabited land) was used as pasture by the surrounding market towns, but not resettled and used for cultivation until the second half of the nineteenth century. By this time, capitalist relations were transforming the Hungarian countryside. Arable land was increasingly scarce. Immigrants to Tázlár were diverse. Some early settlers purchased relatively large holdings of good quality land. Their descendants were classified as rich peasants (*kulák*) by the socialists and vilified in the Stalinist years. Others, more numerous, could afford only small parcels of sandy soil that were insufficient to ensure the basic goal of self-sufficiency. Living conditions were abysmal and widely taken in the 1930s to epitomize the economic backwardness of the entire country. But even the poorest immigrants built their new homes on the land they purchased and embraced the ideology of private property. Schools and churches were constructed in small hamlets, but until the socialist decades the great bulk of the population (almost four thousand in the 1940s) lived and worked on scattered farmsteads.

This history and settlement pattern made the farmers of Tázlár unusual in the national context. In other regions of the Great Plain the isolated farmstead was a supplementary building used only in the agricultural season and the main dwelling was located in a large village or town. But the peasant ideology was pretty much the same everywhere. In the inter-war decades, following the dismemberment of the historic kingdom, the crisis of the nation was perceived as a crisis of the peasantry. This was true of populists on the left as well as the right. Among the former, Ferenc Erdei documented the poverty of Tázlár and the surrounding district in the 1930s (Erdei 1937). He later analysed its deeper causes in the distortions of uneven capitalist development and semi-feudal social structures. Erdei initially imagined that solutions could be found through adopting Western forms of cooperative farming, as a route to embourgeoisement (*polgárosodás*). However, the majority of his rural constituents could never support policies which would compromise the ideals of the self-sufficient peasant farm. These ideals had been firmly implanted since the demise of serfdom. They were represented by the Independent Smallholders Party, the most popular party in the 1940s in Tázlár, as in the country as a whole. The Smallholders were deeply committed to the cause of national restoration, not to the international revolution of the proletariat. A map of historic Hungary (as opposed to the 'mutilated' Hungary imposed at Trianon) was a potent symbol, to be found on the wall of many a kitchen or living room in Tázlár. During the Second World War, villagers with non-Hungarian surnames came under strong pressure to replace them with a Magyar equivalent. The Smallholders, leaders and followers alike, were also deeply committed to their churches. The *református* (Calvinists) had long constituted a national church. In spite of the Habsburg legacy, the dominant Roman Catholic Church also tried to emphasize its national character, notably in 1938 when orchestrating nationwide celebrations of the nine-hundredth anniversary of the death of King Stephen, who for Catholics was also Saint Stephen.

What little support there was in Tázlár for socialist ideals dwindled even further when the poorest peasants left the community in the first phase of industrialization. However, after collectivization, and especially in the liberal economic climate which prevailed after 1968, those villagers who remained began to prosper. They were encouraged to give up their isolated farmsteads for a modern house in the rapidly expanding village centre, where the socialist authorities had invested in electrification, a piped water supply, a culture house, shops and other institutions. In a sense, the pre-socialist embourgeoisement agenda set out by Ferenc Erdei was realized, but in the context of socialist rural development rather than voluntary cooperatives as in Holland or Denmark. Through the establishment of 'specialist cooperatives' (initially three, which united to form the Peace specialist cooperative in 1974), Tázlár villagers were given incentives to remain active in those sectors of agricultural production where the family-labour farm enjoyed basic advantages, notably in raising pigs but also in grape and wine production. With the proceeds of their labour, villagers could buy cars and invest in bathrooms and other comforts for their homes. They worked extremely hard, but willingly, motivated by the material gains. Some individuals bought tractors and other equipment, rivalling the cooperative as a supplier of agricultural services to their neighbours. Some invested in their children's education and in urban real estate. These were common topics of conversation during my fieldwork in 1976–77. The collective core of the cooperative experienced major problems at the time, but private farming activities, not to mention the construction sector, were flourishing. My landlady belonged to a *kulák* family. She attended church daily and deplored communism and the nationalization of church schools. But I do not recall any conversations in which she evoked historic Hungary. The wrongs done to the nation at Trianon were taught in the village school on the basis of socialist history textbooks, but it seemed to me in the 1970s that they were no longer on anyone's emotional agenda because just about everyone was oriented towards a brighter future. Even politically, optimism increased after the corrupt Council Chairman was removed from office and replaced in 1987 by a local teacher who, though still at this time a member of the ruling Communist Party, enjoyed the respect of the community.

All this changed very quickly after 1989. The Independent Smallholders' Party was reformed and dominated the local political stage for the next decade. In Tázlár the Christian Democratic People's Party also formed a local branch, while the Hungarian Socialist Party (formerly the Communist Party) lost most of its members and attracted very few votes. Why were villagers so ungrateful, in view of the prosperity that socialist rural development had brought them? The answer hinges on the continued strength of the old ideology of private property. This was evident in the number of persons who pressed claims for the restitution of their land in the 1990s. Even though many households had been able to continue utilizing their former plots, and even though most had benefited from the services provided by the cooperative, they had nonetheless remained doggedly opposed to it in principle. Those whose use rights were affected when the cooperative consolidated fields in later decades were generally aghast, even though the socialist institution had always offered ample compensation elsewhere for all plots it appropriated. In the early 1990s, it was obvious to many villagers that, with the collapse of the COMECON markets and the abolition of socialist subsidies for cooperatives, regaining full private property rights was unlikely to be profitable. Yet to members of the older generations, emotional ties to the soil purchased and tilled by one's ancestors were more powerful motivations than any narrow economic calculation (Hann 1993).

Attachment to one's own patrimony in the community was reflected in the revival of a larger concern with the patrimony of the nation. As the local rural economy declined (many plots were abandoned because their cultivation was unprofitable), the rhetoric of nationalists proved more persuasive than that of socialist politicians whose party had committed the cardinal sin of violating property rights. The misfortunes of the sector were blamed by the new generation of populist politicians on foreign capital, and sometimes on Brussels. After Hungary's accession to the European Union in 2004 the situation improved slightly, since some villagers became eligible for European Union subsidies. However, these are bureaucratically quite complex and do not compare favourably with the attractive and relatively secure conditions enjoyed in the best years under Kádár. Some of those who were highly critical of the 'specialist cooperative' before 1990 now say they would like to 'cry it back' or to reinvent some form of collective institution, if only to facilitate marketing. Small-scale wine producers face particular problems. Many villagers have simply given up attempting to produce for the market, though they still cultivate their gardens in order to eke out modest pensions.

The present Mayor is one of the largest wine producers of the village. He does not belong to any party but was elected in 1994 with the support of the Smallholders and has been in office continuously ever since.[12] Soon after his election, he designated a strip of land near the main asphalt road as an industrial estate. However, following the discovery of a medieval cemetery, mandatory archaeological excavations have precluded the commercial development that was supposed to bring new jobs. The population has continued to decline as unemployment has risen. Some villagers depend on remittances from their children, who work in Austria, northern Italy, or London, and who usually prefer to remain in these locations if they can. Because the cost of housing is significantly lower in Tázlár than in neighbouring market towns, a few Roma families have moved in. They are not made to feel welcome.

The specialist cooperative in Tázlár organized a number of auxiliary workshops, in which most of the jobs were taken by local women. These are certainly missed, perhaps as much for their sociality as for the additional income they generated. Most people worked extremely hard during those years. They recall not only the intense conviviality of mutual aid in house building and lavish wedding parties, but also toil and stress. Today they are more likely to have 'time on their hands'. In a sense, this is a return to pre-socialist times, when most people had time, outside the peak periods of the agricultural season, for relaxed sociality with kin and neighbours. Their temporal subjectivities today are different, however, as a consequence of the accumulation of the intervening socialist decades in which many villagers rushed home from a socialist factory and then went to work at once on the household plot, or on some extension to their house or outbuildings. Today, they spend much more time at home watching television, or playing cards at a pensioners' club in the Culture House. Foreign travel is now theoretically much easier, but in practice it remains out of reach for the great majority. There has been a spate of amateur publications about the community, including the history of the institutions established during the socialist decades; people had no time for such activities before 1990, but now they look fondly at old photographs in these publications and feel some pride in what was accomplished. Critical attitudes towards the former communist Council Chairman and to the now defunct cooperative have softened.

Compared to their forebears in the pre-socialist era, villagers today are more likely to see themselves as relatively deprived. Their nostalgia definitely has a material basis, even in the case of those who have not become worse off in absolute terms. Thanks to the modernization process described above ('socialist embourgeoisement', in the terminology of Erdei and sociologist Ivan Szelényi, 1988), these former peasants were integrated into the national community. Populists of every political hue had proclaimed under Horthy that the peasants were the essence of the nation, but it was the socialists who actually brought their social isolation to an end. Nonetheless, no one is grateful to them for this civilizing contribution, because of their violation of property precepts. These socialists failed to provide any convincing alternative to the established myths that the peasants had learned to live by. Kádár's social contract was welcomed but it was an instrumental compromise, deficient in the symbolic dimension. The upshot is that, although many Tázlár villagers may mutter positive things in private about the latter decades of socialism, in the public sphere anything less than unqualified denigration of the silences and hypocrisy of those years is unacceptable. I turn in the final section of the chapter to illustrate these ambiguities by looking more closely at two non-peasant individuals whose biographies reveal the complex entanglements of personal and collective memory.

Dispossession, Material and Moral[13]

I first met Sanyi in May 1976, when I was nervously walking around the region for the first time in search of a field site. He picked me up in his Trabant in the late afternoon and offered me a lift back to the railway station in Kiskőrös, the district centre. It rapidly emerged that he was the ideal person to help me to understand the tensions of the unusual form of cooperative described in the previous section, and to mediate my residence and research in the village where he worked. Sanyi was an agronomist, employed by the Tázlár specialist cooperative to facilitate the independent household farming of its members; he was not involved with its (rather limited) collective activities. Sanyi had not grown up on a farm, but in small towns (his father was a watchmaker). He was a member of the Communist Party. He had joined not for careerist reasons but rather because he was a believer in socialist ideals. I had ample opportunity to witness this over the next ten months, during which Sanyi was my principal companion in the village. For example, I recall him arguing vehemently with elderly peasants still resident on isolated farmsteads who resented the appropriation of their plots to form larger fields for the cooperative. It was Sanyi's job to persuade them to accept alternative plots elsewhere. He pleaded for the rational advantages of mechanized cultivation, but he knew that he could never win these arguments, because he understood the emotional loyalties of the older generation to the land of their ancestors.

His own role underwent changes in the last decade of socialism, when he was appointed to be the first full-time secretary of the local cell of the Communist Party. This required him to give up his job as an adviser to smallholder producers, but he remained a member of the cooperative's leadership and argued pragmatically for flexible policies that would benefit all of its members. He also served as manager of a small 'auxiliary economic unit' devoted to the manufacture of shoe uppers, which provided jobs (mainly for women) and helped to keep the cooperative solvent during the last years of socialism. Meanwhile, like almost everyone else in rural

Hungary (as well as many city dwellers), Sanyi worked on his own plots in his spare time. Thanks to this additional income (mainly from vineyards), he was able to modernize his house in the market town and to purchase and maintain his Trabant.

The end of socialism was a catastrophe for Sanyi. It coincided with the breakup of his first marriage. Following his divorce, he had to give up his home in Kiskőrös and private vineyards to his ex-wife. By the time he remarried, he had lost his job in Tázlár and was left with no regular source of income. He was not the only cooperative leader to suffer in this way, but Sanyi's case was much more serious because of his divorce settlement. For some years, he and his new wife had to endure atrocious unhygienic conditions while living at the cooperative's central pig facility. Eventually, with the health of his infant children as the justification, the post-socialist council helped him to construct a new house. He was never able to finish the building properly; his house and yard remain conspicuous for their untidiness and obvious signs of poverty. Some villagers comment on this as evidence of moral failure, and project a mysterious connection between the breakdown of his first marriage and his loyalty to the Communist Party. But my impression over the years is that a large majority sympathizes with Sanyi as a victim of the transition; villagers respect the fact that (almost alone among Party members) he has not switched allegiance but has remained committed to the Hungarian Socialist Party. His previous record of assistance to small farmers is not forgotten and the continued civil engagement of the former Party secretary (e.g., with the theatre group of the upper hamlet), is widely appreciated.

Sanyi became an old age pensioner himself in 2008. After 1990, transfers from the state (mainly child allowances) were the principal source of income in his household. To make ends meet, he has pursued a range of small-scale farming activities, butchered pigs and undertaken other casual jobs for neighbours. One key element in his retirement strategy was to hold on to the shares he received in the cooperative when it was restructured in the early 1990s. Indeed he and his wife bought up shares disposed of by others as cooperative membership shrank. They did so in part because they wanted to show their loyalty to this socialist institution, but at the same time they were convinced that its real estate, including the auxiliary economic units established at the end of the socialist era, would make their investment secure. However, long drawn-out litigation instigated by the former Chief Agronomist eventually resulted in a compensation award that nullified the value of the shares. The cooperative was defunct by 2008, its last remaining properties having been sold to pay off the major creditor, the state. With this, the material dispossession of those who had remained ideologically sympathetic to the specialist cooperative was complete.

Sanyi is clearly a victim; indeed it is hard to imagine a more dramatic case. He has lost much of the ebullience I recall from the socialist era, which he must at least on occasion 'cry back' bitterly in private. Occasionally he attaches blame to particular individuals, notably the cooperative chairman who chose not to rehire him as an agronomist when it would theoretically have been possible to do so in 1990. However, he does not indulge in self-pity and I have never heard him or anyone else in the village use the terms victim or scapegoat; but that is how I see him myself. I admire the fact that he has stuck to his principles. Alone in the village, Sanyi pays a small annual subscription to a county-level association of former cooperative cadres, whose annual meeting he enjoys attending. He still believes deep down that socialist ideals are the key to a more just society. He generally keeps these views to himself, though they slip out occasionally in light-hearted, ironic exchanges at the village clubs, which he organizes, when chatting with those who will understand and perhaps share nostalgic allusions. Unlike the children of his first marriage, those of the second (primarily because of the enthusiasm of their mother) go to church every Sunday and have gone through the standard Catholic life-cycle rituals. Sanyi was baptized and brought up *református*, but it has been made clear to him that some members of that congregation in the village would not welcome his participation in their services. However, in the eyes of the majority, he does not need to attend church services to hold on to his place in the moral community.

With its well-tended garden and tidy yard, the luxurious house of Feri is indicative of the stark contrast between himself and Sanyi. Feri is some five years younger but within the same social generation. At the time of my first fieldwork in 1976–77 he shared a yard with his grandmother, who was my landlady. She was the daughter of one of the first immigrants to resettle the *puszta* of Tázlár in the late nineteenth century. The family had accumulated a substantial acreage, and then lost most of it after being branded *kulák* in the 1950s. Young Feri did not go to church like his grandmother, but he shared her basic political views and had evidently inherited the family's entrepreneurial energies. After completing vocational school, he had applied his skills as a mechanic to profit from the opportunities available in the relaxed climate of the time. It was relatively easy to acquire a private tractor and the additional equipment necessary for a full range of farming services, which he was able to offer more promptly and efficiently than the tractor drivers of the cooperative. Later he added a combine harvester to his private machine park. This dynamic success continued after the end of communism, when he opened the village's first (and only) petrol station and acquired a haulage fleet for long-distance freight transport. When the cooperative began to dispose of its assets, Feri used his shares and those of his grandmother to buy a bus for a knockdown price, reselling it promptly for a substantial profit. In the early 1990s he was the ultimate market entrepreneur, rejoicing in the effective demise of the cooperative through the definitive privatization of all its farmland; he himself showed no interest in regaining ownership rights over expropriated family plots, because he could see that farming had no future.

On the face of it, Feri is a 'winner' of the Hungarian *rendszerváltás*, though in his case the very notion of a rupture is problematic. There was perhaps a slight acceleration in the early 1990s, but his capital accumulation had its roots in the market socialism of the 1970s. Feri was a nominal member of the cooperative (as was his grandmother), but even under socialism, when the cooperative required its members to provide labour inputs (six days per year), he preferred to pay a small financial penalty instead. He employed others to work for him, mainly as drivers. This was initially part of the 'black' economy, since it obviously contradicted the socialist norm, though by the time of my first fieldwork it was tolerated. In the 1990s, his chief assistant and drivers were fully legal: Feri conscientiously paid the employer's prescribed insurance and pension contributions. He has never played any significant role in politics or the public sphere in the village, but he certainly has friends and his material success commands respect. With Sanyi, the former Party Secretary, I recall a teasing, joking relationship in the 1970s. Feri, like his grandmother, made no secret of his distaste for the wasteful bureaucracy of the *kommunisták*. Sanyi countered with banter, nicknaming Feri '*sumák*', a term that implied a moral rebuke for avarice, with implications of cheating.

During my visit in 2008 I could not help but notice changes in Feri's lifestyle, compared to the assertive entrepreneur I had known previously. The change had begun in the late 1990s and was closely linked to the sudden loss of his wife through leukaemia in 1999. Since then he has gone to church more often and lived alone in his large house. One daughter lives and works in Budapest. Another, who has married and given him grandchildren, lives in a nearby market town; she visits regularly and assists him with his accounting. Feri had a new companion who cooked and looked after the house. During my 2008 visit we talked about his business interests and the general social and political climate. He complained that the haulage market was saturated, and that for several years it had been an uphill struggle to balance the books. Although the Hungarian Socialist Party was in power at this point, Feri did not blame this government or its leaders (many others were more critical). Instead, he ventured more sweeping generalizations about the era of *demokrácia*, comparing it unfavourably to the late socialist era. I made the obvious riposte. I suggested that he, of course, had rosy memories of the Kádár years, but only because he had been one of the most astute in exploiting new economic niches. Now such opportunities were few and far between, because there was market competition in all sectors; but surely he would admit that the consolidation of the market was a good thing, even though it made future windfall profits for himself less likely?

'No, no, no,' he explained. I had misunderstood. In his opinion, the economic society of the late socialist era was still fundamentally humane (*emberi*) in a way that the cut-throat competition of the new market society was not. Mistrust was now far more prevalent, the opportunities for village youth had been greatly reduced, and the high incidence of unemployment was tragic. To put it in the terms of Karl Polanyi (1944), Feri offered me a narrative of 'disembedding', in which the very nature of human social relations had been transformed. Despite his very different family background, values and politico-economic profile, his views about the socialist era seemed quite similar to those held by Sanyi. Winner and loser alike hold Kádár's version of socialism to be basically decent, though their own positions in that system had been utterly different. This, I suggest, is evidence of a new 'hidden transcript' among Hungarian villagers. It modifies the dominant rural narrative, which emphasizes the material dispossession of collectivization and the violence done by socialism not only to persons, but to the nation. This hidden transcript opens up a space for nostalgia for the socialist past beyond the economistic, analogous to the ways in which the hidden transcripts of those earlier decades rested on a positive evaluation of that which the socialists had ruthlessly swept aside.[14]

These various elements of social memory, the national narrative that dominates in the media and the local narratives of villagers, fit uncomfortably together in individual heads, as do the Eastern and Western elements within the national mythomoteur, as described above. My impression is that private nostalgia for the Kádár era has risen over the years, at least in the social generation to which Sanyi and Feri belong. Some of the most vociferous detractors of socialism – those who were most active in the Independent Smallholders' Party until its ignominious collapse in 2002 and who were ideologically opposed to *any* form of cooperative – have come to concede that socialist job security and support policies for agriculture compare favourably with the situation today. It is very unlikely that Feri will ever cast his vote for a candidate of the Hungarian Socialist Party; but neither he nor Sanyi have much time for elite contestations of the national past and symbols such as the turul.[15]

Subjective temporalities are affected by intimate personal circumstances. I hinted at the significance of domestic misfortune in the cases of both Sanyi and Feri. Their children, most of whom have no personal recollection of life under socialism, certainly see many matters quite differently (as noted, Feri's daughters have left the village; Sanyi's five children with his second wife remain in Tázlár). But it seems to me that both generations have experienced what I have elsewhere theorized as the destruction of the socialist moral economy (Hann 2003) or 'moral dispossession' (Hann 2011). Although the loose form of cooperative in Tázlár differed from the standard models of socialist agriculture, the end of the old moral order was very much the same throughout the rural sectors of the former Soviet bloc. Some post-socialist nostalgia for that collective order can be expected everywhere, since the countryside has been one of the major losers of the transformation processes. Compared to the ex-USSR, rural nostalgia is a more complex phenomenon in Eastern Europe because it conflicts with strong ideologies of private ownership, still powerful elements in the recollections of older generations. Within Eastern Europe, the propensity for nostalgia is further modified by the particular forms of collective farming adopted, the Hungarian path being one of the most flexible and successful.

Conclusion

> Nostalgia can be defined, from the sociohistorical viewpoint, as a persistent image of a superior way of life in the distant past. It is, therefore, a kind of 'collective memory' with intense affect implications. (Armstrong 1982: 16)

In contrast to the case of the former East Germany, where *Ostalgie* is to a large extent the manipulative creation of new external elites, post-socialist nostalgia in Hungary has been almost a taboo for the new, endogenous political elites (Nadkarni 2010). When one considers the dynamism of the Kádár era, the many positive social, economic and even political indicators of the 1970s and 1980s, this reticence seems paradoxical. The explanation must be sought in the *longue durée* national memory. John Armstrong provides a useful corrective to short-term temporalities by analysing nostalgia in the context of the rise of agrarian empires and urban civilizations across Eurasia over millennia. He argues that modern national identities derive from ancient mythomoteurs, the constitutive myths of pre-national polities. The Hungarian case is of particular interest because, alongside the western Christian legitimization sought by Stephen for a newly sedentarized people, traces lingered of an alternative mythology, that of Finno-Ugrian (or 'Turanian') steppe nomads. This alternative withered in the course of the Middle Ages, but it was spectacularly revived (arguably a clear-cut case of elite 'invention') in the age of nationalism and is still available for invocation today.

When a government is unwilling or unable to address unfavourable socioeconomic trends, accentuated by a global crisis, a resort to the mytho-moteur is perhaps the only way forward. The term 'world nation' does not exist in the dictionary. The speech at Ópusztaszer, from which I quoted above, was Viktor Orbán's way of expressing belligerent Hungarian exceptionalism. The Magyars are not just another small people of East-Central Europe. They have a unique origin and enjoyed a glorious history, at any rate until the end of the Austro-Hungarian Empire, when millions of Magyars became the subjects of other states. It seems that Hungary is still struggling to come to terms with the loss of imperial power (which was not untarnished, because inferior to that of Austria, but more than vicarious). Its contemporary leaders would like nothing more than to blot out the entire twentieth century and return to the nineteenth, when they constructed their splendid capital city and the key elements of the richly ambiguous mytho-moteur that remains in place today. If socialism figures in contemporary public symbolism, it is primarily with reference to the 1950s, a decade which can only be demonized. The later decades of socialism were more successful but not in such a way as to lend themselves to incorporation in the national mythology. However, as I have shown, villagers in places such as Tázlár may still cry them back privately, and not only for economistic reasons.

Acknowledgements

I am grateful to the editors, to the anonymous reviewers, and to Ildikó Bellér-Hann, Krisztina Kehl-Bodrogi, László Kürti and Mihály Sárkány for their comments on an earlier draft of this chapter. I am also grateful to Sanyi, Feri (who passed away in 2013) and many other long-term friends in Tázlár, Budapest and elsewhere in Hungary. Of course none are responsible for the views I express, but all will surely understand how hard it is for an ethnographer to write about nostalgia in the country of his first fieldwork without the constant encroachment of his personal nostalgia.

Notes

1. In Hungarian: 'zsebravágott minket a történelem'. This is a chorus line in a song by Feró Nagy, the title of which provides the epigraph for this chapter. Feró Nagy (born in 1946) is an iconoclastic rock musician of working-class background, best known for introducing punk styles into Hungary from the late 1970s. He had numerous awkward encounters with socialist power holders.

'I hate the entire twentieth century' (1991) was the most successful album of his band, *Beatrice*; this was surely the first time Miklós Horthy, Adolf Hitler, and Josef Stalin featured together in a pop lyric.

2. Armstrong acknowledges Ramon d'Abadal i de Vingals as the originator of this concept, which was later popularized in numerous works by Anthony Smith (e.g., Smith 1986). Although specifically referring to representations of collective identity, mythomoteur has an affinity to Sahlins's more general notion of 'mytho-praxis' (Sahlins 1985). Whereas all of these authors place the emphasis on long-term cultural continuities extending throughout the society, in this chapter I emphasize that the modern mythomoteur of the Hungarians was largely the creation of elites in the age of nationalism; full dissemination throughout the population is incomplete even today.

3. This party, too, faded in the second post-socialist decade, and Csurka himself died in 2012. However, very similar policies and positions are held by the members of *Jobbik*, which polled almost as strongly as the *Hungarian Socialist Party* in the general elections of 2010 and 2014. Besides the alleged internal threat posed by Jews and Roma, these parties rail against foreigners in general, including officials of the European Union.

4. This government has sought to implement a radical reorientation of Hungarian politics and society. Though ostensibly committed to the values of Christian Europe, its policies have led to very strained relations with the European Union.

5. In spite of this formal equivalence, this institution (located on Andrássy Street, previously People's Republic Street) devotes much more of its space and resources to commemorating the 'victims of communism'. It is prominent in the public sphere, with effective outreach to school parties as well as to tourists. On 25 February 2013, the Day for the Commemoration of the Victims of Communism (*A Kommunizmus Áldozatai Emléknapja*) was celebrated with guided tours led by well-known musicians, among them Feró Nagy. For the perfect antidote to this museum (not featured in the tourist guides and so discreet that no name is displayed outside the premises), the reader is advised to walk down Andrássy Street to the 'Terv' cafe-bar at 19 Nándor Street. Here the aura of Hungary's great football team of the 1950s (the 'gold team') and consumerist memorabilia stimulate customers to look back with curiosity and even genuine nostalgia on the early years of central planning.

6. The Hortobágy National Park to the north-east was included in the UNESCO World Heritage list in 1999. The justification read 'The Hungarian Puszta is an outstanding example of a cultural landscape shaped by a pastoral human society'. See Albert 1999 for further discussion of the Great Plain as a national symbol.

7. For subtle comparison of Árpád with King Stephen in the iconography of the nation, see Sinkó 1989.

8. The previous name was the nondescript 'Sövényháza'. 'Ópusztaszer' has an immediately patriotic ring. The first letter means 'old' and was necessary to distinguish this settlement from Pusztaszer, the rival northern settlement

promoted by Kecskemét. *Puszta* refers to uninhabited plain, generally used as
pasture (like that of Tázlár until the nineteenth century), while *Szer* was the
fragmentary link to Árpád provided by *Anonymus* in his manuscript. In addition
to the scholarly inputs of archaeologist Gyula László, the driving force behind
the initiative was Ferenc Erdei (1911–1971). Erdei was a 'left populist' who published pioneering analyses of the pre-socialist countryside (see the next section
of this chapter) and was passionately committed to an 'embourgeoisement' that
would allow the persistence of Hungary's unique folk culture. He was closely
allied to the reformers in 1956 and came close to paying for this stance with his
life. However, his peasant origins made him useful to János Kádár's regime and
he played an important role during the 1960s in ensuring the flexible imple-
mentation of collectivization (see Huszár 2012).

9. The complex was opened to the public in 1995, under the socialist-led government of Gyula Horn. For more information about the site and its programmes
   (in English and German as well as Hungarian), see <www.opusztaszer.hu>.

10. As reported in the newspaper *Pester Lloyd* / 40 – 2012 (Feuilleton), 5 October
    2012. My translation.

11. This is not so self-evident: when it comes to the study of temporal subjectivities,
    there may also be dangers and disadvantages. The foreign anthropologist in
    period t who believes he has shared some experiences with village informants
    in period (t – 1) is not thereby well informed about period (t – 2), which must
    have shaped local subjectivities in (t – 1) and may have more direct impact than
    (t – 1) on nostalgia, or the lack of it, in t. If the fieldwork experience is recalled
    positively, with exhilarating personal moments, leading eventually to a PhD
    and a career, the elderly anthropologist's recollections of (t – 1) may be signifi-
    cantly out of line with those of local people, despite the year or two in which
    certain experiences were ostensibly shared. In short, a younger colleague free of
    such distorting factors might be a more trustworthy guide in grasping how the
    villagers in period t recall (t – 1), even if he or she may not be able to comment
    on the accuracy of certain memories, which the earlier researcher feels better
    able to assess in the light of concrete encounters and what was committed to
    paper in (t – 1).

12. Following bitter internal disputes, that party disintegrated around the turn of
    the century. Its rural constituency has since tended to vote for Viktor Orbán's
    FIDESZ party, though more extreme right-wing parties also attract a significant
    following.

13. This section of the chapter is based on a field trip in summer 2008. It is adapted
    from a lecture given at a Workshop at the University of Bielefeld, which was
    later published electronically (Hann 2011). The context was a *Graduiertenkolleg*
    with a focus on the concept of generation; my thanks to workshop conveners
    Jeanette Prochnow and Caterina Rohde.

14. I borrow the concept of 'hidden transcript' from James Scott (1990). Friends
    in Budapest frequently suggest similar analogies to the one I make here. Some
    suggest that, in certain respects, there is actually less scope to challenge the

views of today's FIDESZ government than there was to criticize government policy in the last decades of socialism; it is certainly wise to keep critical opinions (or any sentiment that might be construed as nostalgia for socialism) to oneself if one wishes to remain employed in the public sector.
15. This does not imply that they are not normal, patriotic citizens. In Feri's case this consciousness is not diminished in any way by the fact that he is of Slovak descent on his father's side; their Slovak surname was Magyarized in the early 1940s.

References

Albert, R. 1999. 'La Grande Plaine hongroise, symbole national. Genèse d'un imaginaire, XVIII–XX siècles', in Rose-Marie Lagrave (ed.), *Villes et campagnes en Hongrie XVI–XX siècles*. Budapest: Les Cahiers de l'Atelier 1, pp. 11–37.
Armstrong, J.A. 1982. *Nations Before Nationalism*. Chapel Hill: University of North Carolina Press.
Berdahl, D. 2010. *On the Social Life of Postsocialism: Memory, Consumption, Germany*. Bloomington: Indiana University Press.
Boyer, D. 2010. 'From Algos to Autonomos. Nostalgic Eastern Europe as Postimperial Mania', in M. Todorova and Z. Gille (eds), *Post-Communist Nostalgia*. New York: Berghahn, pp. 17–28.
Erdei, F. 1937. *Futóhomok. A Duna-Tiszaköze*. Budapest: Athenaeum.
Gal, S. 1991. 'Bartók's Funeral: Representations of Europe in Hungarian Political Rhetoric', *American Ethnologist* 18 (3): 440–58.
Hann, C. 1980. *Tázlár: A Village in Hungary*. Cambridge: Cambridge University Press.
———. 1990. 'Socialism and King Stephen's Right Hand', *Religion in Communist Lands* 18 (1): 4–24.
———. 1993. 'From Production to Property: Decollectivization and the Family-land Relationship in Contemporary Hungary', *Man* 28 (3): 299–32.
———. 2003. 'Introduction: The Moral Economy of Decollectivisation', in C. Hann and the 'Property Relations' group (eds), *The Postsocialist Agrarian Question: Property Relations and the Rural Condition*. Münster: LIT, pp. 1–46.
———. 2011. 'Moral Dispossession', *InterDisciplines* 2 (2): 11–37. Retrieved from http://www.inter-disciplines.de/bghs/index.php/indi/article/viewFile/36/31 (accessed 12 October 2012).
———. 2012. 'Transition, Tradition, and Nostalgia: Postsocialist Transformations in a Comparative Framework', *Collegium Antropologicum* 36 (4): 1119–28.
Huszár, T. 2012. *Ferenc Erdei 1910–1971; politikai életrajz*. Budapest: Corvina.
Kürti, L. 2001 *The Remote Borderland: Transylvania in the Hungarian Cultural Imagination*. Albany: State University of New York Press.
Lampland, M. 1995. *The Object of Labor: Commodification in Socialist Hungary*. Chicago: Chicago University Press.

Nadkarni, M. 2010. '"But it's Ours" Nostalgia and the Politics of Authenticity in Post-socialist Hungary', in M. Todorova and Z. Gille (eds), *Post-communist Nostalgia*. New York: Berghahn, pp. 190–214.

Polanyi, K. 1944. *The Great Transformation: The Political and Economic Origins of Our Time*. Boston: Beacon Press.

Rady, M. 2009. 'The Gesta Hungarorum of Anonymus, the Anonymous Notary of King Béla: A Translation', *Slavonic and East European Review* 87 (4) : 681–727.

Sahlins, M. 1985. *Islands of History*. Chicago: University of Chicago Press.

Scott, J. C. 1990. *Domination and the Arts of Resistance: Hidden Transcripts*. New Haven, CT: Yale University Press.

Sinkó, K. 1989. 'Árpád versus Saint István. Competing Heroes and Competing Interests in the Figurative Representation of Hungarian History', *Ethnologia Europaea* 19 (1): 67–83.

Smith, A.D. 1986 *The Ethnic Origins of Nations*. Oxford: Basil Blackwell.

Striker, S. 1984. 'The Dancehouse: Folklorism in Hungary in the 1970s', *Folklore and the State: Contemporary Eastern Europe Conference*, Bellagio, 27 August 1984.

Swain, N. 1985. *Collective Farms which Work?* Cambridge: Cambridge University Press.

Szelényi, I. 1988. *Socialist Entrepreneurs: Embourgeoisement in Rural Hungary*. Cambridge: Polity.

Todorova, M. and Z. Gille (eds) 2010. *Post-Communist Nostalgia*. New York: Berghahn.

Zempléni, A. 2002 'Sepulchral Land and Territory of the Nation: Reburial Rituals in Contemporary Hungary', in A.G. András (ed.), *A nemzet antropológiája (Festschrift for Tamás Hofer)*. Budapest: Mandátum, pp. 73–81.

Chapter 5

Consuming Communism

Material Cultures of Nostalgia in Former East Germany

Jonathan Bach

Ostalgie is perhaps the most high profile case regarding the phenomena of sympathetic sentiments for the vanished socialist republics of Central and Eastern Europe. Many years after the film *Good Bye Lenin* made *Ostalgie* – the German neologism for nostalgia for the former socialist German Democratic Republic (GDR), also known as East Germany – into a household word, the phenomenon has not faded but rather become a stable part of the tourist and commercial landscape. Today, Berlin's tourist office promotes the GDR Museum, where 'the kitchen still has the cooking smells of way back when', and the Trabi Safari where you can drive the cult cars from old days. The old East German street-crossing signals known as *Ampelmännchen* are not only the rare GDR vestige adopted in the West, but are a growing international brand with a chain of shops from Berlin to Tokyo, where the Japanese website presents them as the 'symbol of traffic safety, German unification, and resurrection' and sells their image on everything from lamps to noodles (Ampelmann-Japan 2013). 'Eastern product' shops like Ostpaket do a respectable business in the mid six figures, plying over seven hundred items from mundane household goods to novelties such as the Young Pioneers condom with the original Pioneer motto: 'Be prepared – always prepared!' Tourists can stay in Berlin's GDR-themed hotel 'Ostel' and take in the hit East–West love story musical *Beyond the Horizon*,

124Jonathan Bach

while more determined visitors can celebrate the GDR's anniversaries in rural Tutow's DDR Museum with dancing and Soljanka soup served in genuine Mitropa bowls.

In the early years after unification the appearance of nostalgic themes struck critics as misguided or naive in the wake of the failed dictatorship. The few initial stores that sold 'Eastern' products, such as Intershop 2000, became the focus of media curiosity and occasional scorn for trivializing the GDR dictatorship. Ironic appropriations, such as nostalgia parties, seemed acceptable as long as they mocked the failed regime, yet any serious expression of longing for the GDR was commonly derided as delusionary and ungrateful. The term *Ostalgie* itself carries connotations of a stereotypically narrow-minded Western view of former Easterners. While colloquially used, it is seldom preferred by those in what we can call the nostalgia industry. For example, the proprietor of a successful Eastern products store 'flew into a rage' at a journalist's mention of the word, countering that 'when someone in the West uses Nivea cream one doesn't call him *West*algic' (Trappe 2012). An annoyed contributor to a recent online forum about Eastern products complained how '*Ostalgie* is a Wessi [i.e., Western] concept for defaming people whose right to their home [*Heimat*] is resented for arrogant, ignorant, bigoted, consumption-addled, socially insensitive and politically charged reasons' (Viktor 2010). Yet whether it is called *Ostalgie* or not, commodified material manifestations of the GDR era – what we can call nostalgia objects – are currently part and parcel of the German cultural and memory landscape.

This chapter contributes to the investigation of *Ostalgie*, with specific focus on the material dimension of nostalgia.[1] While nostalgia is thought of primarily as a form of longing for something no longer attainable – a longing for a style of longing, as I explored in an earlier article (Bach 2002) – it is made manifest primarily through material objects that are, in one form or another, obtainable. Objects and images, as Dominik Bartmanski (2011: 9) writes, 'need to be approached as constitutive, not epiphenomenal of nostalgia'. I argue here that what we call nostalgia is a collective phenomenon that emerges *through* the effects of commodification, which transforms everyday objects into nostalgia objects and thus makes them capable of transmitting cultural knowledge. Commodification marks representative items from a past era, usually from everyday life, as valuable (both literally and figuratively). This allows them to remain in or re-enter circulation and, most importantly, pushes objects into the domain of what Michel de Certeau (1984) calls secondary production, where consumers 'produce' new symbolic meanings that were not originally intended. In their new guises, the symbols, slogans and styles of the old regime are dislodged and recombined in ways that make them effectively contemporary. In this way nostalgia objects are kept alive and gradually turned into a 'normal' part of the landscape.

I am not arguing that commodification is somehow a good in itself, or making a statement about the relative value of cultural knowledge transmitted through nostalgia objects. Rather, the examples in this essay explore the relation between nostalgia and materiality. Understanding this relation might help explain why *Ostalgie* did not wane with the coming of the first post-unification generation, but rather became seemingly entrenched. Beyond the example of Germany, it might also help explain how nostalgia functions as a form of cultural transmission. Further, as the above comments critical of the term *Ostalgie* indicate, I also hope to convey some of the quandaries that accompany the widespread use of the term to refer to the phenomenon of nostalgia for socialism. There is a constant slippage in the discourse between *Ostalgie* as a descriptive, derogatory, or defiant term, depending on who is speaking and under what circumstances. In the first part of this essay, I examine a form of redemptive discourse, in which collectors salvage objects of discarded everyday life and give them new values as they find their way into private museums. The second part follows former GDR era products that are sold today, often with cult status, showing how what began as a defiant reappropriation of symbolic value became part of an established market for regional products. The conclusion suggests why *Ostalgie* has become an accepted but not acceptable part of contemporary German culture.

Collecting Communism

In the immediate years after unification, all across the former GDR citizens purged their products, appliances, clothes, cars and documents. This massive cleansing was the corollary to a collective effervescence of consumption that had accompanied the currency union between West and East Germany in February 1990, when Eastern stores switched their inventories to Western products literally overnight. For months shelves were stocked and restocked at breakneck speed in response to the massive pent-up consumer desire endemic to socialist economies of scarcity. As a consequence, fully functional everyday GDR objects instantly became culturally obsolete and wended their way into the bins or attic. In that first unification year residents of the GDR territory produced 1.2 tons of rubbish per capita, three times that of the West (Ahbe 2000). Anything Eastern seemed suddenly inferior. Items that once occupied high status in the East were suddenly next to worthless.

As a joke went at the time, a man stops at a garage on the highway and asks the mechanic for two windshield wipers for his (East German) Trabant car. The mechanic replies: 'That's a fair trade'.

As the material life of a dead nation state disappeared into dumps, attics and storage spaces, a motley crew of mostly middle-aged males, gripped by anxiety at the suddenness of change, began to collect remnants of everyday life from rubbish heaps, flea markets, abandoned buildings, friends and neighbours. This often took the form of a consciously desperate attempt to grasp the past as it slipped away before their eyes. Stretching out his arms with clenched fists, one collector illustrated to me how, during the unification year, he would collect bags and bags of DDR 'stuff' from the streets and shops on his way to and from his night shift at a light bulb factory, fretful because he 'knew it would soon disappear'. Collectors combed flea markets, stores, rubbish bins, buildings and industrial sites for packages of dry goods, Communist Party-related paraphernalia, certificates, postcards, bottles of soda, appliances, cups and saucers, furniture, record albums and instruction manuals, doing the hard work to wrench the everyday out of the fringes.

The first phase of the afterlife of GDR objects of everyday life is inseparable from this collector culture. The inveterate collector, Jürgen Hartwig, was a former East German locksmith who found his calling during an epiphany over Christmas 1989 when he realized the past – his past – which had been preserved behind the Wall, was on the verge of disappearing, and he must begin to collect it. Hartwig was living in West Berlin at the time, having been forcibly expelled after serving two years in a GDR jail for trying to leave the country illegally. Suddenly, preserving for posterity the country that ejected him became a major motive. He co-founded and continues to serve as the president of the Association for the Documentation of GDR Everyday Culture, which has run a swap meet every month at the formerly prominent GDR Café Sybille for over twenty years. Similar acts of collecting gave the everyday objects a combination of two values that began to transform trash items to nostalgia objects.

The first value that accrued to the object through collecting was survival. With the 'death' of the GDR came a widespread sense of people becoming strangers in their own land or permanently estranged from a past that defined their identity (as with Hartwig 1994). One form of the work of mourning is to survive what amounts to a form of living death through the act of collection (Baudrillard 2005 [1968]). The collectors engage in salvage as a way of ordering time and space, of reorganizing the suddenly drastically disorganized present. One collector explained the heady rush of salvage as an irresistible impulse 'to hoard and to hoard, because time is running

out . . . I want above all to brutally collect and unsystematically hoard everything' (Faktor 1999). In a context where many Eastern Germans felt that,
'There was no time to say goodbye' (the title of a 1995 collector's exhibit),
objects become, as Baudrillard (2005: 104) wrote, 'the thing with which we
construct our own mourning' and thus symbolically transcend death.

Beyond the value of personal and cultural survival, once the objects
began to be the focus of collections they acquired intersubjective worth –
the value of recognition of another's desire for your object. Collectors began
to understand how their own past could literally fetch a price, and learned
to play their own sense of self-worth in the dance around monetary value.
The monetary value of GDR items remains unspectacular compared with
antiques from earlier periods, with the priciest objects falling into conventional categories such as coins, currency and stamps. Yet the very notion that
one's material past can fetch a price began to change self perception, allowing for knowingly ironic reversals and new-found fluency with commodity
culture. For example, an East Berliner recalled how, shortly after unification, he saw a Westerner buying badges at a flea market and realized with a
sudden flash of insight that his own old school badges and medals, buried in
boxes somewhere to which he had never given a second thought, might fetch
hard cash. More or less on a whim he invited the Westerner to his home to
show him his badges (Krawczyk 1996). When the Westerner asked, 'How
much for everything?', the response was a mixture of melodrama, irony and
business acumen:

> I stood up, breathed deeply, sat down, and whispered: 'That is my past, how can
> you convert it into money?'
> 'How much?'
> 'You tell me.'
> 'Hundred.'
> I laid a cloth over the objects. The effect was stunning. As soon as he
> couldn't see what he desired, he increased his offer by two and half times.
> I said: 'I won't let it go for under three hundred'. Fast as a pickpocket he drew
> three bills from his pocket, and covetously withdrew the cover from his freshly
> acquired possession.

The point, of course, is not that some GDR everyday items can, as with
the badges, fetch some small cash, but that desire by others produces an
enhanced sense of the worth of one's own past, and that the clever deployment of this sense can lead to playing with role reversals and notions of
value. This suggests a process of self-inscription in objects, similar to what
David Parkin (1999) observes among persons whose sense of social self is disrupted by displacement. Yet unlike Parkin's examples, where self-inscription

happens in 'non-commodity, gift-like' objects such as mementos that refugees carry with them when they flee, in this example the re-articulation of identity happens through commodification. Commodification of one's own past allows people to access what Parkin, in another context, has called their 'temporarily encapsulated personhood', otherwise stored in the objects that survive from one setting to another.

Object Lessons

These early collections formed the impetus for the two trajectories that GDR nostalgia objects have taken since unification: museums of everyday life and the rebranding of products with commercial distribution. Back in 1994 Hartwig fantasized that 'one day former East Germans will have a similar experience as I have had with things from forty years of GDR history, and a museum that documents history and everyday culture will later awaken a great interest' (Hartwig 1994: 3). While there is no one such museum (though the GDR Museum in Berlin comes close), nearly twenty years later there are over two dozen private GDR museums of varying size and quality dedicated to socialist everyday objects, and publically funded museums regularly incorporate everyday objects into their exhibits.

With some difficulty at first, collectors began to find permanent homes for exhibiting their collections, and their museums sprouted in basements, garages, homes, barracks and former factories. With no access to public money they usually formed private non-profit organizations, in the German sense of 'common-use societies', that allowed them to raise funds through membership fees, contributions and admissions. In addition to their own collections they placed public calls for the donation of artefacts. Among the very first of these museums was the Open Depot, which turned into the Documentation Centre for Everyday Culture of the GDR in Eisenhüttenstadt (independent from Hartwig's similarly named association), emerging originally from a short-lived collaboration between the less orderly Hartwig and the scholarly West Berlin curator Andreas Ludwig. More typical of the dozens of private museums is the GDR Museum Pirna, where the founder, Conny Kaden, began collecting numismatics in 1993 and realized a few years later that his small (fifty square metres) apartment resembled a museum – 'everywhere stood radios, toys and medals, the bookcases were piled with GDR books, and on the walls in the corridor and kitchen hung GDR and Pioneer flags and every morning our former politicians smiled down at me' (Kaden 2012). In 2004 he opened the museum, which today occupies two thousand square metres in a former military barracks.

The museums are a qualified success. Some are haphazard collections in cramped spaces, others are multi-story mainstays of their local tourist economy. Over 120,000 visitors to date have sought out the recreated dentist's office, schoolroom and kitchen in Apolda, and over 50,000 visitors a year trek to the Time Travel (*Zeitreise*) museum in Radebeul near Dresden. The Berlin GDR Museum tops them all with over half a million visitors a year.[2] All of the museums claim that showing life 'as it really was' is their main task, educating people too young to remember the GDR and providing an identity-affirming experience for the older generation who, judging by conversations and the many entries in guest books – 'the museum awakens memories of our childhood' is a typical example – are generally appreciative of the trip down memory lane.

The private museums themselves mostly conform to a general format that places emphasis on experience and interactivity, most pronounced in the Berlin GDR Museum with its motto of 'history to touch'. Nearly all of them place emphasis on quantity, with rooms full of radios, watches, strollers, or over-stocked *Konsum* grocery stores conveying a sense of scale and fullness in distinction to the sense of the GDR as a small state defined by scarcity. In contrast to the image of the GDR as grey, the exhibits are colourful and homey, as with the 1960s diorama in Wittenberg, complete down to the details of a chocolate bar and cookies on the table, a Stempke vacuum cleaner, a homemade antenna for receiving Western TV, and Igilit shades on the lamps illuminating books in the modular shelving units.[3]

The term *Ostalgie* is generally avoided to describe the museums or used sparingly and with qualifications. Nearly all museums make a point of saying that they do not yearn for the past, they only wish to dignify people's lived experience. 'Dear visitors', asks an open letter at the GDR Museum in Tutow (Görß 2013), 'is it *Ostalgie* to long for the scents of childhood?' This reference to childhood is not random, rather it points to a major trope in the GDR museums, where objects are presented mostly as innocent carriers of personal memory. As Shevchenko and Nadkarni (this volume) note, nostalgia gains its force by depoliticizing memory into something apolitical, non-partisan and seemingly objective and neutral, such as childhood memories. In the complex case of the socialist everyday, everyday life was mercilessly politicized and private life was officially delegitimized and made inherently suspect. For both public and private museums, then, the representation of mundane objects is more treacherous than it might seem at first glance because it invites and confounds attempts at historical objectification.

The private museums' defensive claim that it is *not* nostalgic to objectively show life 'as it really was' can therefore itself be seen itself a political move to correct a perceived hegemonic Western narrative that devalues East German lives, consigning them to a past where life was either a lie or a crime. Directors of some of the private museums expressed in conversations their contempt for professional exhibits that they saw as a hegemonic, Western, self-serving, state-supported 'demonization' of East Germany. The favour is returned by historians and curators, however, who see such museums as trivializing the very lies and crimes that trapped East Germans in a corroded, paranoid netherworld. While the Time Travel (*Zeitreise*) museum in Radebeul ('Zeitreise' n.d.) declares up front that the museum 'is not about the usual portrayal of the GDR and its mechanisms of repression', the historian Martin Sabrow (Sabrow 2009: 13) counters gravely that denying the complicity of everyday life with dictatorial rule 'would not be the first time in the history of Germany's grappling with dictatorships that the self-validation of one's own experience represses a regime's violence'.

Beyond debates over whether the museums trivialize the past, their relentless and repetitive focus on the world of everyday goods quietly embodies the vexed role of consumption at the heart of the socialist experiment. Consumption functioned as both a core identity of late socialist modernity and the Achilles' heel of the system.[4] Today it plays a further ironic role in reifying (literally) the past. This is reinforced by the significant role the gift shop often plays, becoming in some ways an extension of the museum (and often the entrance itself), presenting GDR-era items ranging from replicas of typical colourful rooster-shaped egg cups to novelty items celebrating the fictitious 'sixtieth anniversary' of the GDR (which only lived till forty). This abundance and variety of GDR goods on display and for sale provides a further irony: socialism was supposed to overcome the alienation caused in part by the loss of meaning in 'things' due to commodity fetishism, but now it is precisely the socialist 'thing' that restores meaning as a commodity.

Products of the Past

This brings us to a discussion of the second trajectory emerging from the transformation of everyday items into nostalgia objects. The collectors' linking of commodities with identity was reinforced in the museums, and also materialized in the steady reappearance of GDR-era brands and associated products, so-called *Ostprodukte* (East products). Tapping into what Hartwig called a 'reservoir of memories deeply anchored in the consciousness of the ex-GDR citizen about the positive side of the GDR and one's own lived past', once unloved GDR items became displaced sites for emotions

(Hartwig 1994: 3). 'I broke into tears of joy, good old Rondo', pronounced a customer upon the reintroduction of a GDR coffee brand in 1997 (Ahbe 2005: 50).

Similar to the move of everyday objects from the trash to private museums, commercially available products came to affirm the 'positive side' of lived experience for Eastern Germans against a general atmosphere of inferiority and insecurity. In the 1990s the rap group A.N.T.I. sang 'Eastniggers . . . /are what we all are. / The color of our skin is white / yet in Germany we are the last shit' (in Roth and Rudolf 1997: 119), an extreme version of a sentiment that is still present in the stubborn inequality in income and employment rates between the former West and East. This binary discourse was to a significant extent internalized in the early years, when the same pent-up consumer desire that drove East Germans to toss their material culture into the rubbish bin conversely overvalued Western products as synonymous with the seemingly superior value. In the wake of unification, GDR products conveyed inferiority in both production quality and taste, a sentiment widely shared in the West.

Yet the shame that surrounded GDR products simultaneously served as a form of cultural intimacy in Michael Herzfeld's (1997) sense, where a set of objects define insiderhood through their disapproval by powerful outsiders, in this case West Germans. The products of everyday life that returned to or remained on the market – detergent, pickles, mustard, beer – were intimate also in the literal sense of being ephemeral products that came into close contact with the body. Some people stockpiled goods out of practicality, like the man who recalled hoarding a year's supply of *Spee*-brand detergent when he realized that stores suddenly considered it worthless. But soon a few stores began to hang signs saying 'We sell Eastern products', offering certain popular GDR brands to appeal to consumers exhausted by the task of trying new items and seeking to save money.

In a short time certain brands developed cult status, in part because they were still available, familiar and inexpensive, and in part because of their design, which emphasized the retro directness of socialist era advertising. Admired in the West largely for their novelty value, these brands also provided a way for Easterners to symbolically undermine the West/East binary by refusing supposedly self-evidently superior Western goods. In conversations with friends, in stores and in online forums Eastern Germans began to regard Eastern products as better tasting in part because they were more authentic: some considered them purer in substance (less preservatives) and soul (less marketing gimmicks), even if this was not always the case. 'Good old' East German products became vehicles of unsubtle defiance, for example, Club Cola – 'our Cola' – came with the tag 'belittled by some, it can't be killed' (*Von einigen belächelt, ist sie doch nicht tot zu kriegen*), or Juwel cigarettes, which addressed its target audience with the slogan: 'I smoke Juwel because I already tested the West. One for us' (*Ich rauche Juwel, weil ich den Westen schon getestet hab'. Eine für uns*). The reference to testing the West alludes not only to the obvious but to a famous slogan for an older Western brand of cigarettes called 'West'. Eastern products became a political strategy for Easterners to resist speechlessness in a discursive field of cultural production dominated by the West.[5]

One of the reasons why so few East German brands survived unification had to do not only with consumers' perceptions of quality (real or imagined), but with the inability of East German firms to compete in the new unified German market. The federal trust agency in charge of privatization liquidated or sold most of the 'people's own' firms that produced East German consumer products, with the result that the best selling major GDR-era brands today are mostly owned by Western companies, even if in some cases they still produce locally. Juwel, for example, is owned by Phillip Morris, while Club Cola is owned by a Hessen-based (West German) beverage company. F6, the Phillip Morris subsidiary that produces Juwel, cheerfully explains how its product 'stands for what's good and trusted from days past and helps with the self-conscious articulation of East German identity' (Lay 1997). However accurate the clever, critical, advertising slogans of Eastern products are in capturing the sentiments of a lost identity, they are also a marketing strategy for capturing market share in the former East.

Today a standard repertoire of GDR-era brands follow specific marketing strategies aimed at regional identities (except for alcohol brands, which are among the few to have nationwide recognition).[6] In some cases products are redesigned to seem even more local, like mustard from Bautzen, known in the GDR as Bautzener Senf, and rebranded after being purchased by a Bavarian company as 'Bautz'ner Senf' with the apostrophe suggesting a colloquial, folksy image. Following a national trend towards buying local, GDR-era brands successfully give the impression of helping the struggling local economy, which is an oft-cited reason given by consumers for purchasing them.

The sense of regional identity and authenticity of quality and heritage is deepened by a renewed emphasis on the pre-war roots of many 'GDR' products, such as the Spreewald brand pickles made famous by the film *Good Bye Lenin*, which, it turns out, had received a very early product endorsement in the writings of Theodore Fontane at the end of the nineteenth century. Nudossi hazelnut spread was already enjoyed, as one irked Easterner claimed in a 2010 online discussion, in the Weimar Republic.

Under the heading *Do Western Germans Have No Sense of Quality?* he asserted that, in comparison to Nudossi, the better-known brand Nutella is a 'cheap sugar paste', and implicitly compares it with Goethe and Schiller, who also 'spent much of their time in "East Germany"' (Ruediger 2010).

If certain Eastern products such as Radeberger beer or Rotkäppchen (Little Red Riding Hood) sparkling wine have found their way into the standard supermarket repertoire, the largest concentration of Eastern products is to be found in the specialty stores. The largest of these, such as Ostpaket and Ostprodukte Versand, have substantial physical stores and a robust online presence.[7] Similar to the private museums, which they resemble in many ways, the specialty stores disavow *Ostalgie*, claiming simply to give the people what they want and keeping alive 'affectionate memories of how', as the store Ostprodukte-Versand puts it, 'alongside the Wall, there was much loveliness [*so viel Schönes*] in our own country' (Ostprodukte-Versand 2013). Similar to the museums, they see themselves as providing a vital social function of transmitting history to the next generation. Accordingly, their websites contain history sections with photos, guides to GDR currency or official abbreviations, and lyrics to the GDR national anthem, in addition to trivia contests, editorials and links to GDR-themed sites. Ostpaket (the store whose proprietor flew into a rage at the mention of the word *Ostalgie*), has created its own mini museum called 'East Times' (*Ostzeit*) that seeks 'to keep alive memories of forty years of living and working in the GDR' (Ostpaket 2013). To this end, the store asks to borrow objects from former GDR citizens for its exhibit, preferably accompanied by stories such as 'on my turntable is the record by the band AMIGA, like it had when I got my first kiss!'

Ostpaket, whose logo is a Trabant against a silhouetted map of the GDR accompanied by the motto 'good things from the East!' plays in its name (literally 'East Package') on an inversion of the well-known phenomenon of West Packages sent to the GDR from West Germany during the Cold War. Similar to other stores it offers several ironic varieties of 'East Packages'. As a profit-making business engaged in an earnest historical mission, Ostpaket and other similar stores seek distinction through their use of irony. Similarly to the private museums, who often use an ironic background soundtrack of songs like *The Party is Always Right*, the self-conscious irony that pervades the Eastern products industry serves to dislodge the slogans, symbols and styles of the regime and make them usable as contemporary persiflage.

In one of dozens of possible examples, the company Ostprodukte Versand offers a 'Hero of Labour' set, of six 'Hero of Labour' products, including shower gel, bottle opener and a certificate that adapts socialist language, for example: 'The superhuman and exemplary tasks rendered by the bearer of this honorary title are worthy of emulation and continuous improvement. To learn from the hero is to learn victory'. This last sentence echoes the famous GDR slogan 'To learn from the Soviet Union means to learn victory'. In the early years of unification such irony functioned to strip official symbols of once feared power (cf. Shevchenko and Nadkarni, this volume). More than twenty-five years later the effect is to 'retrofit' the symbols, to use Serguei Oushakine's term, to 'offer a recognizable outline without suggesting an obvious ideological strategy of its interpretation' (2007: 456). As a result, the symbols are redeployable in new contexts and for new generations.

Conclusion

In Schevchenko and Nadkarni's excellent treatment of nostalgia in post-socialist Hungary and Russia (this volume), they locate its power within the ability of politicians to generate political capital out of nostalgic content. In the German case, the *Ostalgie* phenomenon has been decidedly less directly connected to the machinations of party politics. What the above examples suggest is how nostalgia functions to create a popular-cultural form of knowl-edge transmission. In this essay I am not concerned with the substance of the knowledge (e.g., whether the representations are historically accu-rate), but in understanding how everyday objects become nostalgia objects through acquiring new forms of value. In the process of acquiring value and re-entering circulation, consumers appropriate the symbolic capital of the objects in new ways. The case of socialist-era symbols is particularly rich when it comes to semiotic re-appropriations, not least because, as Vladislav Todorov (1995) writes, the socialist deficit of goods was accompanied by the overproduction of symbolic meaning, offering a potentially large domain for creating new double meanings, 'retrofitting' and other forms of second-ary production in the post-socialist era.

Through commodification and new forms of representational value, *Ostaglie* has become recognized, if grudgingly, as a fixture in the larger land-scape of German memory politics. This recognition manifests itself often in strong rejection of the term as at best insufficient, and at worst inimical, for the task of doing justice to the lived experience of the GDR. The younger generation – ostensibly the beneficiaries of the private museums and spe-cialty shops' educational efforts – seem to agree. An initiative called Third Generation East expresses dissatisfaction with the lack of voices of those who grew up after 1989: 'We don't want to choose anymore between the

GDR as an unjust state (*Unrechtsstaat*) and a plaintive *Ostalgie*', writes one member, 'we third generation, of all people, have the responsibility to make our own image of the past' (Staemmler 2011; see also Hacker 2011).

Different actors thus project onto *Ostalgie* and its material forms a different set of meanings, definitions and emotional investments. In this essay, I have focused on everyday objects as they are transformed into symbolic carriers of 'positive' aspects of the former GDR as nostalgia objects. Their widespread presence, whether in the private museums, supermarket shelves, or specialty shops, combined with a robust nostalgia industry in the form of tourist attractions, fixes *Ostalgie* in this objectified form in the German memory landscape. In this sense, we may be able to speak of *Ostalgie* as a social fact. Yet, however socially recognizable *Ostalgie* becomes, it is unlikely to ever to become fully socially acceptable and transcend its negative connotations as trivializing, camp and kitsch. In the German case, where national identity is founded on a 'will to memory' (Eyal 2004), *Ostalgie* functions as an insolent interjection to the 'injunction to remember'. Through its alternately innocent and ironic representations, *Ostalgie* subtly undermines the redemptive quality of collective memory as a national project under the guidance of professional historians and State commissions. As Eyal (2004) has analysed, collective memory in Germany is central to the state and its institutions as a guarantor of identity and a healer of wounds. *Ostalgie* dislodges symbols of this project so that a digitized Lenin can wink at you in the Berlin GDR museum, prodding established identities and scratching at the wounds. Nostalgia allows the symbolic content of collective memory to be re-appropriated by collectors, companies and consumers, rather than the hermeneutic guardians of culture and history. Thus does nostalgia tug at our conscience, even as we enjoy its (guilty) pleasures.

Acknowledgements

This research is part of a larger project that explores how materiality is integral to the practices and discourses of memory and cultural production through the case of contemporary Germany and the material remains of socialism. It draws on regular research visits to Germany over the last two decades, including extended stays for ethnographic research in 2009 and 2013 supported, respectively, by the German Academic Exchange Service and the Czech National Science Foundation as part of a collaborative grant from Masaryk University, Brno, Czech Republic on the post-communist city and collective memory. Thanks to the editors of the volume, the reviewers and Yukiko Koga for their helpful comments.

Notes

1. For existing literature on *Ostalgie* see, inter alia, Berdahl and Bunzl 2010, Boyer 2006, Cooke 2005 and Todorova and Gille 2010. See also Betts 2001, Rethmann 2009.
2. This data comes from the museums' respective websites: for the Berlin GDR Museum see <http://ddr-museum.de/de/presse/statistiken>, for Zeitreise see <http://www.ddr-museum-dresden.de/>, for Apolda see <http://www.olle-ddr.de>.
3. For a fuller discussion of private GDR museums see Bach, 2014. See also Scribner 2003. For a discussion of the Open Depot, the forerunner of the Documentation Centre for GDR Everyday Culture in Eisenhüttenstadt, see Kuhn and Ludwig 1997. See also the catalogue for the Centre's first major exhibit, Ludwig, Stumpfe and Engelhardt 1996, and Berdahl 2010.
4. See, among others, Pence and Betts 2008, Reid and Crowley 2000 and Rubin 2008.
5. See Bach 2002 for these and other examples. On *Test the West*'s reception in the East see also Norman 2000.
6. The top Eastern brands, not all distributed in the Western states, include alcoholic beverages (Rottkäppchen Sekt, Nordhäuser Doppelkorn, and Köstritzer, Wernesgrüner, Hasseröder and Radeberger beers), sweets (Halloren Kugel, Grabower Küsschen, Frischli cookies, Komet desserts, Nudossi spread, Schlager chocolates), baked goods (Kathi baking mixes, Burger Knäckebrot, Filinchin crackers, Teigwaren Riese), detergents (Spee, Fit), body and bath (Florena cream, Badusan soaps), Bautz'ner Senf, Halberstädter sausages, Vita Cola, Werder Ketchup, coffee (Rondo Coffee, In Nu malt coffee), and of course Spreewald pickles. See Trappe 2012 and Willmroth 2010.
7. The major specialty stores of GDR products in 2013 include Ostpaket, Ossiversand, Ostprodukte-Versand, Ossiladen, Allerlei Ostprodukte, Kaufhalle des Ostens (KdO), Ostprodukte.de, Ostprodukte Verkauf, and Ostshop.com.

References

Ahbe, T. 2000. Hammer, Zirkel, Kaffeekranz. *Berliner Zeitung*, February 5.
———. 2005. *Ostalgie: Zum Umgang mit der DDR Vergangenheit in den 1990er Jahren.* Erfurt: Landeszentrale für politische Bildung Thüringen.
Ampelmann-Japan. *Concept.* Retrieved from <http://ampelmann.co.jp> (accessed 27 January 2013).
Anon. *Ostalgie-Kabinett.* DDR Museum 'Ostalgie-Kabinett'. Retrieved from <http://www.ostalgie-kabinett.de> (accessed 30 June 2009).
———. 2013. *Ostalgie-Shop.* Ostprodukte-Versand. Retrieved from <http://www.ost produkte-versand.de/cnr-28/Ostalgie.html> (accessed 7 January 2013).
Bach, J. 2002. '"The Taste Remains": Consumption, (N)ostalgia and the Production of East Germany', *Public Culture* 14 (3): 545–56.

——. 2014. 'Object Lessons: Visuality and Tactility in Museums of the Socialist Everyday', in P. McIssac and G. Muller (eds), *The Past on Display: Museums, Film, Memory*. Toronto: University of Toronto Press.

Bartmanski, D. 2011. 'Successful Icons of Failed Time: Rethinking Post-communist Nostalgia', *Acta Sociologica* 54 (3): 213–31.

Baudrillard, J. 2005 [1968]. *The System of Objects*. New York: Verso.

Berdahl, D. 2010. 'Expressions of Experience and Experience of Expression: Museum Re-Presentations of GDR History', in M. Bunzl (ed.), *On the Social Life of Postsocialism: Memory, Consumption, Germany*. Bloomington: Indiana University Press, pp. 112–22.

Berdahl, D. and M. Bunzl. 2010. *On the Social Life of Postsocialism: Memory, Consumption, Germany*. Bloomington: Indiana University Press.

Betts, P. 2001. 'The Twilight of the Idols: East German Memory and Material Culture', *Journal of Modern History* 72 (3): 731–65.

Boyer, D. 2006. 'Ostalgie and the Politics of the Future in Eastern Germany', *Public Culture* 18 (2): 361–81.

Cooke, P. 2005. *Representing East Germany Since Unification: From Colonization to Nostalgia*. Oxford: Berg.

de Certeau, M. 1984. *The Practice of Everyday Life*. Berkeley: University of California Press.

Eyal, G. 2004. 'Identity and Trauma: Two Forms of the Will to Memory', *History and Memory* 16 (1): 5–36.

Faktor, J. 1999. Mitglieder stellen sich vor, *Rundbrief*. Berlin: Verein zur Dokumentation der DDR-Alltagskultur e.V., 7.

Görß, K. 2013. *Liebe Gäste*. Retrieved from <http://ddr-museum-tutow-mv.de> (accessed 18 August 2013).

Hacker, M. 2011. *Die Vergangenheit ist ein Ort, an dem Du nicht warst*. Retrieved from <http://www.dritte-generation-ost.de/blog/entry/0> (accessed 29 April 2013).

Hartwig, J. 1994. *Einleitung, Rundbrief*. Berlin: Verein zur Dokumentation der DDR-Alltagskultur e.V., 3.

Herzfeld, M. 1997. *Cultural Intimacy: Social Poetics in the Nation-State*. New York: Routledge.

Kaden, C. 2012. *Chronik des DDR-Museum Pirna*. Pirna: DDR Museum Pirna. Retrieved from <http://www.ddr-museum-pirna.de/index.php/chronik.html> (accessed 5 February 2013).

Krawczyk, S. 1996. Mitglieder Stellen sich vor, *Rundbrief*. Berlin: Verein zur Dokumentation der DDR-Alltagskultur e.V., 12.

Kuhn, G. and A. Ludwig. 1997. *Alltag und soziales Gedächtnis: die DDR-Objektkultur und ihre Musealisierung*. Hamburg: Ergebnisse Verlag.

Lay, C. 1997. 'Der Siegeszug der Ostprodukte: Zur Mentalitäts- und Produktgeschichte der deutschen Vereinigung', *Kommune* 1: 6–10.

Ludwig, A., Stumpfe, M. and J. Engelhardt. 1996. *Alltagskultur der DDR: Begleitbuch zur Ausstellung 'Tempolinsen und P2'*. Berlin-Brandenburg: Be.Bra Verlag.

Norman, B. 2000. 'Test the West: East German Performance Art Takes on Western Advertising', *Journal of Popular Culture* 34 (3): 255–67.

Ostpaket 2013. *Ostzeit Design und Konsum.* Retrieved from <http://www.ostpaket-berlin. de/ostzeit.htm> (accessed 21 October 2013).

Ostprodukte-Versand 2013. *Startseite: Ostalgie.* Retrieved from <http://www. ostprodukte-versand.de/cnr-28/Ostalgie.html> (accessed 30 April 2013).

Oushakine, S.A. 2007. '"We're Nostalgic but we're Not Crazy": Retrofitting the Past in Russia', *The Russian Review* 66: 451–82.

Parkin, D. 1999. 'Mementoes as Transitional Objects in Human Displacement', *Journal of Material Culture* 4 (3): 303–20.

Pence, K. and P. Betts. 2008. *Socialist Modern: East German Everyday Culture and Politics.* Ann Arbor: University of Michigan Press.

Reid, S.E. and D. Crowley (eds). 2000. *Style and Socialism: Modernity and Material Culture in Post-War Eastern Europe.* New York: Berg.

Rethmann, P. 2009. 'Post-communist Ironies in an East German Hotel', *Anthropology Today* 25: 21–23.

Roth, J. and M. Rudolf. 1997. *Spaltprodukte: Gebündlete Ost-West-Vorurteile.* Leipzig: Reclam.

Rubin, E. 2008. *Synthetic Socialism: Plastics and Dictatorship in the German Democratic Republic.* Chapel Hill: University of North Carolina Press.

Ruediger 2010. *Haben Westdeutsche kein Qualitätsbewusstsein?* Retrieved from <http:// www.spiegel.de/wirtschaft/unternehmen/0,1518,718647,00.html> (accessed 23 August 2012).

Sabrow, M. 2009. 'Die DDR erinnern', in M. Sabrow (ed.), *Erinnerungsorte der DDR.* Munich: C.H. Beck, pp. 11–30.

Scribner, C. 2003. *Requiem for Communism.* Cambridge: MIT Press.

Staemmler, J. 2011. 'Wir, die Stumme Generation', *Die Zeit,* Zeit Online Edition, August 18.

Todorov, V. 1995. *Red Square, Black Square: Organon for Revolutionary Imagination.* Albany: State University of New York Press.

Todorova, M. and Z. Gille. 2010. *Post-communist Nostalgia.* New York: Berghahn Books.

Trappe, T. 2012. 'Boom bei Ostprodukten: Ein Hauch von DDR', *Süddeutsche Zeitung,* Süddeutsche Online Edition.

Viktor 2010. 'Jeder Mensch kann zurück in seine Heimat, wenn es ihm hier nicht gefällt … DDR-Bürger nicht'. Retrieved from <http://www.spiegel.de/ wirtschaft/unternehmen/0,1518,718647,00.html> (accessed 14 August 2013).

Willmroth, J. 2010. 'DDR-Marken: Schluss mit der Ostalgie', *Der Spiegel,* Spiegel Online Edition.

'Zeitreise' n.d. *Zeitreise, Lebensart DDR 1949–1989.* Radebeul: DDR-Museum Zeitreise.

Chapter 6

The Key from (to) Sefarad

Nostalgia for a Lost Country

Joseph Josy Lévy and Inaki Olazabal

A key will be my dwelling.
    – Char, *Effacement du peuplier.*[1]

One of the earliest references to nostalgia can be found in Book V of the *Odyssey*. In it, Homer describes a discussion between Calypso and Ulysses, prisoner of the nymph, which underscores the impact of homesickness as a psychological phenomenon: returning home weighs heavier than reaching the immortality offered by the goddess. Ulysses refuses this opportunity, so desperate is he to return home to his wife Penelope:

> Calypso, the beautiful goddess, was the first to speak, and said: ... Son of Laertes, sprung from Zeus, Odysseus of many devices. Yet, even so fare thee well. Howbeit if in thy heart thou knewest all the measure of woe it is thy fate to fulfil before thou comest to thy native land thou wouldest abide here and keep this house with me, and wouldest be immortal, for all thy desire to see thy wife for whom thou longest day by day. Then Odysseus of many wiles answered her, and said: 'Mighty goddess ... I know full well of myself that wise Penelope is meaner to look upon than thou in comeliness and in stature, for she is a mortal, while thou art immortal and ageless. But even so I wish and long day by day to reach my home, and to see the day of my return. And if again some god shall

smite me on the wine-dark sea, I will endure it, having in my breast a heart that endures affliction.

This concept of homecoming, *nostos* in Greek, was used by Johannes Hofer (1688) in his *Medical Dissertation on Nostalgia*, a medical neologism describing the feelings of suffering related to *mal du pays* or homesickness. Hofer notes the frequency of this condition in displaced people, students, domestic help and servants and Swiss mercenaries living far from home. Associated with mental disorders, including visual and auditory hallucinations and physical symptoms, nostalgia could even lead to suicide. These behaviours were reported in other European populations, such as the Russians in the eighteenth century, but absent in other cultural settings. By the nineteenth century, the concept of nostalgia was found in contexts beyond the medical use, including philosophy, poetry and literature, becoming a significant theme of reflection and evident in diverse applications (Boym 2002).

Psychology, history and sociology also embraced this theme, exploring its different expressions among groups of immigrants from different regions of the world. For example, we find it among the Chinese living in Canada (Sakamoto and Zhou 2005), women of Turkish descent expelled from Bulgaria and relocated in Turkey (Parla 2009) and Italians living in Argentina (Schneider 2000). The social functions of nostalgia in these contexts are also described, revealing how important this concept becomes in constructing a collective memory and personal and social identity (Bellelli and Amatulli 1997). The idea of nostalgia in the Jewish world has also been studied in its occurrences in diverse historical and sociological settings, such as Vienna at the end of the century (Beller 1996), the city of Harbin in China, where a Jewish community settled towards the end of the nineteenth century (Ben Canaan 2007), orthodox groups in the United States (Finkelman 2009), Holocaust survivors in Czernowitz, Poland (Hirsh and Spitzer 2002) or the Jews of the Mzab living in Alsace (Raphael 1979). These studies reveal the divergence between historical analysis and ambivalent personal and collective memories. Another example of this discrepancy can be found in the case of the Sephardi Jews and their descendants who were expelled from Spain in 1492. Through a review of literary sources, novels, poetry and songs, as well as an analysis of the importance of the Sephardi heritage in contemporary Spanish tourism, we will explore some aspects of nostalgia, conveyed by the symbolic reference to the key of the house, as a metaphor for the longing for the lost country.

Following the complete *Reconquista* of the Spanish territory after the fall of Granada, the last city occupied by the Arabs, the Catholic Kings

Ferdinand and Isabella decided to unify religiously the kingdom by giving their Jewish population the choice between conversion and expulsion. A segment of the population opted to convert to Christianity to escape uprooting, but many of them kept their primary faith hidden, developing Marrano identities and cultures that influenced the culture of Spain as well as other countries such as Holland and South America (Wachtel 2001, 2011, Yovel 1992, 2009). Others decided to leave the kingdom and the *Edict of Expulsion*, preserved to this day, describes the harsh conditions surrounding the departure or those who refused to be baptised and the sanctions to be applied if orders were disobeyed.

> Having taken deliberation about this matter, resolve to order the said Jews and Jewesses of our kingdoms to depart and never to return or come back to them or to any of them. We command that by the end of the month of July next of the present year, they depart from all of these our said realms and lordships, whatever age they may be, and they shall not dare to return to those places, nor to reside in them, nor to live in any part of them . . . and should in any manner live in them, they incur the penalty of death and the confiscation of all their possessions . . . And we command and forbid that any person or persons of the said kingdoms, of whatever estate, condition, or dignity that they may be, shall dare to receive, protect, defend, nor hold publicly or secretly any Jew or Jewess beyond the date of the end of July.[2]

This event had a very powerful traumatic impact on the first genera-tions of Spanish Jews who left Spain, and this painful memory was transmit-ted to many of their descendants. This traumatic legacy can be construed as a post-memory experience, a concept developed by Hirsch (2008: 106) and defined as 'a structure of inter- and trans-generational transmission of traumatic knowledge and experience. It is a consequence of traumatic recall but, unlike post-traumatic stress disorder, at a generational remove'.

Tens of thousands of Jews left by land or sea and spread out in the Mediterranean region and North and Central Europe, becoming, as expressed by Angel Pulido (1905) Spaniards without a homeland (*Españoles sin patria*). Their forced departure was a major trauma, underlined by both the exiled and Spanish witnesses. Abrabanel, a community leader, recorded the extreme emotions experienced at the time (Gerber 1992: 138): 'The people heard this evil decree and they mourned . . . There was great trembling and sorrow the likes of which had not been experienced since the days of the exile of the Jews from their land to the land of foreigners'. The historian André Bernaldez, who witnessed the exodus, recalled its heart-breaking conditions and emphasized the hardships that affected all segments of the population (Gerber 1992: 140): 'In the first week of July, they took the route for quitting their native land, great and small. Young and old, on foot and horses, in carts, each continuing his journey to his destined port. They experienced great trouble and suffered indescribable misfortunes on the road'.

Although Jews had been deeply rooted in Spain for a thousand years and despite the fact they were forced to leave the country, the exiled failed to reject the culture of their forefathers. They spread out to Europe, the Mediterranean basin and South America, proudly calling themselves by the endonym Sephardi, the Hebrew word for Spain. They reorganized their communities, maintained and enriched their religious, linguistic, folk and musical heritage, which was replete with Iberian references. Through this retention, the nostalgia for Spain and its memory could be kept and reactivated in rituals and everyday life. This served as a reminder of a collective trauma but also of the memory of an Iberian space where Jews had had an impact on Muslim and Christian societies, as evidenced in poetry, philosophy, sciences, linguistics and architecture. Nevertheless, as in the case of other Jewish migrations, they maintained an ambivalent relation to Spain, as analysed by Romeu Ferré (2011: 107–8), a Catalan specialist of the Sephardi world, with a 'mythification of the historical past', focusing particularly on the Golden Age of the Middle Ages, and otherwise 'the bitter face of this same past', with the events of the Inquisition and the traumatic period of the Expulsion.

These communities came to develop a complex identity that integrated cultural elements of their host countries that were slowly modified with the passage of time and by sociological and historical constraints. This resulted in a dilution of the original characteristics, varying by region, but many traces still remain today in liturgy, food, customs and folklore. The upholding of certain cultural traits over a long period of time harks back to the concept of 'restorative nostalgia' proposed by Boym (2001: 49), which aims to 'reconstruct emblems and rituals of home and homeland in an attempt to conquer and specialise time'. By recalling tragedy, drama and pain, nostalgia provides both a cognitive and emotional meaning to memorial sites. Among the cultural reminders of Spain, the house key (*yave* in Judeo-Spanish, *llave* in Spanish) plays a central role. It is a recurring theme linked to a concrete, imaginary and symbolic object that embodies the country of origin, the lost 'ancestral home' (Olazabal and Lévy 1999), the departure and the possible return. The reference to the key becomes a prism through which the nostalgic relationship to Spain can be re-enacted.

Historically, the evidence that exiles and their descendants kept a key of the family home remains slim. Some observers doubt how widespread this practice was or reject it entirely. According to Israeli historian Mordechai

Arbell, an expert in the history of the American, Asian, European and Caribbean Sephardi world, who informed the Columbian anthropologist Horacio Calle (1996), there exist 'Rare cases where Jews from Toledo kept their house keys. Personally, I have not seen such keys, but I know people that have seen large house keys from Toledo, but not from other locations'. For Romeu Ferré, it is a myth, a 'construction of family legends on the presumed holding of keys of houses abandoned at the beginning of the expulsion' (2011: 107). Miguel Ángel Nieto Solís, a Spanish journalist and producer, director of the documentary *El ultimo sefardi*, which explores Sephardi migrations, has stated in an interview with Rodriguez Mata (2003) that:

> There does not appear to be any documentary evidence that the Sephardi Jews left with their house keys; the main reason being that they were not permitted to take any kind of metal, objects or furniture. They had to exit empty handed . . . It is logical to assume that these Jews believed at that moment that this would be a temporary expulsion.

However, testimony given by descendants of expelled Jews confirms that at least one key from Toledo is indeed a reality and passed down from generation to generation, as reported by Haim Lévi (2008), a rabbi who recalls, when young, following the daily ritual of contemplating the family object with his grandmother, which becomes an obsessive reminder of the trauma, linked to a repetitive nostalgia:

> I spent many years with my maternal grandmother, Amalia, the one who took very special care to teach me the history of the Jewish people. Every day I would go into her bedroom to see 'la *llave* de la casa en España'. . . . This key was in fact a very large iron key taken from the family home in Toledo, Spain. My brother Leon, who now lives in Albany, New York, is the person who now acts as the keeper of this key.

In addition, Horacio Calle (1996) reports the story of a Colombian professor who came to lecture in the United States and overheard one of his students singing ancient Ladino romances. She invited him to meet her family who showed him a small box containing a key from the house in Seville.

The theme of the key in musical folklore is not widespread, but it can be found in a Judeo-Spanish song composed by Flory Jagoda, a modern American singer and songwriter of Sephardi origin from Bosnia, famous for her wide repertory. Entitled *Llave de Espanya*,[3] *The Key from Spain*. This song emphasizes the idea that nostalgia for the lost country is disappearing with the indifference of the contemporary generations. Not only is this indifference felt towards the key, forgotten in a drawer, but also for the past generations that maintained a close and sentimental relationship with Spain marked by feelings of pain, then love. The link to Spain faded and is only kept alive by tenuous references. The theme of the key is also found in a poem by Jorge Luis Borges published in 1964 with the title *Una llave en Salonica*, a city that had a large number of Sephardi Jews who had settled there following the expulsion, a great majority of whom were subsequently deported and died in the Nazi camps.[4]

The poem begins by quoting names of Jewish Spain, like Abrabanel, one of the great statesmen and scholars from this period, reminding the reader of the city of Toledo. It again underscores the initial trauma of the persecution and expulsion. The attachment to the Toledo ancestral home, whose door has turned to dust, nevertheless survives and is upheld by a bronze key whose contemplation is reminiscent of a ritual. This idea is reinforced by the image of another key, this one associated with the Second Temple of Jerusalem, destroyed by the Romans. Borges thus emphasizes the continuity of a traumatized collective memory in the Diaspora, but beyond hope and terror. The key appears also in many novels written by Spanish and French authors. A first example is found in the historical novel *La gesta del marrano* (1991), by Marcos Aguinis, a Jewish writer from Argentina, which tells of the travels of Francisco Maldonado Da Silva, a Marrano physician from Portugal living in the seventeenth century and persecuted by the Inquisition in Lima because he publicly revealed his Jewish identity. Jailed and tortured for years, he held steadfast to his ideals and deflected his detractors by his argumentation and writings, composed in secret during solitary confinement to affirm his freedom of thought and religion. He ultimately was executed by auto-da-fe in 1639. As underlined by Lopez-Calvo (2008), this complex novel:

> ... is the story of a travel from oblivion to memory. The protagonist's life represents a song not only to the freedom of the Jewish people, but also of humankind – especially of marginalized groups – against religious obscurantism and totalitarianism ... Although Catholic institutions make him feel like an undesirable, he gains consciousness of the injustice suffered by his people, at the same time that the odyssey of his family and his Sephardic past opens before his eyes. The stories that he hears are his history and he learns to love it by contrasting two different perspectives: that of José Ignacio de Sevilla, who loves it with all its consequences, and that of Diego López de Lisboa, who has been forced to hate it, hence negating himself.

Through his acknowledgement of history and memory, for the protagonist in this story, Francisco, then a young child living in the Argentinean city of Ibatin (the Tucuman of today), the key to the Spanish house, lost and imagined, plays an essential role, as shown in the novel's first chapters. Conversations between him and his mother, then with his father, frame the emotional relationship to the key, keeper of the family memory in a privileged Spanish environment and whose secret is revealed. This episode begins with Francisco's unexpected discovery of a big trunk under a pile of his father's clothes, in which he finds an adorned box. Inquisitive, he brings the object to his mother and questions her about its contents. She refuses to answer him, claiming that a wife must not question her husband. When his father returns, he asks him the same question. Surrounded by his family, the father places the box on a table, and by the light of a candle he opens it, disclosing the object inside, an iron key, decorated with an engraved torch, and emphasizing its deep spiritual value. The father then reveals to his son the history of his family heritage. He had received the key from his father who had lived in Portugal. This was the key of a magnificent house, owned by his forefathers who kept it for generations, and hoped to return to it one day after their expulsion. Full of manuscripts and documents, this residence was frequently visited by high-ranking nobles and dignitaries. His father took this key from the hand of his own father on his deathbed, and in order to avoid the repetition of this difficult gesture he put it in a box. The narrator thus explained to his son that he will inherit it to maintain an unbroken chain of transmission.

When the son asks whether returning to Spain is a possibility, the father responds with a cautious 'I don't know', expressing the uncertainty and anxiety related to the precarious condition of the Marrano. In this excerpt, the reasons for the departure from Spain are not described, nor are the Jewish origin of the family, which ultimately is revealed. Nevertheless, nostalgia is ever present, as expressed in its transgenerational transmission from father to son, contrary to other literary occurrences where this responsibility falls on the grandmother and mother. This is revealing of the changes in inheritance rules and the significant role of women in socialization processes and the passing down of family history. In accordance with the hypotheses formulated by Romeu Ferré (2011: 107), we find in this novel the expression of an 'aristocratic feeling' found among Sephardim but also associated with the Marrano identity. This is evidenced by holding on to a key that, it is said, opened a majestic home visited by princes and scientists and by the sense of a family with a high social status whose genealogy is considered prestigious. Thus nostalgia does not exclusively stem from the loss of home and country, but also from the loss of a respectable social position projected on ancestors involved in valued intellectual endeavours.

The previous historical novel describes the situation of Marranos a few generations following the expulsion, when their memory is still fresh and fanned by the Hispanic environment of Latin America at the height of colonization. In the other two novels discussed below, the relation to nostalgia is treated in more contemporary contexts. *Vingt ans et un jour*,[5] a novel published in French in 2004 by Jorge Semprun, a Franco-Spanish author who was deported to Buchenwald, sets the plot in Spain, during the time of Franco in the 1950s, but harking back to the history and memory of the Spanish Civil War of the 1930s. One of the main characters, Michel Leidson, is an American historian who came to study this event and is introduced as a descendant of Jews from Riga and Toledo. However, he is apparently not very interested in the origins of his family. By contrast, his mother is still attached to Sephardi Spain but refuses to visit the country while Franco is alive, although she is keeping abreast of its situation through the media. She has taught her son Spanish and the history of the Jews, talking very often about the legends of Sefarad, a faraway country but close to her heart. The intergenerational transmission of the Sephardi memory does not go through men as in the case of the novel by Aguinis, but rather through women as in the case related by Haim Lévi described earlier. Travelling to Toledo and reading the *Voyage en Espagne* by Théophile Gauthier, which describes the most ancient synagogue of the city, the Santa Maria de la Bianca, Leidson remembers the medieval key kept by his family who came originally, as in other texts, from Toledo and displayed it on the walls of his living room, despite many moves.

The memories evoked by his readings compel him to explore the old Jewish quarter of Toledo, using the details provided by his mother to locate the ancient streets where his ancestors might have lived. But the original house has disappeared, destroyed a few centuries following the expulsion, thus revealing a hidden face of the relationship to the key whose function is now to awaken memories, full of legends. This novel introduces for the first time, to our knowledge, a protagonist whose nostalgia is no longer simply nourished by the simple evocation of the memory of the Sephardi past. The actual physical location in an architectural space gives body to the memory by returning to places where historical events occurred, but that no longer correspond to the nostalgic images transmitted by community and family myths. This return to Sefarad appears also as a transgression of the royal injunction inscribed in the expulsion edict that compelled Jews to never return to the kingdom. Leidson exemplifies, through his experiences in Spain, the metamorphosis of the relationship to this country, heralding a new type of nostalgia linked to elements of tourism, as we describe below.

A more recent novel with a direct ethnonymic title, *Séfarade* (2009), written by Éliette Abécassis, a French novelist, describes the journey of a young Moroccan Jew born in Strasbourg, who, through the nostalgia for the countries where her ancestors lived, Spain and Morocco, rediscovers the various facets of her mixed identity and her link to a tormented history. The Sephardi dimension of her identity appears in the initial pages of the novel where the female protagonist, Esther Vidal, reconnects with the lost Spain via her choosing Spanish as a foreign language at school, briefly describing the attachment to this country and the uprooting that followed the expulsion, akin to a sentimental break up, noting the types of grief and nostalgia that the perception of the exile accentuates. For her, this choice is a way to reconnect with her forefathers, who left the country with only a few belongings including the key to their house, hoping to return one day, expressing by their songs their distress and pain. But when these displaced persons realized that their return would not take place, their language, the Ladino, became their homeland.

The symbol of the key at the beginning of the novel is recaptured in the conclusion, where a wedding that will never take place is being organized. Esther's intended spouse offers her a package given to him by his father, which contains an old chiselled key, transmitted from generation to generation, the sign of the last link to the Spanish house.

The image of the key to the Spanish house thus appears inter-textually in works by authors from various backgrounds, but in a stereotyped fashion. This begs the question whether this repetition does not in the end exhaust its nostalgic potential, becoming a cliché that no longer elicits any specific emotion. Miguel Ángel Nieto Solís, the Spanish journalist mentioned above, deconstructs this process, deeming it a sterile contemporary literary device (Rodriguez Mata 2003):

> The problem is that the use of the key . . . by this Spanish author from the early twentieth century, has become like a funeral for this people. Éliezer Papo has strenuously complained of this situation. The legend was superimposed on the reality of a culture. As such, the legends of the key and Sephardi music have somewhat masked the Sephardi reality. In this way, we did not have to say what we had done to them . . . When something is converted to a memory, it is not painful, and becomes harmless. And the legend of the key, invented by a writer, was a politically correct way to avoid having to talk of other things when the issue of Sephardim came up.

This function of diversion, if not of entertainment, appears confirmed when we consider the representations of the key in modern national and international strategies of tourism in the Spanish and Sephardi world, where nostalgia becomes a marketing tool. The key, closing an abandoned house, is transformed into an accessory symbolizing openness and

welcoming. These changes are related to the political and social changes
seen in Spain following the death of Franco in 1975 and the re-establish-
ment of the monarchy. The kingdom's policy of openness is characterized,
among others, by the adoption of a democratic Constitution that abolished
references to a state religion, the reconciliation between the state and the
small Jewish communities living in large Spanish cities since the 1960s
and the official apology presented by the King of Spain in 1992 at the time
of the five-hundredth year commemoration of the expulsion of the Jews.
This request for forgiveness was also accompanied by the possibility for
Spanish descendants of Sephardi Jews to quickly obtain Spanish national-
ity. Together with this, links were re-established with the Muslim world,
harking back to the Spain of the Three Cultures of the Middle Ages. These
policies resulted in the reintegration of the Jewish heritage in the Spanish
landscape, spearheaded by cultural and tourist institutions, a major asset
in the international competition to attract tourists but also as a way for the
Spanish people to re-engage with this period of their history they do not
know deeply. The project of Caminos de Sefarad, established in 1997 by the
central government in cooperation with the mayors of several towns where
Jews had lived, highlights the willingness to recapture the different facets
of the Spanish past by linking a network of cities in order to recapture a
missing part of the history of Jews of Spain. These routes where a Jewish
presence remains in different forms and artefacts (*juderías*, houses, streets,
synagogues, ritual baths, famous figures, cemeteries and funeral head-
stones), modernize a forgotten heritage and highlight it in museums and
intellectual and cultural events. Tourists could follow in the footsteps of
well-known poets and philosophers retained by the literary or intellectual
history or delve into the atmosphere of some cities known for their spiritual
past, such as Gerona.

In this context, the key becomes a significant product in marketing
strategies used by both local and international Spanish and Sephardi
organizations involved in tourism endeavours and the advancement of this
heritage. Several examples of this use can be found on Spanish and English
Internet sites, which become a new space, albeit virtual, where the theme
of the key is introduced and spread. The marketing of the key can be seen
at various levels. The Spanish organization Tarbut Sefarad, which aims to
promote and broadcast Jewish culture in Spain, uses the key as 'a symbol
of the remembrance and memory of the Jews of Sefarad, of those who were
killed, persecuted and forced to flee to defend their identity and beliefs;
a symbol of reconciliation to keep alive the flame of the struggle for the
defence and promotion of Jewish culture'.[6] The World Sephardi Congress
chose the key as its logo, while Spanish high authorities insisted on the

significance of this symbolic object as a proof of loyalty to Spain and its culture, while angling the idea in a modern way to emphasize openness and collaboration. The Spanish Prime Minister José Maria Aznar (2002), in a speech given at a world meeting organized by the World Sephardi Congress in Spain, thus stated:

> The World Sephardi Congress has chosen as its symbol an ancient key, like the one many Sephardi families still have today, from their houses in Toledo, Gerona, Segovia or Cordoba, abandoned during the Diaspora of 1492. The image of the key also represents the extraordinary heritage that the Jews carried out with them after the expulsion, and that they kept in their new destinations all around the Mediterranean ... I encourage you to ensure that the key that symbolizes this congress opens the door to a future of liberty and coexistence. And I say that those who aspire to such a future will always be welcomed in Spain.

The reference to this symbolic object is also present at the municipal level. Luis Campoy Zueco, the President of the Rutas de Sefarad network and mayor of the city of Tudela, a city of Navarre, at the beginning of his speech given on the same occasion (Campoy Zueco 2002) repeated the same arguments as the Prime Minister on the legend of the key, but emphasized the connection between the key and the local history of his city, to then focus on describing the tourist development projects of the Rutas de Sefarad. In concluding his speech, while revisiting the image of the key, he invited Jews to seek out a new Spanish home and welcomed them: 'I give you this key, ... a symbol of the houses that had to be closed five hundred years ago ... With this key, you can open the home that awaits you in Sefarad'. This welcoming tradition was repeated in 2011, when Alfredo Sánchez Monteseirín, the Mayor of Seville, gave the President of the American Sephardi Federation the Jewish key to the city with these words: 'With this Jewish key to Seville, we open all doors for you, not only those recognized historically, Puerta de la Carne, Puerta del Mesón del Moro y Puerta de San Nicolás, but all of the doors of the city'.[7] The Llave del calle de Tarragona (the key of the Jewish quarter of Tarragona) whose original bronze model was designed and created by a jeweller from Tarragona, Joan Blazquez, features a Star of David on the handle and a menorah (a reproduction of the seven-branched lamp stand used in the Temple in Jerusalem) on the key bit along with a Hebrew inscription, *Shalom Tarragona*, on the stem. This symbolic key was given to descendants of Sephardi Jews that lived in the city, as happened in July 2010. The use of this artefact reveals a new dynamic. By losing its symbolic function connected with a particular ancestral home, it becomes a community object replete with various Jewish cultural motives adopted by the Spanish population to express its welcoming of the Jews returning to visit the cities or to reconnect with their heritage.

These speeches and rituals seem to emphasize the existence of two distinct countries: a 'real' country, modern Spain, and a superimposed one, an imaginary country, Sefarad, which could be retrieved by recreating the spirit of the locations. Tourism contributes to the amplification of the components of a restorative nostalgia by projecting visitors into a Sephardi past that remains replete with evocative traces. The example of Gerona, a Catalan city where the remembrance process has been brought forward by a major project, the renovation of the Call, the ancient *judería*, is a striking example (Olazabal and Lévy 1999, Lévy and Olazabal 2004, 2007). Heart of the Provençal Kabbalistic centre between the twelfth and fourteenth century, homeland of Nahmanide, one of the most eminent Jewish thinkers of that period, this neighbourhood, with its small streets and houses, aims to recreate the atmosphere of a *judería* of the Middle Ages, a model that was imitated in other Spanish cities.

In addition to the architectural renovations, several cultural activities are offered to tourists, from exhibits to organized tours and musical events, as it is the case in Toledo. Once again, the key plays a role as evidenced by their display in museums or the fascination for doors and locks of this city. One of its guides, Oscar Monterreal (2012), in a text on the relevance of the visit to the *judería*, finds both 'an immaterial evocation and a worldly satisfaction' to it: 'At each step, an interesting detail grabs your attention, but if I had to choose something, it would be the locks of the oldest houses, to remind ourselves of the legend . . . that says that the Sefardi in Exile took the keys to their houses in Toledo, with the hope of returning one day'. One of the walking tours of the city, Toledoth La llave de Sefarad, proposed by a travel agency, offers also a discovery of the 'secrets of Jewish Toledo, of mysterious and unknown corners of the *judería*',[8] emphasizing the legend of the key.

The recurrence of this theme throughout the examples provided here, but also available in texts, videos, images and websites on the Internet, reveals that its use has spread beyond the family framework and community that had dominated until recently. It has reached national and international dimensions in the promotion of the Sephardi past, becoming a trademark for attracting tourists with diverse interests, curious to visit places where their ancestors may have lived. As stated by Juris (2006: 246) in his review of Spanish travel guides highlighting these itineraries, nostalgia, nevertheless, remains a primordial motivation for modern tourists: 'Patrimony is something that particularly attracts post-tourists because through it is found a type of dynamic historical voyeurism, with fantasy elements and nostalgia for the past. It is this nostalgia, and not only the need to understand the past, that converts patrimony into something this fascinating'.

Conclusion

Replete with various meanings, symbol of openness and closure, the key summarizes the attachment to the ancestral home and its history, but also, in its handing down, points to a generational interaction laden with memory traces. In the case of Sephardi history, the significance of this reference can in great part be explained by the major trauma caused by the physical and cultural uprooting related to the expulsion from Spain and the nostalgia linked to this country ever since. This nostalgia is evidenced by the attachment, during generations, to the language and cultural heritage of Spain but reinvented during the complex processes of integration and acculturation to the various host societies, in particular in the countries of the Mediterranean region. Historical reality for some, legend for others, the theme of the key of the Sephardi house is found throughout folklore and novels in versions that emphasize the suffering, the nostalgic memory, and the impossible hope of return. This is found both in historical and modern novels, transforming itself in a repetitive theme more rhetorical and illustrative than emotional.

The trivialization of the concept of the key extends to the modern world with the imparting of heritage status on the Sephardi patrimony in Spain, thrust forward by the convergence of national and international cultural and tourism interests. The key has become one of the elements of marketing strategies used by both Spanish and Sephardi organizations, leading to several uses from logo conception to themes of musical events. In this way, it has taken a collective and international dimension, amplified by the Internet and its various tools. Nostalgia is no longer held up by an imaginary place. It is also found in the actual locations where history took place, superimposing the real country of Spain on the reconstructed and phantasmagorical 'Sefarad', with its multiple narratives that tourists can, in a certain way, reconstruct according to their likings. These tourist marketing strategies contribute to fuel the modern nostalgic quest of the past and to stimulate it by using and manipulating emotional and symbolic components, at the risk of trivializing and weakening the complex and rich historical past of Spain.

Notes

1. Unless otherwise indicated, translations from Spanish and French to English are provided by the authors.
2. Foundation for the Advancement of Sephardic Culture and Heritage. Retrieved from <http://www.sephardicstudies.org/decree.html> (accessed 15 September 2012).
3. Song lyrics are available from the album *Return to the Land of Your Soul*, p. 8. Retrieved from <http://www.wayofthesun.com/nightfires/CDInfo/ReturntoSoul Lyrics.pdf> (accessed 15 September 2012), p. 8.
4. This poem has been translated by Willis Barnstone (2000: 15–16).
5. This novel has not been translated into English.
6. Retrieved from <http://www.tarbutsefarad.com/es/portada-inicio/viaje-a-israel /4091-tarbut-sefarad-entrega-a-isaac-navon-la-llave-de-sefarad.html> (accessed 15 September 2012).
7. Retrieved from <http://www.esefarad.com/?p=22345> (accessed 15 September 2012).
8. *Toledoth: la llave de Sefarad.* <http://www.rutasdetoledo.es/index.php/rutas/toledo-judio.html> (accessed 15 September 2012).

References

Abécassis, E. 2009. *Séfarade*. Paris: Albin Michel.

Aguinis, M. 1991. *La gesta del marrano*. Buenos Aires: Planeta.

Aznar, J.M. 2002. 'Palabras de salutación del Presidente al Congreso Sefarad Mundial'. Retrieved from <http://www.worldsephardicongress.org/congress/ponencias/ponencia3.htm> (accessed 5 September 2012).

Barnstone, W. 2000. *With Borges on an Ordinary Evening in Buenos Aires: A Memoir*. Champaign-Urbana: University of Illinois Press.

Bellelli, G. and M.A.C. Amatulli. 1997. 'Nostalgia, Immigration, and Collective Memory', in J.W. Pennebaker, D. Paez and B. Rimé (eds), *Collective Memory of Political Events: Social Psychological Perspectives*. Mahwah, N.J.: Lawrence Erlbaum Associates, pp. 209–20.

Beller, S. 1996. 'The World of Yesterday Revisited: Nostalgia, Memory, and the Jews of Fin-de-siècle Vienna', *Jewish Social Studies* 2 (2): 37–53.

Ben-Canaan, D. 2007. 'Nostalgia vs. Historical Reality'. Retrieved from <http://kehilalinks.jewishgen.org/harbin/nostalgia_vs_historical_reality.pdf> (accessed 5 September 2012).

Boym, S. 2001. *The Future of Nostalgia*. New York: Basic Books.

Calle, H. 1996. 'Las Yaves', La Pajina Djudeo-Espanyola. Retrieved from <http://www.aki-yerushalayim.co.il/ay/085/085_09.htm> (accessed 5 September 2012).

Campoy Zueco, L. 2002. 'Recuperación y preservación del legado Sefardí en España proyecto de cooperación international'. Retrieved from <http://www.

worldsephardicongress.org/congress/ponencias/ponencia5.htm> (accessed 5 September 2012).

Char, R. 1964. *Effacement du peuplier*. Paris: Gallimard. Retrieved from <http://www. florilege.free.fr/florilege/char/effaceme.htm> (accessed 15 September 2012).

Finkelman, Y. 2009. 'Nostalgia, Inspiration, Ambivalence: Eastern Europe, Immigration, and the Construction of Collective Memory in Contemporary American Haredi Historiography', *Jewish History* 23 (1): 57–82.

Gerber, J.S. 1992. *Jews of Spain: A History of the Sephardic Experience*. New York: The Free Press.

Hirsch, M. 2008. 'The Generation of Post-memory', *Poetics Today* 29 (1): 103–28.

Hirsch, M. and L. Spitzer. 2002. 'We Would Not Have Come Without You: Generations of Nostalgia', *American Imago* 59 (3): 253–76.

Hofer, J. 1934 [1688]. 'Medical Dissertation on Nostalgia', *Bulletin of the Institute of the History of Medicine* 2: 376–91.

Homer [1919]. *The Odyssey* (Book V). Translated by A.T. Murray. Cambridge, MA: Harvard University Press; London: William Heinemann, Ltd.

Juris, J.S. 2006. 'Los Caminos de Sefarad', *Revista de Antropología Social* 14: 241–79.

Lévi, H. 2008. 'Dawn of the Sephardic Revival'. Retrieved from <http://www.scribd. com/doc/3320164/dawn-of -the-sephardic-revival> (accessed 5 September 2012).

Lévy, J.J. and I. Olazabal. 2004. 'Les Routes Juives d'Espagne Réveillent une Mémoire Oubliée. L'Exemple de Gérone', *Les cahiers Espaces* 80: 59–65.

——. 2007. 'Le Développement du Tourisme Culturel à Girona (Catalogne) Dans le Cadre du Réseau des Routes Juives d'Espagne', in J.-C. Lasry, J.J. Lévy and Y. Cohen (eds), *Identités sépharades et modernité*. Québec: Presses de l'Université Laval, pp. 31–46.

Lopez-Calvo, I. 2008. 'The Decolonization of Jewish Cultural Identity in the Works of Marcos Aguinis', *Bardulia*. Retrieved from <http://ignaciolopezcalvo.blogspot. ca/2008/11/decolonization-of-jewish-cultural.html> (accessed 5 September 2012).

Monterreal, Ó. 2012. *Toledo, capital de Sefarad*. Retrieved from <http://www.aurora-israel.co.il/articulos/israel/Mundo_Judio/44829/> (accessed 5 September 2012).

Olazabal, I. and J.J. Lévy. 1999. 'Représentations Contemporaines de la Réinscription du Patrimoine Juif dans la Ville de Girona: une Étude Exploratoire', in *La Cultura del Llibre: Herencia de Passat, Vivencia de Futur*, Actes del Congrès Internacional Cultura sefardita al Mediterrani, Girona, 26–28 mars 1998. Ajuntament de Girona, Collecio Historia de Girona 24, pp. 221–43.

Parla, A. 2009. 'Remembering across the Border: Postsocialist Nostalgia among Turkish Immigrants From Bulgaria', *American Ethnologist* 36 (4): 750–67.

Pulido, A.F. 1905. *Intereses Nacionales, Españoles sin Patria y la Raza Sefardi*. Madrid: E. Teodoro.

Raphael, F. 1979. 'Nostalgie de la Fête chez les Juifs du M'zab (Sud Algérien)'. Retrieved from <http://www.revue-des-sciences-sociales.com/pdf/rss08-raphael. pdf> (accessed 5 September 2012).

Rodríguez Mata, S. 2003. 'Entrevista a Miguel Ángel Nieto Solís'. Retrieved from <http://www.quintadimension.com/televicio/index.php?id=130> (accessed 5 September 2012).

Romeu Ferré, P. 2011. 'Sefarad ¿la 'Patria' de los Sefardíes?', *Sefarad* 71 (1): 95–130.

Sakamoto, I. and Y. Zhou. 2005. 'Gendered Nostalgia: The Experiences of New Chinese Skilled Immigrants in Canada', in V. Agnew (ed.), *Diaspora, Memory and Identity: A Search for Home.* Toronto: The University of Toronto Press, pp. 209–29.

Schneider, A. 2000. *Futures Lost: Nostalgia and Identity among Italian Immigrants in Argentina.* Oxford: Peter Lang.

Semprun, J. 2004. *Vingt Ans et Un Jour.* Paris: Gallimard Folio.

Wachtel, N. 2001. *La Foi du souvenir. Labyrinthes marranes.* Paris: Seuil.

———. 2011. *Mémoires marranes.* Paris: Seuil.

Yovel, Y. 1992. *Spinoza and Other Heretics, Volume 1: The Marrano of Reason.* Princeton: Princeton University Press.

———. 2009. *The Other Within: The Marranos: Split Identity and Emerging Modernity.* Princeton: Princeton University Press.

Chapter 7

Nostalgia and the Discovery of Loss

Essentializing the Turkish Cypriot Past

Rebecca Bryant

While we usually associate nostalgia with memory, this chapter explores the relationship between nostalgia and forgetting. Indeed, I propose here that contrary to what we usually think, the object of nostalgia has the status of the forgotten – the lost, the irretrievable, the impossible object of memory. Nostalgia emerges from the impossibility of return, representing a lost home, lost community, lost innocence. Moreover, it appears to emerge with the break represented by a lost dream – a dream that has beguiled us away from our former selves while making us into something new from which we cannot return. Whether this is the dream of the immigrant who longs for a country that has changed in her absence, the dream of capitalism whose collapse results in post-Soviet nostalgia, or the dream of modernity whose alienation leads to a longing for some imagined former *Gemeinschaft*, nostalgia seems to be predicated on collapsed hope. Nostalgia, then, may be said to represent a type of everyday disenchantment, the sort of awakening after which everything appears differently. We look back on the innocence of our former selves even as we can no longer retrieve or relive that innocence. It is in this sense, then, that nostalgia represents the forgotten, as an innocence or perfection that we acknowledge we no longer remember or know.[1] I would also suggest that this is why nostalgia is often viewed as the symbolic ailment of modernity (Pickering and Keightley 2006, Turner 1987): both because modernity signals a linear temporality from which there is no return, and also because modernity is the temporal home for disenchantment.

Seeing nostalgia in this way I think also allows us to account for another oft-noted aspect of nostalgia, namely, its tendency towards reductionism, sentimentality, even kitsch. This is because, as I wish to argue here, one of nostalgia's basic functions is to essentialize, to portray ourselves to ourselves in ways that we would like to see. Nostalgia portrays to us some (imagined) essence that has been irretrievably lost. And this is why, I will claim, nostalgia emerges most at times of liminality and identity confusion: because nostalgia represents not a longing for a forgotten past, but rather a *longing for essentialism*, a longing for a simplified representation of ourselves that is no longer available to us. In other words, it is at times when we do not know who we are that nostalgia represents not a longing for simplicity and innocence *per se*, but rather a longing for a time when we were innocent enough to believe we knew who we are.[2]

My ethnographic site for thinking about this problem is the divided island of Cyprus, and specifically the Turkish Cypriot community, which in the past decade has experienced a wave of nostalgia. Because more than half the community has been displaced, one aspect of this wave is nostalgia for lost homes and villages, today expressed in memoirs, television programs and village festivals. This new nostalgia has burgeoned at a particular historical moment, one that follows the opening of the island's checkpoints in 2003 and the subsequent visits of Cypriots to their homes and villages after almost thirty, or in some cases almost forty, years. It also followed an island-wide referendum in 2004 on a UN-sponsored plan that would have united the island, and Greek Cypriot rejection of that plan. This nostalgia arose, then, in a period when Greek Cypriots and Turkish Cypriots are able to move about the island with little restriction but ultimately return to their homes in two separate states.

It is important to note that these new nostalgic practices emerged in a political context in which 'return' has historically been understood as return to one's former home and, by implication, return to a prelapsarian, pre-conflict past. Within the context of large-scale displacement, official discourse in the Greek Cypriot community since 1974 has emphasized remembrance, and the idea of 'not forgetting' one's homes and villages in the island's north has been reproduced in schools and embraced by refugee associations in ways that indeed have created a 'post-memory' of those places and their loss among the children and grandchildren of displaced persons.[3] The moral demand not to forget has been reproduced in families and schools and has become a familiar part of public discourse about the island's north. Very simply put, in public discourse and everyday language, the island's north is under occupation and must be remembered as it was until the day when the occupation will end and Greek Cypriots will return to their lost homes to re-establish their communities there.

In contrast, Turkish Cypriot official discourse has emphasized 'remembering to forget', or the impossibility of return to the past and the permanence of the island's division. And for almost three decades after 1974, the finality of that discourse was rarely challenged by Turkish Cypriots who, for the most part, expressed no desire to return to their former homes and preferred the safety of the space where they had gathered in the island's north. That discourse, as 'state' discourse, has instead been called into question by the fact that the Turkish Cypriot de facto state established in the island's north after 1974 has never been recognized by any international body or country besides Turkey. This failure to gain recognition for their state has, in turn, left Turkish Cypriots in a perpetual state of liminality, neither citizens of a recognized state nor stateless, in which the current state of the island's division has been declared unacceptable by the United Nations and other international bodies and so by definition must change.

As we will see, in contrast to a Greek Cypriot nostalgia that emphasizes change as rupture and the past as future, Turkish Cypriots are nostalgic today for a past that they stress will not return. Nostalgic practices underscore the irretrievability of the past, and this nostalgia has emerged at a historical moment when Turkish Cypriots highlight Cypriot identity while at the same time having lost hope for reunification with their former Greek neighbours. But more than simply an interesting case, I think that Turkish Cypriot isolation and political liminality may give us new insight into the relationship of loss, liminality, nostalgia and essentialism. The shift from more than two decades of forgetting to pervasive practices of nostalgic remembrance points us to ways of understanding the relationship between memory, loss and gain. Today in north Cyprus, nostalgia has pervaded all aspects of life to such an extent that words used, foods eaten and places visited are all experienced nostalgically. What it means to 'experience nostalgically' will be the subject of the final part of the chapter, where I will discuss the relationship between this practice and predictions of their own cultural demise. This will also allow me to reflect in the conclusion on the ways in which nostalgia may be used to emphasize purity and produce boundaries.

On Forgetting and the Forgotten

The scene is a heart-warming one: on the divided island of Cyprus, Turkish Cypriots return to their formerly mixed village for a wine festival. The

Mallia village in the Troodos mountains of Cyprus had been a predominantly Turkish Cypriot village with a small Greek Cypriot minority until
Turkish Cypriots fled the village in 1964, at the beginning of an intercommunal conflict that would culminate ten years later in the division of the
island. Their departure from the village had been a violent one: because
Turkish Cypriots were an 18 per cent minority on the island, it was unusual
for a village to have a Greek Cypriot minority. As a result, when violence
began in late 1963, Turkish Cypriots who were minorities in surrounding
villages took refuge in Mallia, only to find themselves under attack by Greek
Cypriot forces in early 1964. A number of young men were killed, and the
rest of the village and those who had taken refuge there fled. Although half
of the Mallia Turkish Cypriots returned to their homes several years later,
they were displaced again in 1974. The rest have not been able to return to
their homes since their initial displacement. Before 1974, they had feared for
their safety, while after the division of the island they had made their way to
the north and were not able to cross back to the south. After the easing of
movement restrictions in the island in 2003 they began to visit, and in 2010
initiated what they hope will become an annual festival. As the organizer
of the festival said to me: 'The place where a person is born, where he has
his memories, is holy. We're trying to give people that experience this way.
Believe me, today everyone has a smile on their faces'.

The festival is carefully coordinated: the several hundred villagers who
attend take donkeys to the vineyards to collect grapes, which they bring with
them in straw baskets to the village. In the square, men in traditional costumes
stamp the grapes with their feet in stone basins. Fresh zivania (a local alcoholic
drink) flows, and souvlaki turns on spits. Folklore groups have been brought
from the island's north to perform, including children and grandchildren of
those displaced from the village. The Greek Cypriot Minister of the Interior
is in attendance, and he makes a speech that emphasizes coexistence and the
reunification of the island. But at the same time that he is making his speech,
one of the Mallia Turkish Cypriots turns to me and says, 'Greek Cypriots
tend not to come. It's mostly a chance for us [the Mallia Turkish Cypriots] to
get together. Some of us live in Aydınköy [a village in the island's north], but
a lot of us were scattered. It's a chance to see people I haven't seen in a long
time, maybe to see someone's grandchild that I haven't seen yet'. And indeed,
when I look around, I notice that most of the village's current Greek Cypriot
population hovers at the edges of the crowd, remaining in the coffee shop on
one side of the square. Almost all of the original Greek Cypriots of the village,
who as a minority spoke Turkish, have stayed at home.

This is only one example of a burgeoning of village festivals celebrating attachment to former villages. The number of festivals should not

be surprising given that in 1975, one year after the division of Cyprus, almost 60 per cent of the Turkish Cypriot community was displaced or had experienced long-term displacement. Their displacement began as early as 1956, when the first tensions arose following the 1955 beginning of a Greek Cypriot struggle against British colonial rule that was intended to unite the island with Greece. Turkish Cypriots opposed the idea of union, and by 1957 they had formulated their own counter strategy, a demand for division of the island and union of its two parts with the respective 'motherlands', Greece and Turkey. In that scheme, Turkish Cypriots would move to the north, which was the area closest to Turkey and so would 'naturally' be united with it in the event of such a partition. After Turkish Cypriots formed their own guerrilla organization to pursue this goal in 1958, intercommunal clashes led to the displacement of 1,900 Greek Cypriots and 2,700 Turkish Cypriots.

When this struggle resulted in neither union with Greece nor division of the island, and instead leaders of the two communities were called upon to put down their arms and unite in a new Republic of Cyprus, around half of those displaced returned to their homes. They lived there in relative peace between the establishment of the Republic in 1960 and its subsequent breakdown in 1963. As a result of a struggle over power sharing, Turkish Cypriots withdrew from the government in December of that year, and afterwards the Republic of Cyprus became a de facto Greek Cypriot state. Intercommunal violence broke out, and in the last months of 1963 and first months of 1964, almost 25,000 Turkish Cypriots were uprooted from their homes, including almost all of those who had been displaced in 1958. When the Republic was established, there were 106,000 Turkish Cypriots scattered throughout the island, living in 114 mixed towns and villages and 117 wholly Turkish villages.[4] By 1964, only 8,000 Turkish Cypriots were living outside of armed enclaves, and reports from the time emphasize that even this small number did not receive government services, as they refused to submit to government control (Patrick 1976: 463–65). The enclaves were put under siege, and exit from them was considered a dangerous endeavour.

Turkish Cypriots remained in their enclaves for almost a decade, despite a period after 1968 in which the siege against them was lifted, and they were able to leave the enclaves to visit their villages.[5] It was only after the junta government in Greece sponsored a coup against President Makarios in 1974 that Turkey intervened militarily. This intervention resulted in the division of the island and a large movement of populations, in which approximately 145,000 Greek Cypriots from the island's north moved to the south, and approximately 45,000 Turkish Cypriots from the south made their way to the north. This movement of populations occurred in some cases spontaneously, as when Greek Cypriots fled advancing Turkish troops, and in other cases more gradually, as Turkish Cypriots over the course of a year made their way over the mountains and by sea to the north. Including those Turkish Cypriots who were already displaced in the north, the total number of Turkish Cypriots who had fled their villages during the conflict reached 62,000. Of these, more than 50,000 were unable to return to their homes.

For many Turkish Cypriots, the division of the island was simultaneously the culmination of a decade of trauma and the realization of a political goal. As I discuss elsewhere (Bryant 2010), Turkish Cypriots' movement to the north was accompanied by a period of triumphal looting, as they broke out of their ghettoes to find that Greek Cypriots had grown prosperous in their absence. Greek Cypriot properties were distributed to displaced persons and to those whose homes had been destroyed in the conflict. In addition, Turkish Cypriots moving into Greek Cypriot villages and neighbourhoods ransacked houses, taking furniture and refrigerators. They took over Greek Cypriot businesses, factories, orchards and hotels, and they imported peasants from Anatolia to work the land and boost the demographic balance. For most Turkish Cypriots at the time, this was the last stop, seen both in the phrase used to describe their displacement (*özgürlük göcü,* or 'freedom migration') and in the ways that they narrate the period leading up to this migration.

I have noted elsewhere that until about a decade ago, the writing of history in the Turkish Cypriot community may be seen as what I call a 'retrospective apocalypticism'. By this I mean that much both official and unofficial history in the island's north was written as though it inevitably led to the Turkish military intervention and division of the island. Within such a history, nostalgia itself became eschatological, anticipating a homeland yet to be constructed (Bryant 2008). One finds this in other liminal communities, where 'home' appears to represent an endpoint rather than a lost beginning (see also Fillinghim 1997: 77). A generically nostalgic view of 'home' comes to represent an ideal not yet realized. And prior to the past decade, we see that in much Turkish Cypriot writing and representation of their villages and life before division, nostalgic images of home are primarily used to mourn destruction and to advance an understanding of community as one constructed out of conflict.

The writing of a new homeland, then, entailed the construction of 'home' as goal and the forgetting of actual homes left behind. In the period after 1974, Turkish Cypriots were engaged in a project of constructing a new community, and they did so out of collective trauma and dispossession, as well as the experience of having committed both physical and material violence against another community. For the first time, they were gathered together into a physical space that they claimed as their own, and over the course of time, their identity as a community became linked to that space and to the act of living together. Should it be surprising, then, that rather than mourning the past, they chose to forget it?

Forgetting, like remembering, is of course an act engaged in by individuals, not by communities.[6] However, the attempt to find terms for our collective erasure of the past is handicapped by the negative connotations of many of the words available. Peter Burke, for instance, has written about 'social amnesia' (Burke 1989). And while Burke points out that amnesia has an etymological relation to amnesty and so may be something necessary and desirable in order to maintain social harmony, at the same time the word 'amnesia' has acquired in popular culture the meaning of an undesired and undesirable loss of memory, a loss against which innumerable heroes of film and print have struggled. This further reflects what Paul Connerton refers to as 'the view, commonly held if not universal, that remembering and commemoration is usually a virtue and that forgetting is necessarily a failing' (Connerton 2008: 59). Forgetting is one of those peculiar faculties that is usually seen as desirable when it is impossible and the result of failure or even repression when it occurs. One sees this, as well, in the antonyms that we employ: memory versus amnesia, remembrance versus forgetfulness, both of which sets imply an active faculty against a passive lack. As forgetting is the only gerund that we have and so the only noun implying wilful activity, I will use it here to refer to both individual and collective processes of electing to forget.

One may argue that there are surely certain pasts that cannot or should not be forgotten, and this is surely as true as to say that memory is never stable or certain. But it seems to me that this also confuses public forgetting with individual forgetting; after all, certain events may be fully erased from public memory while remaining as individual traumas. However, I would also draw a heuristic distinction here between what I will refer to as public forgetting, social forgetting and individual forgetting. While what I will call public forgetting refers to the concrete ways in which the past may be erased from public life, often as a state or institutional project, individual forgetting refers to the varying degrees to which memories are erased from consciousness. Social forgetting, on the other hand, is the more nebulous area where these two intersect, the realm of literature, popular culture and public discourse, where we may experience ebbs and flows of remembering and forgetting. Moreover, it is at the level of social forgetting that we define identity and hence moral community, and as a result it is at this level that processes of remembering and forgetting are given a moral tone.

For more than two decades after the division of Cyprus in 1974, Turkish Cypriots engaged in all these forms of forgetting. Public remembrance of communal traumas, as seen in school books, museums, monuments and ceremonies, called for individual forgetting of anything good about a past lived with Greek Cypriots. Public remembrance emphasized rupture, a break with the past, and asked Turkish Cypriots to go on with the task of building a new homeland. At the social level, there is a lack of writing, a historical hole, when it comes to the enclave period between 1963 and 1974, what is simultaneously considered the most important period for the community and about which one might expect there to have been novels and memoirs written and songs composed. And there is evidence that individuals engaged in a fair share of forgetting, at least to the extent that their individual traumas and losses were not transmitted to their children and grandchildren, who today have little knowledge of their ancestral homes in the south and experience none of the 'post-memory', or secondary trauma, of Greek Cypriot youth.

One indication of the extent of this forgetting amongst displaced persons was the fact that, at a certain moment, a handful of Turkish Cypriot poets (not themselves displaced) began to castigate refugees for choosing to remember so little. One of them poetically asked, for instance:

You say the past is past, my nomadic soul.
Do you not miss at all the earth that you still smell on your skin?
Two unfamiliar eyes have settled in your face
Unseeing of the vineyard dying from an untended fate,
Your heart has turned a corner,[7] around you are clouds of forgetfulness.
Were you able to find the equivalent value[8] of all those things you erased and forgot?

(Quoted in Kızılyürek 2011)

The kind of forgetfulness described by the poet is what Paul Connerton usefully calls 'forgetting that is constitutive in the formation of a new identity'. He notes that in such instances forgetting may not be a loss but a gain, and he remarks:

The emphasis here is not so much on the loss entailed in being unable to retain certain things as rather on the gain that accrues to those who know how to discard memories that serve no practicable purpose in the management of one's current identity and ongoing purposes. Forgetting then becomes part of the process by which newly shared memories are constructed because a new set of memories are frequently accompanied by a set of tacitly shared silences ... What is allowed to be forgotten provides living space for present projects. (ibid.: 63)

While Connerton does not discuss the specific circumstances under which such forgetting is possible, we may speculate that not all political, economic and social circumstances would be conducive to or allow such forgetting. In the Turkish Cypriot case, we have a group that experienced what at the time it considered a 'victory'[9] and that consequently experienced a prolonged period of isolation in which there were few convincing challenges to official versions of past events.

Moreover, all of this was considered a 'gain'. Certainly, my own formal and informal interviews with several hundred displaced Turkish Cypriots who were adults when they fled their homes show that at least for the first two or so decades after 1974, there was a calculation of having gained what they perceived at the time as freedom and safety, an unwillingness to dwell on loss, and a desire to 'put the past behind us', as they would say. I should also note that for some there were material gains, as approximately 100,000 Turkish Cypriots, only around 50,000 of whom were homeless, built their new statelet in an area from which around 150,000 Greek Cypriots had fled. The number of homes and properties left behind by Greek Cypriots far exceeded the capacity of Turkish Cypriots to absorb them. As a result, many Turkish Cypriots received more than they had left behind, adding to the already triumphal atmosphere that existed after the war.

In general there seems to have been, then, a perception of gain rather than loss. But Connerton also emphasized the role of forgetting in what he calls 'the construction of a new identity'. In his own attempt to distinguish various forms of forgetting, Ankersmit (2001) has similarly discussed a type of forgetting in which as communities[10] we enter new epochs and lose the identity we once had. To illustrate this, he uses the examples of the French Revolution and the birth of modern science, both epochal events that changed the way we see ourselves. He distinguishes this type of forgetting from the more official repression that takes place as a result of historical trauma, even though he views this type of forgetting as a particular type of trauma, one destined to remain unresolved. Moreover, he asserts:

> The historical transformations occasioning it [this form of forgetting] are always accompanied by feelings of a profound and irreparable loss, of cultural despair and of hopeless disorientation. In this sense such historical experiences are undoubtedly traumatic. But the stake of the traumatic experience is far more dramatic in such cases: for here one really loses oneself, here a former identity is irrevocably lost forever and superseded by a new historical or cultural identity ... The new identity is mainly constituted by the trauma of the loss of a former identity – precisely *this* is its main content. (Ankersmit 2001: 302)

However, unlike Connerton, who views the shedding of a former identity as a potential gain, Ankersmit observes: 'Moving to a new and different world really *is* and also *requires* an act of violence, in fact nothing less than an act of suicide' (Ankersmit 2001: 316, emphasis in original). Although both authors appear to be discussing the same phenomenon – namely, a type of forgetting in which the erasure or silencing of the past is incorporated into a new identity – Connerton's more upbeat take could not contrast more strongly with Ankersmit's invocation of the violence of such an act. While Ankersmit calls it a suicide, Connerton seems to see this act as a matter of clearing away dead branches to make room for new ones to grow.

The problem appears to lie in their equally unproblematized use of the word 'identity', which could obviously mean many things, including 'self sameness', as in our own individual identities, or 'sameness with others', as in group identity. Ankersmit seems to use 'identity' in the first sense, to refer to self sameness through time. At the same moment, he appears to elide communal and individual identity, taking one to stand for the other. 'Identity', then, is Ankersmit's way of encapsulating both the remaking of community and the remaking of self that accompanies rapid social change. Connerton, on the other hand, seems to understand 'identity' in the sociological sense, as 'sameness with others'. In Connerton's sense, we are able in certain cases to remake society, casting away pasts and persons who may not fit the mould we wish to shape.

This detour into the distinction between Connerton and Ankersmit's approaches is important for understanding the historical trajectory of Turkish Cypriot forgetting that I would like to follow. Rather than speaking of the role of forgetting in the construction of a new identity, I find it more useful to speak of the role of forgetting in the construction of a new moral community, as the idea of a moral community clearly refers to a group without specifying how the group represents its unity. In the philosophy of ethics, the moral community is often explained as including those persons who merit 'regard', i.e. those persons we 'see' and consider worthy of our moral consideration. In recent years, much discussion in the philosophy of ethics has centred on our ethical responsibilities to non-humans. One of those who argues in favour of animal experimentation, Michael Allen Fox, uses a 'hard' definition of moral community to justify his claims. Fox describes a moral community as 'a group of beings that shares certain characteristics and whose members are or consider themselves to be bound to observe certain rules of conduct in relation to one another because of their mutual likeness. These rules create what we call obligations and derive in some intimate way from the characteristics which the beings composing the moral community have in common' (Fox 2006: 184). Here I intentionally use a 'hard' definition to emphasize that, like 'identity', moral communities are based on inclusion and exclusion. Fox says that obligations derive from a perceived mutual likeness, in other words, from 'identity', and from the characteristics that those in the community have in common. Remembering and forgetting play an important role in helping us define those persons worthy of 'regard,' those persons to whom we have obligations and those to whom we do not.

I draw the distinction between moral community and identity here to make a specific point. Because although 'identity' is not a *substance* but a *representation*, it describes something that groups perceive as their 'essence', that thing that ties them together, and it describes it both to themselves and to others. 'Identity', then, is taken to be a particular essence or accretion, something that everyone and every group 'naturally' has. In the particular case in question, this distinction is important to understand that while a process of forgetting was important for the construction of a new moral community after 1974, Turkish Cypriots have for a long time been much less certain about their identity.

While a complete explanation of the reasons for this uncertainty is beyond the scope of this chapter, much of it is attributable to the twin and related factors of immigration and non-recognition. Both of these represent to Turkish Cypriots what it means to live in a de facto state. The state that they declared after 1983 has been recognized as sovereign only by Turkey, which despite that recognition continues to maintain around thirty thousand troops in the island and has a significant say in Turkish Cypriots' domestic affairs. As with the patron states[11] of other unrecognized entities, Turkey is North Cyprus's military protector, while the Turkish Cypriot economy is sustained by a yearly Turkish aid package. And because of Turkey's role as banker and protector, north Cyprus often appears more as Turkey's province or colony than as a separate state that Turkey has recognized.

Moreover, after 1974 an agreement between the Turkish Cypriot leadership and Turkey facilitated the migration of approximately thirty thousand Anatolian peasants to the island's north, both as a workforce and to boost the island's Turkish population. This feat of demographic engineering has been internationally condemned as the consolidation of an occupation. And for a couple of decades, despite Turkish Cypriots' initial complaints about the cultural difference of those immigrating, those immigrants and especially their children and grandchildren were for the most part absorbed into the social fabric. In the 1990s, however, the visa requirement was lifted for Turkish nationals entering the island, and as a result many Turkish nationals from poorer regions, especially Turkey's southeast, which was suffering from conflict, flooded into the island seeking work. Most of them found it, and they created chains of immigration. In addition, universities began to open in the island's north, catering to around thirty thousand students from Turkey annually. As a result, in the 2011 census, persons of Turkish origin outnumbered persons originally from Cyprus by four to three.

This has led to a 'discourse of demographic danger' (Hatay 2007, 2008; see also Kurtuluş and Purkis 2008) similar to other such phenomena resulting from globalization, though in this case the immigration is from the country that is banker, protector and generally dominant over a small population in an unrecognized state. One result has been a widespread belief that Turkish Cypriot culture is being eroded by food, music and other trends coming from Turkey, and that the Turkish Cypriot community is in the process of a gradual extinction. This has caused much soul searching, as well as a turn to nostalgia, even as, interestingly, Turkish Cypriots emphasize that they do not know what their identity means. While the most common identity discourse today is that of the 'Turkish Cypriot', and almost all emphasize ties to Cyprus and difference from Turks from Anatolia, there is much division over what the content of that identity might be.

Fractures over meaning, of course, are common to every identity, as no designation means the same thing to every individual or subgroup. The problem today in north Cyprus, however, is that if you ask almost any person of Cypriot origin, they would say that they are not certain about their identity. Young people ask: 'Who are we in the world?' and invoke the uncertainties of living in an unrecognized state. And recently a close friend asked me: 'Do you know how difficult it is not to know who you are? I mean, if someone asked you to tell them what it means to be an American, you would be able to do that, right?' I had to disappoint her by telling her that I have absolutely no idea what it means to be an American, but the interesting point here is her expectation that one should be able to explain the content of the identity that one claims or that is assigned to one.

I refer here to this anxiety over not knowing 'who one is in the world' as a *longing for essentialism*. Gayatri Spivak has of course used the notion of 'strategic essentialism' to describe the ways that groups, especially minority groups, use fixed images to represent themselves in a strategic way (Spivak 1984/5). Michael Herzfeld expanded this idea to describe the ways that the nation state and its institutions, as well as average citizens, may strategically use stereotypes and essentialized notions of themselves in daily life (esp. Herzfeld 2005). As should be clear from these critiques of the strategic value of essentialism, we may see essentialism as a form of representation, a way of strategically representing oneself in order to achieve certain ends. But we also know from social theory at least since Hegel that there is an inherent connection between identity and recognition, in that we need to be recognized by others in order to recognize ourselves. Hegel's original insight has recently been revived by political theorists such as Axel Honneth, who sees the struggle for recognition as being at the heart of social conflict (Honneth 1995).

We return, then, to the issue of non-recognition, which is internalized as an anxiety over 'Who are we in the world?' This anxiety has increased over the past decade, with lawsuits in the European Court of Human Rights that erode the de facto sovereignty of the state in the north; the 2004 failure of a UN reunification plan, which would have given that state some legitimacy; and the increasing regional and economic power of Turkey. The failure of both recognition and reunification, as well as the increasing effects of globalization, have resulted in what I am calling here a 'longing for essentialism'.[12] So while Turkish Cypriots were able to recreate a new community in a newly defined territory after 1974, and while one of the defining features of this community was that it incorporated forgetfulness into its being, the failure of Turkish Cypriots to gain recognition, along with immigration and other effects of globalization, have left them less certain about identity. And it is in this context that a new nostalgia has emerged.

Nostalgia's Threshold

My second ethnographic example is a museum, the Melandra Culture House, which stands as a monument to a lost village life. The displaced owner of the property is from the village of Melandra, another wine-producing area of the island's south, and he built a monument to his displacement in a replica of his village house, placing it incongruously on one of the main coast roads in the Famagusta area, opposite the sea. Although the house is supposed to be a replica, the owner admits that it was actually constructed by a builder from Mardin, in Turkey, who used stones in the Mardin style. The two-story stone house is surrounded by outbuildings, including a kitchen and toilets. Signs explain the function of each, and visiting parents point out to their children how 'primitively' Cypriots lived in the past. The family has collected antique furniture, clothing, photographs and household items, and these are on display in various rooms. In a small room off the entrance, they also sell 'original' Cypriot bakery items, such as village bread with halloumi and olives. On the day that we first visited the museum, the wife of the owner, known in her own right as a memoirist, encouraged us to sit at a picnic table while she brought lemonade. As we sipped our lemonade, she plucked jasmine from a vine near us and held it out to us. 'Sniff it!' she encouraged us. 'This is the way Cyprus used to smell!'

The house itself and the owner's nostalgic gesture represent only one part of a new identity industry in the island's north, one that emphasizes Cypriotness and localism, seen in the explosion in 'Cypriot' products – from homemade cheese to woven baskets – an insistence on using names and words from the Cypriot Turkish dialect; and roaming television programs that test villagers' knowledge of Cypriot culture. While in one sense this new localism is a now-common response to the destabilizing effects of globalization, north Cyprus, as I remarked above, has been peculiarly affected by globalization as an unrecognized state. For many years, north Cyprus' only door to the world was through Turkey, but it was a door that swung both ways: while it allowed Turkish Cypriots to travel on Turkish passports and to export goods via Turkey, it also brought Turkish military and political interference, as well as large numbers of Turkish labour migrants. Culturally reactionary responses to high levels of immigration are now familiar, but in north Cyprus such a response has taken the particular form of a reaction against the Turkish culture that had once been a model for and source of Turkish Cypriots' understanding of their own cultural identity.

But we see in the examples I have given that the nostalgia employed is both essentializing and contradictory. While Turkish Cypriots from Mallia organized an event in their formerly mixed village, it was clearly their own event and did not encourage the participation of their former Greek neighbours. Neither did it signal a desire to return. A similar contradiction may be seen in the recent meeting of displaced Turkish Cypriots from Limassol, a picnic held in the Boğaz area between Nicosia and Kyrenia, but not in Limassol itself. And while the Melandra Culture House is a space that engages specifically in an essentializing nostalgia, it is also explicit about memorializing a way of life that no longer exists.

And yet all of these nostalgic events and spaces are filled with a particular type of longing, which I have called a longing for essentialism. This longing was summarized quite well by the owner of the Melandra Culture House when she described in one of the local newspapers the reasons that they had decided to pursue the project. Both she and her husband, she said, had felt like plants that had been uprooted when they arrived in the north. They anticipated that they would go back to their homes, and they longed for them, she claims:

> This longing sometimes penetrates to the depths of our hearts like a sharp knife. As the years passed, the hope that we would be able to return to our homes, to our original places, diminished. As our hope diminished, hopelessness increased.

On 23th April 2003, when the rusted lock on our cell and the barbed wire that had prevented us for twenty-nine years from returning to our homes parted slightly,[13] we were able to return to our places. Both Greek Cypriots and Turkish Cypriots experienced the same trauma. We were shaken! We were disappointed! Our childhoods, our youths, our neighbours, our relatives, most importantly our mothers and fathers . . . our memories, our remembrances . . . were gone! They were all gone! My village was in darkness! Complete darkness! Even the shadows had been erased . . . Melancholy wound up like a ball in our hearts. A storm gathered in my thoughts . . . This was always repeated, every time I went to my village.

I am surrounded by a growing population with its own way of speaking, its own customs, its own dress. There are new customs, new traditions, new cultures in my country. I am going extinct as the days pass. To accept extinction while living is worse than death . . . And so, precisely because we did not accept to die while living, five years ago we began the construction of the Melandra Culture House. (Kıralp 2010)

In the island's north today, it is quite common to hear similar expressions of their own impending cultural demise: the idea that in twenty years, or fifty years, Turkish Cypriots as a group will be extinct. In a recent series of interviews that I conducted for a different project, I asked interviewees where they saw Cyprus in ten years' time.[14] All but one of them said that they had trouble seeing a future. One left-wing academic remarked: 'I think that Turkish Cypriots are in the process of being wiped off the stage of history in front of our eyes. I don't know if it will be in ten years, but certainly in forty or fifty years I don't think it will be necessary to talk anymore about the existence of Turkish Cypriots'. And one business woman commented: 'The Cypriot Turkish community was reduced in the 30s and 40s and again in the 60s and 70s and 80s because of migration,[15] but it still managed to survive. At the moment, Turkish Cypriots think that they're going to have a hard time surviving from now on'.

I have outlined some of the reasons for this fear of extinction above, but I should note here that the anxiety is clearly not only one of numbers, whether migration out or migration in. The anxiety is concerned with *cultural* extinction, with the idea that something called a 'Turkish Cypriot' is disappearing, losing its essence. This is why, in another context, political scientist Niyazi Kızılyürek referred to Turkish Cypriots as 'a group of exiles with the ghost of extinction hovering over them' (Kızılyürek 2011). The counterpart of the fear of extinction, I am claiming, is a longing for essentialism, and the boom in nostalgic practices represents such a longing.

And here my reasons for drawing a distinction between moral community and identity should become clear. Because while Turkish Cypriots may today fear losing their cultural identity and may be experiencing an identity crisis to the extent that they are unable successfully to represent themselves in the world, the recent rise in nostalgic practices should make it clear that they are still able to delineate a moral community, even if they struggle to describe what holds it together. And here I might open yet another parenthesis to note that a number of social theorists, most recently Jean-Luc Nancy, have described nostalgia precisely as longing for a lost, ideal community or communion. In other words, nostalgia tends to point to a solidarity and even goodness that we believe we once possessed and have lost.

Indeed, as a co-author and I note elsewhere, one form that this wave of nostalgia has taken is a longing for the period between 1963 and 1974, when Turkish Cypriots lived in isolated ghettoes, and when for almost five years they were under a military and economic siege (Bryant and Hatay 2011, Hatay and Bryant 2008). Although Turkish Cypriots today describe this period as the most difficult of their lives, it was also a time of solidarity, when the community worked together in pursuit of a common goal. As such, this nostalgia bears many resemblances to *Ostalgie* and other forms of post-Soviet nostalgia that long for times perceived as simpler and less morally complex. We may, indeed, follow Nancy Ries (1997) in noting that certain periods of rapid social change produce a sense of liminality, a disorientation as anchors are lost or cast aside and goals are not yet clear. Narcis Tulbure has used the term 'liminal nostalgia' to describe 'a particular form of social imagination through which meaning is created, practices are resignified and positions are renegotiated during periods of epochal change' (Tulbure 2006: 85). Tulbure argues that liminal nostalgia represents a search for moral direction and purposefulness, something that we see in the Cyprus case, as well.

But as the owner of the Melandra Culture House demonstrated with her offer of jasmine, and as any number of television programs, memoirs and festivals show, nostalgia pervades everyday life as a way of marking boundaries. While on the one hand festivals celebrate villages that in fact have been lost, Cyprus still smells of jasmine, and halloumi and olives are still eaten everywhere. In other words, while the first example that I gave demonstrated nostalgia for a village life that was lost and would not return, many other aspects of the current wave of nostalgia call upon Turkish Cypriots to experience their own culture nostalgically as both reminder and foreshadowing of their own future extinction. To experience nostalgically the loss of something that has not yet disappeared is an expression of a longing for essentialism and a way of drawing boundaries.

We see clearly the type of boundaries drawn in the case of the wine festival in Mallia. Villagers in this festival enact and embody nostalgia, picking grapes in vineyards where their parents once harvested, dressing their children in folkloric costumes, drinking zivania in the village square and watching folklore troupes brought with them from the north perform throughout the evening. At the same time, as noted earlier, only a small number of the Greek Cypriots originally from the village come to the festival, and those living now in the village maintain their distance. This is clearly an exclusionary festival, despite the political overtones that try to lend it a 'bicommunal' or 'reconciliatory' facade. And while the spirit of the festival is jubilant, its attempt to re-enact ways of life that have long passed also appears to mark it as a memorial to a past that cannot return.

In other types of nostalgia that call on Turkish Cypriots to experience what they smell, eat and speak as though it has already been lost, they are asked to essentialize their culture and to long for it as though it is already extinct. In this sense, experiencing their culture nostalgically becomes a way to preserve boundaries and to prevent its loss.

Conclusion

Svetlana Boym's oft-quoted statement that 'modern nostalgia is a mourning for the impossibility of mythical return' (Boym 2001: 8) is often taken to mean that nostalgia is an always unfinished and, as Boym calls it, 'insatiable' project, one in which purveyors of nostalgia struggle against the irreversibility of time. What I have suggested here, however, is that such an understanding of nostalgia presumes a *struggle against* mourning rather than an acceptance of it. In other words, if the lost object becomes a source of nostalgia *because* of its irretrievability, it may be the case that some forms of embodied nostalgia of the sort enacted in my examples in fact emphasize the lost object *as something that cannot be regained*. Nostalgia may, then, be used to finalize the past, to emphasize irretrievability and the impossibility of return while also acknowledging loss.

Indeed, insofar as the performances enacted in Mallia may be seen as a form of 'structural nostalgia', a 'collective representation of an Edenic order' (Herzfeld 1997: 109), they are representations that put emphasis on 'the (historical) Fall', on the moment that makes the past prelapsarian and irretrievable. As such, these performances point to nostalgia's always ambiguous relationship with temporal thresholds and so with liminality itself. In other words, if, as I have suggested here, nostalgia represents a longing for essentialism, this is also a longing for a clearly defined identity with its clearly defined boundaries.

One sees this longing for essentialism not only in the sorts of nostalgic practices I have described here but equally in anthropology's disciplinary melancholy for 'lost' cultures spoiled by outside intrusion (Bissell 2005), and in social theory's mourning for the pre-modern (Turner 1987, also, Pickering and Keightley 2006). Moreover, nostalgia appears to result from those historical circumstances in which loss of a previous identity is, indeed, incorporated into the identity itself. In other words, we can hardly be nostalgic for what we do not realize we have lost, and this is just as true of modernity's longing for the pre-modern as it is of Turkish Cypriots' nostalgia for lost villages.

But what this seems to suggest is that nostalgia may be in a closer relationship to forgetfulness than to memory. Or, to borrow from Paul Ricoeur's notes on power and violence, the constitution of community may have the status of the *forgotten*.[16] Indeed, the very casting off of that past becomes a constitutive part of one's identity, but one perceived as a loss.[17] One may see this in post-Soviet nostalgia, where the transition to a neoliberal order was perceived by many as a type of trauma and produced cultural despair and disorientation. We see this in different ways in both the examples I have given: in the first, an emphasis on loss that emphasizes the impossibility of return, and in the second a use of the nostalgic mode to essentialize what they fear is seeping away and to deny the reconstitution of the community. In the second case, the claim that 'this is the way Cyprus used to smell' is a way of constituting the scent of jasmine as an essence already lost and the Turkish Cypriot community as one that is living its own extinction.

If nostalgia occurs at moments of liminality and rapid social change, I have claimed here, it is because of its essentializing function. Nostalgia represents a longing for essentialism, a longing for a clear and secure representation of oneself that appears to have been lost in the reconstitution of community. And so insofar as we may be able to identify a 'liminal nostalgia', this is because nostalgia may be strategically deployed to define thresholds, boundaries and hence orientations towards the future.

Notes

1. I would also contrast this with melancholia, with which nostalgia is often confused. While there is no space for a full discussion of the differences here, I would note that if I am right that nostalgia emerges from the disenchantment and the desire for, but acknowledgment of the impossibility of, re-enchantment, then this also acknowledges the impossibility of return precisely because of the fact that we ourselves have changed – *we cannot go back*. Melancholia, on the other hand, directs itself at lost objects without fully reconciling ourselves to

their loss (see Brock and Truscott 2012). In other words, if nostalgia represents the impossibility of remembering, melancholia represents the impossibility of forgetting. Peter Fritzsche explains the confusion thus: 'While nostalgia takes the past as its mournful subject, it holds it at arm's length. The virtues of the past are cherished and their passage is lamented, but there is no doubt that they are no longer retrievable. In other words, nostalgia constitutes what it cannot possess and defines itself by its inability to approach its subject, a paradox that is the essence of nostalgia's melancholia' (Fritzsche 2001: 1595).

2. The idea of nostalgia as a memorial to the trajectory of one's life and to a lost past is expressed by a Chinese essayist as a 'right to nostalgia': 'Nostalgia is not only a kind of remembrance, but a kind of right. We all have a longing for the past – lingering over some mundane objects because these mundane objects have become the memorial to the trajectory of one's own life, allowing us, without a doubt, to construct a human archive' (Jinhua and Chen 1997: 144).

3. See especially Hadjiyanni 2002 on post-memory. Memories have also been transmitted to the youth through schools and other media, using the slogan 'I do not forget' (*Dhen xsechno*). On the uses of the slogan in a Greek Cypriot politics of remembrance, see Christou 2006 and Marathefti 1989. On recent fractures within the Greek Cypriot community around this slogan, see Yakinthou 2008.

4. For more information on mixed villages in Cyprus and their gradual homogenization over the course of the twentieth century, see Bryant 2012, and Lytras and Psaltis 2011.

5. For an initial view on this opening and the psychological forces, or 'enclave mentality', that kept them in their ghettoes, see Volkan 1979. For more on life in the enclaves, see Bryant and Hatay 2011.

6. For an excellent discussion of many of the pitfalls of the memory terminology, see Berliner 2005 (also Kansteiner 2002).

7. The phrase used here, 'Yüreğin köşe döndü', has a dual meaning in Turkish. While on the one hand it implies change and forgetfulness, 'to turn a corner' also means to come into wealth.

8. Again, the poet uses a word with a dual meaning, 'eşdeğer'. While it literally means something of equivalent value, amongst Turkish Cypriots the word is more commonly used to refer to Greek Cypriot property that they received from the Turkish Cypriot government after 1974 in compensation for their properties left behind in the island's south.

9. In this regard, Peter Burke remarks, for instance: 'It is often said that history is written by the victors. It might also be said that history is forgotten by the victors. They can afford to forget, whereas the losers are unable to accept what happened and are condemned to brood over it, relive it, and reflect how different it might have been' (Burke 1989: 106).

10. Though he seems to imply not as individuals, which seems a questionable assumption. After all, is not 'going on with one's life' after a disaster, a death, or a divorce all about recreating oneself in the absence of an other (person, place, thing) that had been important to one's identity?

11. 'Patron state' is the term commonly used in international relations to refer to
    those states on which unrecognized states depend in the absence of other forms
    of external support. Nina Caspersen summarizes the relationship thus: 'Due
    to their lack of international recognition, unrecognized states are not spoilt for
    choice when it comes to attracting external support, and patron states therefore
    fill an important gap. Based on ethnic links or strategic interests, these states
    choose to support unrecognized states with diplomatic, economic, and military
    assistance. Such external support helps compensate for the lack of international
    recognition and significantly assists the process of state-building' (Caspersen
    2012: 54–55; see also Kolsto 1996). This is important to note here in the case
    of Cyprus in order to emphasize the non-uniqueness of the Turkish Cypriots'
    dependence on Turkey.
12. The sort of essentialism to which I refer here is summarized by James Clifford
    thus: 'Certainly one can't sustain a social movement or a community without
    certain apparently stable criteria for distinguishing us from them. These may
    be . . . articulated in connections and disconnections, but as they are expressed
    and become meaningful to people, they establish accepted truths. Certain key
    symbols come to define the we against the they; certain core elements . . . come
    to be separated out, venerated, fetishized, defended. This is the normal process,
    the politics, by which groups form themselves into identities' (Clifford 2003: 62).
13. She refers here to the easing of movement restrictions that allowed Cypriots
    to cross to the 'other side' after twenty-nine years in which such crossings had
    been forbidden by the Turkish Cypriot authorities.
14. The project was a coauthored report on Cypriot perceptions of Turkey. Turkish
    Cypriot perceptions of their 'patron state' are, as one would expect, complex
    and were intimately entangled with their own visions of their future in the
    island (Bryant and Yakinthou 2012).
15. In the 1930s and 1940s, as well as in the first part of the twentieth century, many
    Turkish Cypriots left the island for Anatolia because of what were perceived
    at the time as the relative advantages and attractions of the new Republic of
    Turkey. In the 1960s and after, Turkish Cypriots immigrated to the UK and
    Australia, as well as to Turkey, to escape conflict.
16. Ricoeur, of course, sees this forgetting as inherent to living together rather than
    a real past: 'Here is my interpretation: the constitution of power in a human
    plurality . . . this constitution has the status of the forgotten. But this forgetting,
    inherent to the constitution of that consent which creates power, does not refer
    back to any past which could have been lived as present in the transparency of
    a society conscious of itself and of its engendering(s). I insist on this point: a
    forgetting which is not of the past. In this sense, a forgetting without nostalgia.
    A forgetting of that which constitutes the present of our living-together' (Ricoeur
    2010: 25). Ricoeur does not appear to be taking into account, however, instances
    where the violence of the past is self-consciously integrated into the forgotten
    of the community's constitution. Ricoeur's point here does not seem to refer to
    the forgetting of hegemony (Comaroff and Comaroff 1991) but appears closer

to the social suppression discussed by Cole (2001), in which violent events may be pushed to the background of everyday life precisely because they constitute its foundation (see 281–85).

17. 'One has discarded (part of the) past from one's identity, and in this sense one has forgotten it. But one has not forgotten *that* one has forgotten it. For that one has forgotten (what one used to be) is a constitutive part of one's new identity ... To put it provocatively, we are not only the past that we (can) remember (as the historicists have always argued), but we are also the past that we can forget' (Ankersmit 2001: 308).

References

Ankersmit, F.R. 2001. 'The Sublime Dissociation of the Past: Or How to Be(come) What One Is No Longer', *History and Theory* 40 (3): 295–323.

Berliner, D. 2005. 'The Abuses of Memory: Reflections on the Memory Boom in Anthropology', *Anthropology Quarterly* 78 (1): 197–211.

Bissell, W.C. 2005. 'Engaging Colonial Nostalgia', *Cultural Anthropology* 20 (2): 215–48.

Boyer, D. 2006. '*Ostalgie* and the Politics of the Future in Eastern Germany', *Public Culture* 18 (2): 361–81.

Boym, S. 2001. *The Future of Nostalgia*. New York: Basic Books.

Brock, M. and R. Truscott. 2012 '"What's the Difference Between a Melancholic Apartheid Moustache and a Nostalgic GDR Telephone?"' *Peace and Conflict: Journal of Peace Psychology* 18 (3): 318–28.

Bryant, R. 2008. 'Writing the Catastrophe: Nostalgia and Its Histories in Cyprus', *Journal of Modern Greek Studies* 26 (2): 399–422.

———. 2010. *The Past in Pieces: Belonging in the New Cyprus*. Philadelphia: University of Pennsylvania Press.

———. 2012. *Displacement in Cyprus – Consequences of Civil and Military Strife: Report 2: Life Stories: Turkish Cypriot Community*. Nicosia: PRIO Cyprus Centre.

Bryant, R. and M. Hatay. 2011. 'Guns and Guitars: Simulating Sovereignty in a State of Siege', *American Ethnologist* 38 (4): 631–49.

Bryant, R. and C. Yakinthou. 2012. *Cypriot Perceptions of Turkey*. Istanbul: Turkish Economic and Social Studies Foundation.

Burke, P. 1989. 'History as Social Memory', in T. Butler (ed.), *Memory: History, Culture and the Mind*. Oxford: Basil Blackwell, pp. 97–113.

Casperson, N. 2012. *Unrecognized States*. Cambridge: Polity Press.

Christou, M. 2006. 'A Double Imagination: Memory and Education in Cyprus', *Journal of Modern Greek Studies* 24: 285–106.

Clifford, J. 2003. *On the Edges of Anthropology (Interviews)*. Chicago: Prickly Paradigm Press.

Cole, J. 2001. *Forget Colonialism: Sacrifice and the Art of Memory in Madagascar*. Berkeley: University of California Press.

176 *Rebecca Bryant*

Comaroff, J. and J.L. Comaroff. 1991. *Of Revelation and Revolution*, Vol. 1. Chicago: University of Chicago Press.

Connerton, P. 2008. 'Seven Types of Forgetting', *Memory Studies* 1 (1): 59–71.

Ege, S. 2007. *Re/producing Refugees in the Republic of Cyprus: History and Memory between State, Family, and Society*. M.A. thesis. Zurich: University of Zurich.

Fillinghim, D. 1997. 'A Flight From Liminality: "Home" in Country and Gospel Music', *Studies in Popular Culture* 20 (1): 75–82.

Fox, M.A. 2006. 'The Moral Community', in H. LaFollette (ed.), *Ethics in Practice*, 3rd edition. New York: Blackwell Publishing, pp. 181–91.

Fritzsche, P. 2001. 'Specters of History: On Nostalgia, Exile, and Modernity', *American Historical Review* 106 (5): 1587–618.

Hadjiyanni, T. 2002. *The Making of a Refugee: Children Adopting Refugee Identity in Cyprus*. Westport: Praeger.

Hatay, M. 2007. *Is the Turkish Cypriot Population Shrinking? An Overview of the Ethno-Demography of Cyprus in the Light of the Preliminary Results of the 2006 Turkish-Cypriot Census*. Oslo/Nicosia, PRIO Report 2/2007.

———. 2008. 'The Problem of Pigeons: Orientalism, Xenophobia, and a Rhetoric of the 'Local' in North Cyprus', *Cyprus Review* 20 (2): 145–72.

Hatay, M. and R. Bryant. 2008. 'The Jasmine Scent of Nicosia: On Returns, Revolutions, and the Longing for Forbidden Pasts', *Journal of Modern Greek Studies* 26 (2): 423–49.

Herzfeld, M. 2005. *Cultural Intimacy: Social Poetics in the Nation-State*. New York: Routledge.

Honneth, A. 1995. *The Struggle for Recognition: The Moral Grammar of Social Conflicts*. Cambridge: MIT Press.

Jinhua, D. and J.T.H. Chen. 1997. 'Imagined Nostalgia', *Boundary 2* 24 (3): 143–61.

Kansteiner, W. 2002. 'Finding Meaning in Memory: A Methodological Critique of Collective Memory Studies', *History and Theory* 41:179–97.

Kıralp, Leyla. 2010. 'Melandra Kültür Evi'. *Yenidüzen*, December 26.

Kızılyürek, N. 2011. 'Tufan Erhürman'ın 'Halleri' – 24 Saat Kıbrıslı Türk Olmak', *Yenidüzen*, 24 October 2011.

Kolsto, P. 1996. 'The Sustainability and Future of Unrecognized Quasi-States', *Journal of Peace Research* 43 (6): 723–40.

Kurtuluş, H. and S. Purkis. 2008. 'Türkiye'den Kuzey Kıbrıs'a göç dalgaları: Lefkoşa'nın dışlanmış göçmen-enformel emekçileri', *Toplum ve Bilim* 112: 60–101.

Lytras, E. and C. Psaltis. 2011. *Formerly Mixed Villages in Cyprus: Representations of the Past, Present and Future*. Nicosia: Association for Historical Dialogue and Research.

Marathefti, A. 1989. *Den Ksechno, I Do Not Forget: The Greek Cypriot Refugee Experience as Oral Narrative*. Ph.D. dissertation. Austin: University of Texas at Austin.

Patrick, R. 1976. *Political Geography and the Cyprus Conflict: 1963–1971*, ed. J.H. Bater and R. Preston. Waterloo: University of Waterloo.

Pickering, M. and E. Keightley. 2006. 'The Modalities of Nostalgia', *Current Sociology* 54 (6): 919–41.

Ricoeur, P. 2010. 'Power and Violence', trans. L. Jones. *Theory, Culture and Society* 27 (5): 18–36.

Ries, N. 1997. *Russian Talk: Culture and Conversation during Perestroika*. Ithaca, NY: Cornell University Press.

Spivak, G. 1984/5. 'Feminism, Criticism and the Institution', an interview with Elizabeth Grosz, *Thesis Eleven* 10–11: 175–87.

Tulbure, N.S. 2006. 'Drinking and Nostalgia: Social Imagination in Postsocialist Romania', *Anthropology of East Europe Review* 24 (1): 85–93.

Turner, B. 1987. 'A Note on Nostalgia', *Theory, Culture, and Society* 4: 147–56.

Volkan, V. 1979. *Cyprus – War and Adaptation: A Psychoanalytic History of Two Ethnic Groups in Conflict*. Charlottesville: University of Virginia Press.

Yakinthou, Ch. 2008. 'The Quiet Deflation of Den Xehno? Changes in the Greek Cypriot Communal Narrative on the Missing', *The Cyprus Review* 20 (1): 15–33.

Chapter 8

Social and Economic Performativity of Nostalgic Narratives in Andean Barter Fairs

Olivia Angé

This chapter explores nostalgic narratives' performativity in the ethnographic context of barter fairs in the Argentinean Andes. These encounters gather valley cultivators and highland shepherds for exchanging part of their agricultural production via *cambios* (exchange). During their negotiation, the protagonists regularly allude to the equity that would have featured in their elders' transactions, whom they refer to with the Spanish term *los abuelos*. More broadly, they regret the decline of the reciprocal exchanges materializing the solidarity between shepherds and cultivators; thereby lamenting the current erosion of the ideal complementarity that would have formerly tied highland and lowland peasants. Some of them cast their glorious retrospections back to the remoter past of the *tatarabuelos*, the ancestors whose deified figures are embodied in the natural environment. These narratives refer to a time escaping historical situation, and confluent with a mythic past when fundamental reciprocities went without saying. They present the twofold aspect identified by Michael Herzfeld as specific of 'structural nostalgia'. On the one hand, they are replicated by succeeding generations, each cohort blaming the next one for modern degeneration; on the other, they relate to the damage of a once perfect reciprocity 'by the self-interest of modern times' (Herzfeld 2005: 149).

In the Argentinean cordillera, the manifestation of a dualist complementarity through barter transactions has indeed become residual in the course of the twentieth century. I will nonetheless highlight the discrepancy between the nostalgic discursive register and the speakers' actions that refute their intention to re-establish the missed social order. During barter bargains, we will see that the ancestors' code of ethics is usually invoked in order to increase the reward. Clearly, these allusions to past order aim at overcoming current struggles and at procuring the speaker a favourable outcome. That nostalgia serves present purposes has been widely pointed out (e.g., Bissel 2005, Davis 1979, Herzfeld 2005, Pickering and Keightley 2006). Nostalgic formulas during barter transactions are not any exception in this regard. More striking is that many of these narratives exclusively point to the immediate material interest that the speaker might obtain, and they do not necessarily suppose the ardent longing for the past, usually assumed as a fundamental feature of nostalgia. In order to understand the stake of lamentations aimed at setting the normative frame of contingent practices, nostalgia should not be regarded as an emotional attachment fomenting historical distortion. Rather, it will be apprehended as a strategy underlying social interactions. More precisely, the chapter addresses nostalgia's practical dimensions by examining its economic efficacy, in the particular context of barter fairs.

Drawing on Edward Casey's phenomenological approach on commemoration (2011), I also discuss the new form of sociability created by this specific kind of recall. In his landmark essay, Fred Davis (1979) brought out nostalgia's propensity to sustain social identities in the context of rapid social change. In the same vein, I describe how nostalgic utterances at fairs delineate social belongings, drawing the edges of an 'ethnic economy' (Harris 1982) experiencing growing national integration. Altogether, this Andean ethnography teases out the relationship between the social performativity and economic efficacy of nostalgic narratives, as well as shedding light on the mechanism of cultural transmission at stake in the case of instrumentalized nostalgia.

Ethnographic Setting

The fairs I will be examining take place in the northern part of the Argentinean province of Jujuy, adjacent to the Bolivian border. In this South Andean region, the peasants are affiliated to the Kolla people, one of the thirty ethnic groups acknowledged after the 1994 amendment of the national constitution which granted legal status to pre-Hispanic communities. This is in contrast to the Argentinean category of creoles, who are not direct descendants of Europeans and do not identify themselves as indigenous, even if some of their ascendants may have done (Sturzenegger-Benoist 2006). They actually do have autochthons amongst their ascendants, and share cultural practices and representations with them. The creole category therefore suggests a process of racial and cultural métissage, and the boundary between creoles and Kollas is particularly subjective and dynamic. Amongst the creole population, those whose direct European ascendance is attested by the whiteness of their skin are explicitly categorized as gringo. However, the latter are very few in this northern region of the country, mostly migrants who have settled in the main towns for professional reasons.

In their daily lives, peasants actually verbalize more spontaneously their belonging to economic entities articulated upon ecological criteria, rather than their belonging to the Kolla people. Shepherds living in the high plateau name themselves Puneños, as compared to the Quebradeños who cultivate plots in the valley. Such categories extend beyond Kolla people because they are also used by Bolivian shepherds and tillers who are not concerned by Argentinean mappings of 'indigenous people'. Despite massive movement of urban migration, working the land remains essential in the definition of Kolla identity. This is clearly stated by Telesforo, an old shepherd in the community of Chalguamayoc, who was interviewed by a journalist about the meaning of being Kolla: 'Kolla agriculture, we will never abandon it', he concluded, 'because we really are Kolla'.[1] As usual in the Andes (Harris 2000: 30), the importance of land is also related to the veneration of telluric beings, amongst which Mother Earth, or Pachamama, is the overwhelming figure. She is indeed conceived as the mother of every being on earth. Telesforo's words are also very clear on this point as he explained to me: 'The earth is like a mother's breast. The baby sucks it and that's how he grows. The earth is our first mother. The earth raises us as a mother raises her children'. Following this imagined kinship, indigenousness remains firmly associated with the countryside, as elsewhere in Latin America (Radcliffe and Westwood 1996: 112). Such a picture of the Kolla as an Andean peasant, in spite of the massive urban integration during the second half of the past century, erases the heterogeneity of this ethnic category, momentarily freezing an extremely fluid ethnic landscape.

Agricultural production is characterized by a typical Andean 'vertical economy' (Murra 1996) whereby peasants focus their activities according to the position of their plots on the multiple ecological niches of this mountainous environment. In short, this could be mapped as follows: highland breeders tend sheep and llamas in the Puna, a plateau lying 3,500 metres above sea level; lowland cultivators grow maize in the Quebrada, below 2,500 metres; and intermediate tuber cultivators live in between. Reciprocal complementarity between shepherds and cultivators enacted by direct exchanges of agricultural goods, is acknowledged as the core of the Andean socioeconomic order (Lehmann 1982, Platt 1987, Rivière 1979, among others). In the Argentinean region, this organization no longer constitutes the cornerstone of the rural economy, as peasants are firmly integrated within a market economy (Göbel 2003, Karasik 1984, Madrazo 1981).

Although rural Kolla people carry on agricultural exploitation, and their economic identity crystallizes around this activity, domestic units derive a steady income from periodic migrations and public allowances, which gives them access to manufactured commodities. Therefore, and because most of their yield is consumed or sold, the proportion of agricultural production invested in direct exchanges is residual.[2] It hovers around 10 per cent of the production, according to the household's composition, its volume of production, connections with urban centres or cooking habits, among other factors. Since llama and donkey caravans aiming at procuring exotic items have become exceptional, barter exclusively happens through isolated inter-household transactions, or during the fairs at issue here.

8.1 Panorama of a fair. Photo by Olivia Angé

8.2 Highland landscape. Photo by Olivia Angé

8.3 Lowland landscape. Photo by Olivia Angé

Even if direct exchanges are minor in terms of the amount of production involved, they remain fundamental to the way peasants conceptualize their regional economy. This is clearly illustrated by this extract from a speech given by a political authority during the monthly meeting in the valley community of Chosconty: 'The Quebrada has always needed products from the Puna. And the Puna needs the Quebrada as well . . . We share the same culture, the same tradition and the same customs'. This example also hints at the negation of the intermediate zone according to a dualist conception of economic and social organization for, in spite of the transitional zone's empirical existence, 'in symbolic thought it can be "reduced" to a line which opposes and joins two halves' (Harris 2000: 105, see also Platt 1978).

The Fair

In the Southern Andes, barter fairs are usually embedded in broader religious celebrations, called *fiestas*. These events last two to nine days, and bring together hundreds to thousands of participants. Fairs' material circulation centres on agricultural products brought by peasants who are looking for goods that cannot easily be produced in their own fields. 'Mostly, it is an exchange of what we lack for what they lack. They don't have meat, we bring them meat. We have no flour or maize,' glossed one young woman on the purpose of her venture. On the scene of exchanges, each community concentrates on a specific sector. Since Andean peasants usually specialize in a particular production according to their plots' location on craggy slopes compounded of different ecological niches, those sectors also indicate the geographical origin of the protagonists.

Cultivators coming from the valley supply multiple varieties of maize, fruits, aromatic plants and flowers. Shepherds come down from the hills laden with fresh or dried llama and lamb meat, cheese and wool. In the intermediate ecological zone, peasants do tend animals as a complement to the vegetables they are able to grow at this altitude. But craggy slopes circumscribe their narrow plots, making livestock farming disadvantageous, as compared with grazing in the Puna. Because breeding is not the most productive in the intermediate level, people from this zone only provide fairs with the tubers, beans and cereals that grow easily in their fields, and tend to ignore their minor activity of livestock farming. In doing so, the intermediate region's peasants identify themselves with lowland cultivators, although they distinguish themselves by trading the species that do not thrive in the lower valley. Hence, during the fairs, products being exchanged evidence participants' identification with one of the two entities that symbolically complement each other in the Andean peasant economy: namely, highland shepherds and lowland cultivators.

Beside agricultural products, fairs also involve manufactured goods such as shoes and clothes, batteries, candles and industrial foodstuffs.

8.4 Highland shepherds' meat and wool. Photo by Olivia Angé

8.5 Lowland cultivators' multiple varieties of maize. Photo by Olivia Angé

Peddlers trading these items live in urban centres, where such goods are readily available. Most of them are looking for monetary income, although some also make a business out of barter. In many fairs, those transactions involving manufactured goods are overwhelming in terms of the volume of goods in circulation. However, as attested by the phrase 'Barter for the fiesta', direct exchange constitutes a significant feature of the meeting, on the symbolic side at the very least.

In the morning, transactions abound: tillers and shepherds go back and forth laden with meat, fruits and vegetables. In the busy crowd, some of them stand in conversation. These are friends, blood kin or ritual kin who meet after weeks or months of isolation in the countryside. Later, they may join together to share lunch. These festive meals ideally introduce dances and, after having eaten, some go to the tents to sing folk songs or dance *cumbia*. After a few days, the fair is deserted. Laden with the exotic products they coveted, kin get in the vehicles leaving for their village.

Agricultural Goods Exchanges

Among the different kinds of barter (*trueque*), cambio alludes to an archetypal transaction of agricultural products, framed by normative prescriptions peculiar to peasants' interactions. Fixed exchange rates exist for each pair of agricultural products circulating in opposite directions: a dried sheep is equivalent to an arroba of corn, a bag of potatoes equals the same volume of corn on the cob, a clay pot equals its content in foodstuff, to mention only a few examples. These equivalences are called 'measures of the elders' (*medidas de los abuelos*). The voice of the elders is charged with authority because they are seen as prime communicators with the ancestors whose remotest figure is Pachamama. As stated by Telesforo: 'The ancestors have settled [the measures] like that. They used to talk with Pachamama'. This scale of equivalences is regarded as the very objectivization of fairness. This is attested by several formulas circulating at fairs such as: 'After cambio, we all end up equal'. Cambio is imbued with such morality of equity because it is deemed to gauge the effort necessary for producing the goods. As noted by a middle-aged man who grew up in the Puna, during Saint Catherina festival: 'Harvesting also requires sacrifices. If it freezes, crops are damaged. If it does snow in the countryside, lambs die of starvation. This relationship manifests itself between those who conduct cambios: everything is sacrifice'.

At the same time, these measures obviously lack precision since there are no objective criteria for deciding whether a bag of potatoes is full or not. Far from being inviolable, these equivalences actually serve as 'reference

8.6 The elders' measures. Photo by Olivia Angé

points for bargaining to take place' (Mayer 2002: 144). The quality of the goods, the abundance of the harvest, the ecological zone where the fair takes place and the nature of the social relationship between the partners are the main parameters mentioned in the course of the negotiation. When Pancho met with Massimo, an acquaintance from the valley, to exchange two lambs for fruit at Yavi's fair, he began the conversation by recalling the previous events when they had met. As they were chatting, the friends started to bargain the traditional equivalences of exchange. Drawing attention to the quality of his lamb, Pancho launched the negotiation: 'It is not skinny. No, it isn't. How do you want to exchange?' 'I will exchange, brother. I will make up (to the traditional equivalencies)', replied the cultivator. Pancho mentioned that he needed a lot of apples for his nine kids waiting for him at home. He then dwelled on the long way he had to go to supply fresh meat to tillers, highlighting that the fair's location was much closer to Massimo's place. 'In one's place, as I said, everything costs almost double', he mentioned later on. When Massimo shoved extra fruits into the shepherd's bag, the former commented: 'To friends, one must give different treatment'.

This typical interaction shows that the value relationship between the goods comes up as 'a performative moment to be re-created at every transaction' according to its peculiarities, as Guyer put it in her analysis of conversions in Atlantic Africa (2004: 155). Therefore, the ability to evaluate one's goods as compared with those from another ecological zone requires long-term training which is acquired by accompanying elders in their venture. When I enquired about the value of the llama she was transporting, Griselda, who had grown up in the city of Abra Pampa, replied:

> I don't understand barter. Only a little. I don't come [to fairs]. I am just accompanying my grandmother, because she is getting old. If I try to exchange, I can't. I did not grow up with this. My grandmother has been coming every year since she was a kid. She knows: this must be exchanged with such an amount of that stuff. They could give me miserable quantities, and I would not even realize.

Although anyone could in principle be informed about the elders' equivalencies, performing a cambio requires a long-lasting personal engagement, under the teaching of an initiated person. This transaction therefore implies a shared economic intimacy between the partners, and testifies a symbolic filiation to the predecessors from whom its ethic is being transmitted.

Market prices should not influence a cambio's measures, or only as one among the many arguments for bargaining. In between transactions, Julia, a middle-aged woman from the intermediate zone who used to barter potatoes at fairs, explained to me: 'We weigh, "that much . . . for that much . . .", because it's a cambio. Potatoes are not worth as much as grapes, grapes are worth more. But we do not put prices on things. We are making cambios'. However, another system of measurement regarded as freshly adopted but nonetheless widely diffused consists of comparing the products in light of their monetary value on the regional market. As observed by Lola, my 60-year-old neighbour in Yavi, who also used to exchange her potatoes at fairs:

> Of course, now they usually add up how much something is worth. Before, people did not do such sums . . . Most people say: 'How much does your kilo of potatoes cost?' 'Meat costs that much'. And then they add it up. Formerly, they didn't.

According to the protagonists, this system of measure derogates from the principles of the cambio as it would have been practised by the elders. If monetary evaluation departs from the code of cambio as set up by the ancestors, peasants associate it with the logic of business (*negocio*) by which traders aim at generating a quantitative profit from start-up capital. This is the way Perfecto explained it to me: 'Barter enables you to fill your stomach. Business enables you to fill your stomach and to increase your capital'. So, while cambio should raise qualitative benefits through the procurement of use values, negocio is intended to provide quantitative benefits through the accumulation of exchange value. Since *numéraire* reference eases profit management, peasants' glosses generally associate negocio with sales, in contrast with the logic of cambio which should prevail in direct exchanges ideally oriented towards the acquisition of consumption goods. 'When we say "negocio", it means that money is running', I was told during a fair.

However, business does not strictly allude to the circulation of bills but to the *numéraire* calculation underpinning the transaction. Hence, the term business can refer to direct exchanges computed according to prices or, more broadly, any direct exchanges in which one of the parties intends to extract quantitative profits. For instance, Hilda, who is a 55-year-old shepherd from the community of Yoscaba, was complaining at Saint Catherina's fair: 'They [who are bartering maize] cheat a lot. They buy and resell at double price; they do not work like we do. It wasn't like that before: they used to tend their fields and we our flock. Foodstuff for foodstuff. Now, it's a business'. Although profit making is not regarded as immoral in itself, Hilda's indignation shows that it is deemed unfair when one of the partners engages a cambio-minded transaction based upon the quantity of work and effort, while the other strives for appropriating exchange value out of the transaction whereby the equity encapsulated in the elder's measure is substituted by asymmetry in gains. As a general rule, matching with monetary prices is denounced by peasants as a betrayal of the balanced reciprocity that should prevail when local products are bartered. During Easter fair in 2009, a shepherd was complaining: 'Nowadays, they want to give us less than what we give them. They measure with money'. This departs from the ideal of cambio, which should be balanced: 'The same from them, the same from us', as its partakers usually say. Therefore, barter of local production engaged as business globally suffers a negative moral charge.

Opposition and Complementarity: Social Interactions between Cambio Partners

Dense relationships are deemed to provide an ideal social background for engaging in cambios. On the one hand, kin enjoy meeting at fairs to exchange samples of their respective productions. The largesse of these transactions materializes their social complicity. On the other hand, unknown partners tend to repeat successful transactions and weave social ties by means of material and linguistic exchanges, in order to set a positive frame of interaction. In doing so, strangers become acquaintances (*conocidos*) who, in the course of further meetings, can become friends (*amigos*) or even ritual kin (*compadres*). All three are preferential economic partners. From one to the other, the weight of the social relationship increases and, accordingly, economic obligations and expectations. Aware of their respective desires and habits, the closest partners even put aside the best part of their production for the event. When they meet, regular partners greet each other warmly. They engage in personal conversation, in which economic exchange is blended. They like to ask for news about each other's lives and compare the ecological, political or cultural features of their villages. Beside linguistic manifestations, complicity is shown in smiles, laughs, handshakes and embraces.

This convivial framework is also signified through material circulation. To ensure the durability of the relationship, the conditions of exchange should be agreed without meanness, 'according to each other's need' as they say. If a traditional equivalence exists for the goods at stake, it should be applied with only little regard for their prices on the marketplace. In the course of the interaction, one can also invite his or her partner to taste ready-to-eat items, thereby emphasizing both generosity and the strength of the relationship. A few fruits could be spontaneously offered, a handful of toasted corn gifted, or, in order to nurture a cherished relationship, a small bag of potatoes or a piece of meat could have been prepared in anticipation. And, at the end of the transaction, generosity is demonstrated through the *yapa*, which is a small amount of goods given on top of the agreed equivalence (Angé 2011).

Although peasants barter with their kin and strive to establish friendship or even ritual parenthood with their partners, this remains unusual and most transactions occur with anybody. 'Sometimes, yes, you know the partner. Then, you arrive, you deliver and that's done. Better. If not, [you can barter with] anybody', replied Griselda when I enquired about her grandmother's partners. In any case, those social bonds conveying trust and solidarity are considered a normative frame. No matter their personal relationship, protagonists acknowledge their belonging to a shared community based on an imagined kinship they periodically recall. We can see this in the case of some women unknown to each other who, during a cambio, came to question the qualities of their respective lands, separated by some hundred kilometres. Introducing their surname, they nonetheless inferred a shared genealogy. 'My grandmother was Abracaite. Therefore, all Abracaite are my kin. Here, almost all of us are kin', concluded one of them. Hinged upon the institution of ritual kinship between cherished partners, this 'imagined blood community' (I allude to Anderson's famous expression [2006]) calls for a generous reciprocity that should ideally stamp all cambios, whatever the specific tie the partners are linked by. Some participants even justify their transactions by a duty of solidarity towards their counterparts from complementary ecological zones. For instance, a breeder alleged that she engaged in unprofitable cambios because tillers 'also need meat'.

However, even between preferential partners, material and linguistic kindness alternates with harsh defence of personal interest. Interactions are usually composed of bitter dialogues sometimes tinged with humour or irony. At the moment of setting equivalences, discord may arise if the partners turn out to be greedy: 'No. This is worth more. This is worth five pesos and a potato is two. Let's exchange according to prices', complained a peasant to escape the traditional measures. Agonistic interactions are usual, and the transaction could occur in extremis or be aborted. Feeling insulted by a lack of consideration towards his meat's value, Telesforo deemed he would put it to better use by eating it himself. 'Why would I stay here begging? They [cultivators] pretend to be good!', he muttered while packing away the thigh of lama he had slaughtered in the morning for an unknown valley partner.

Another point for potential confrontation concerns the quality of goods. Doubts could be expressed that challenge the partner by calling into question his or her capacity to produce goods of value. It could be well-founded accusations or just a non-cordial way of depreciating the products in order to impose advantageous terms of exchange. 'Your corn is ugly', disparaged a shepherd who nevertheless coveted the cobs. Exchange partners are very quick indeed to use stereotyped accusations aimed at unhinging one another. A good example is that of a shepherd taunting a cultivator: 'You must bring fat meat, not like that'. The latter replied: 'The same for you. Sometimes you provide tough maize, spoilt and eaten by rats'.

Other slanders suggest or explicitly denounce the partner's deceit. Apart from being described as friendly meeting places, fairs are depicted as convenient scenes for cheating (*engaño*). A common trick consists of filling a bag with faulty items and covering them with some good pieces. Others provide incomplete measures. For example, I found stones in some wool balls I purchased. Refusing to apply the equity encapsulated in the elders' measures is also seen as a form of cheating. In the example aforementioned, Hilda considered that maize traders were cheating, as they were making a business out of the exchange of agricultural products. While it is hard to gauge the practical dissemination of fraud, I was nonetheless struck by the pervasiveness of the menace of cheating in the rhetoric of the agonistic moments of interactions.

As these dialogues show, a cambio's terms of exchange are defined through a codified confrontation of stereotyped formulas by which two socioeconomic communities are reified: shepherds from the Puna and cultivators from the Quebrada. Depending on the partners, the nature of their relation and the quality of their goods, each cambio mingles, in a particular fashion, expressions of agonistic confrontation and friendly complicity. Every interaction leading to a cambio hovers between kindly talks in which partners imply their will to complement each other's needs and acrimonious dialogues by which they strive to meet their personal interests, disregarding their mutual values. Through these conventional formulas, each transaction manifests a particular swing between duality and complementarity among peasants coming from different ecological niches.

Nostalgic Utterances: 'All Is Ruined. Fairs Are Vanishing'

Elders and teenagers, cultivators and shepherds, indigenous people, creoles and even white people, though so poorly informed – everybody seems to agree upon the eminent vanishing of barter. Derogation from the elders' equivalences is pointed out as the main cause of fairs' decadence. If peasants baulk at respecting the old weightings, they say it would be because they now barter 'as if it was a business' or 'thinking in money'. This chase for profit is depicted as a modern drift since the elders would have respected their predecessors' etiquette of balanced reciprocity between highland and lowland peasants. As Lola said: 'That's why, as I told you, they used to give three hundred cobs of corn for a lama haunch, or 250. It was a cambio that was not a business. It was a cambio left by our grandparents, our great grandparents'. Because it diverges from the ancestors' measures, seen as fair, direct exchange of agricultural products performed with a logic of negocio is collectively denounced as inequitous. During a fair, a shepherd was complaining: 'Nowadays, they want to give us less than what we give them. They measure with money'.

These lamentations also recount the dissemination of cambios' agonistic tail. While this barter network would have formerly been completely embedded in a dense social fabric hampering dissension, the protagonists depict the contemporary experience of cambio as overrun by its antagonist facet. According to fairs' participants, the elders would have been keener in engaging ritual parenthood, and respecting related social and economic commitment. As regretted by Perfecto: 'Before people had more conscience. They use to give the [old] measure, to make sure that you would leave satisfied. Nowadays they don't. Everyone defends their own interest'. The old Telesforo concluded: 'We can't trust anymore. Like that, barter is useless'. Apart from having corrupted economic transactions, this social crumbling would impinge on the endless parties that they say formerly went along with economic exchanges. Lola remembered that: 'In the past, fairs used to be different. People were not looking for bartering so quickly'. Later she continued recalling that when breeders and cultivators used to dance and exchange extensively, both 'had everything. Nothing lacked'. These discourses present the dense social network between the dwellers of complementary ecological niches as a condition of social balance and economic profusion.

This rhetoric draws the picture of a missed time when the opposition of the partners' interest was fully contained by their complementarity. However, the ahistorical nature of the past to which such rhetoric refers is stressed by the decontextualization of the arguments, and their internal discrepancy. As an example, the young Zara asserted that, in olden days, her mother 'used to undertake exchange journeys and she would procure all kinds of things. Now, it is not like that anymore'. However, she did not identify which fairs her mother used to attend, nor the amount of meat she used to bring. At the same time, Simona groused in a symmetrical narrative that contradicts Zara's complaint: 'Now they [pastoralists] ask more and they bring leaner lamb'. By the same token, it is bewildering to hear shepherds and cultivators accusing each other of disrespecting the elders' equivalences, and of overvaluing their goods at the expense of their partner. As an example, let us listen to Joaquim's complaints:

> We want to respect the old equivalences, but those who have the meat do not want to. They always want us to increase the quantity. For instance, for a sheep, we used to give one of those white bags almost full, but not that much. But now, they want us to give it filled up, with some extra fruits on the top.

And breeders retort likewise.

Broadly, these lamentations allude to the crumbling of the economic complementarity and the solidarity that would have formerly united breeders and tillers. By taking the shape of a *negocio*, the current *cambio* is deemed to reflect shepherd and cultivator's duality, at the expense of the complementarity that would have fostered fertility and abundance in the old days. Those lamentations actually allude to the erosion of the balanced reciprocity drawing the edges of the 'ethnic economy' (Harris 1982). This generalized nostalgia at the fairs laments peasants' inclination to engage in short-term transactions, with no consideration for the long-term sociocosmological order (Parry and Bloch 1989). Thus, at fairs, structural nostalgia points back to a 'time out of time' when interactions were framed by prescriptions guaranteeing both economic and social reproduction of Andean communities, leading some protagonists to the conclusion that 'manhood is vanishing'.

Narratives and Practices

Paradoxically, such laments are verbalized by those who perpetuate the condemned practices. Cultivators deplore that shepherds sell their meat at the market, instead of swapping it for lowland products. For this reason, the latter are accused of favouring business at the expense of old solidarities. But cultivators do not claim as openly their own intention to resell the meat at San Santiago's fair, after they have dried it. Others make a stop at the nearest city on their way back home, in order to sell some bartered sheep. On the other hand, when they complain about the poor quantities of maize obtained at fairs, shepherds do not specify that they have offloaded old or sick animals with no market value. As attested by these few examples, at fairs, not all nostalgic narratives presuppose the mixed feelings of 'loss, lack and longing' (Pickering and Keightley 2006: 921) presented in the literature as specific of nostalgia. Indeed, ethnographic observation shows that it may not be in reverence for their supposed ethics, but rather to take advantage of their moral authority that the ancestors are called upon during economic negotiation. As an example, during the 2010 Easter fair in the village of Yavi, cultivators were lamenting the absence of shepherds, who were particularly few in number. I could hear Perfecto, the leader of a valley community, conferring with Lucio, a counterpart from the highland. He was announcing that the cultivators were planning to give up the fair as well. He dramatically concluded the vanishing of the fair and its barter. Lucio argued that shepherds did not want to barter their meat any more because they could get a better price when selling it in the daily market. Perfecto advocated the rehabilitation of the elders' equivalences, alluding to former jubilation and abundance. Lucio agreed, and concluded diplomatically that he would increase his neighbours' awareness on the matter. And yet, he did know that a significant part of the bartered meat would be reinvested in profit-making transactions. He also knew that Perfecto himself refused to apply the elders' equivalences to some of his fruits that were set aside for sales.

Perfecto, as many other nostalgic speakers, was obviously not intent on putting the ancestral etiquette into practice. Nonetheless, these narrations in praise of the elders' economic code can be successfully summoned for winning the case in an ongoing negotiation. For instance, these formulas can induce the partner to agree upon a balance disregarding market values, even if not exactly tuned up with the elders' one. These formulas can also convince the partner to provide a *yapa*. If it is not the partners' intention to actualize the vanishing transactional ethic, I believe it is in light of the social relationship brought forth by commemoration that the economic efficiency of theses formulas could be understood. As pointed out by Casey, com-memmoration deals 'with overcoming the separation from which otherwise unaffiliated individuals suffer' (2011: 185). During the fair, the co-evocation of the ancestors' economic order gathers the partners within a 'horizon-tal participatory communitas' smoothing out the 'separation' inherent in Andean barter system given the meeting of peasants coming from disparate ecological and economic communities.

This horizontal community lies perpendicular to the 'vertical com-munity' established with the named predecessors. The collective emphasis on the ancestors' economic behaviour assumes the existence of a common descent, which justifies that this behaviour should be regarded as exem-plary (for further details on this shared filiation between cambio partak-ers, see Angé, forthcoming). This imagined genealogy implicitly draws the ethnic boundaries within which members should be granted special treatments that epitomize their economic solidarity. In this case, nostalgic narratives do not ensure continuity of individual identity as much as they 'forge a shared (if illusory) sense of group identity, cohesion, and long-term continuities' (Bissel 2005: 226). This recall of a symbolic genealogy asserts a shared group identity, which is to impel the partners to mate-rialize their solidarity by granting preferential equivalencies. In doing so, peasants pull out of the national market, and seem to periodically reestablish the ideal trust and reciprocity that modern economy would have corroded.

Conclusion

This ethnography of nostalgia has shed light on how the past can be given a transactional role in the present, without the actors necessarily having the intention of setting the conditions for its future actualization. This explo-ration of the economic instrumentalization of nostalgic formulas, hinged upon their social performativity, shows that, while nostalgia tropes express the perception of a rupture with the past, it does not necessarily involve the existence of a sentimental attachment tinged with regrets. In order to understand its practical dimensions, and regard it as a possible feature of social interactions, two modalities of nostalgia should be distinguished. It is, on the one hand, the 'nostalgic disposition', which, in the same vein as Grainge's 'nostalgic mood' (2002; he himself elaborates from Jameson 1991), is verbalized through experiential utterances fuelled by a feeling of loss, lack and yearning. On the other hand, the 'nostalgic discursive device' is verbal-ized through strategic narratives instrumentalized for present concerns such as fashion tactics (Grainge 2002), marketing strategies (Davis 1979, Jameson 1991), political struggles (Herzfeld 2005), self image affirmation (Rosaldo 1989), the making of heritage (Berliner 2012), intergenerational tensions (Berliner 2005) or intra-ethnic economic interplays, as in the present case. Both modalities of nostalgia state discrepancies between an idealized past and a depreciated present situation. However, while the nostalgic disposition supposes longing for a future shaped through the prism of the vanishing past, strategic nostalgia's intentional scope focuses on present affairs. Of course, these analytical figures are not mutually exclusive, since instrumentalization of nostalgic utterances does not preclude sentimental attachment to the past order.

At fairs, the ancestors' code of ethics is not expected to be actualized as such. Rather, the efficiency of commemoration rests upon the acknowledgment of a shared social belonging impelling favourable economic treatments. By performing the solidarity induced by the outlined lineage, the protagonists approve the elders' prescriptions, and its current relevance, even though their overall practices derogate from them. These formulas thereby allow the partners to engage with a present conjuncture with reverence to the elders, while at the same time they infringe the ancestors' norms of exchange. And the subtlety of this discursive stratagem consists of emphasizing considerations regarding the long-term social and cosmological orders, in order to secure personal benefit in the immediate transaction.

I have shown that most speakers do not enact the lamented social order. Still, their narratives foster cultural transmission of this cosmological representation. Indeed such lamentations perpetuate vanishing norms and representations as a past 'available' (Schudson 1995) for framing social interactions. Hence, it is not by a strict conformation that these interactions assent to the ancestral code of exchange, but rather, paradoxically, by lamenting its loss and by denouncing its violation. Thereby, barter between highland and lowland is displayed as a normative ideal, whereas it does not work as a cornerstone institution in this southern Andean economy. Through these nostalgic narratives, transactions at fairs manifest a moral and symbolical continuity with an ancestral past, even when practices shirk the very ideology with which filiation is claimed. By asserting the dualist highland and lowland pattern, the complementary opposition between these entities, or the dense social fabric between their members, the delineated social order relates to the classical structures dwelled upon by Andean ethnologists. Supported by their socioeconomic performativity, nostalgic narratives therefore constitute one of the mechanisms through which these structures are replicated, and reworked, during the complex interplays characterizing these economic scenes.

Acknowledgements

This paper was written during a postdoctoral fellowship financed by Wiener Anspach Foundation, at the University of Oxford. It is based on ethnographic data gathered during long-term fieldwork carried out in northern Argentina since 2005. I am grateful to David Berliner who supervised this postdoctoral research and provided insightful comments on this text. I also wish to thank Anne Marie Losonczy and Gilles Rivière who have supported my work since I started to investigate the Andean barter system.

Notes

1. Extract from *Pueblos originarios. Kollas*, <http://www.descargas.encuentro.gov.ar>. All translations from Spanish to English are mine.
2. In the department of Yavi where I conducted fieldwork, shepherds usually travel each month to the city of La Quiaca where they sell one or two heads of cattle; a few other animals are eaten monthly and a similar quantity is bartered each year. With regards to tillers, they cultivate around two hectares from which approximately half of the harvest is sold at the market, 35 per cent consumed, 5 per cent spared as seeds and the remaining 10 per cent bartered.

References

Anderson, B. 2006. *Imagined Communities. Reflections on the Origin and Spread of Nationalism.* London: Verso.

Ange, O. 2011. 'Yapa. Dons, échanges et complicités dans les Andes méridionales', *Social Anthropology* 19 (3): 239–53.

Ange, O. Forthcoming. 'The Elders' Measures. Barter, Value and Kinship in the Argentinean Andes', *Journal of Latin American and Caribbean Anthropology*.

Berliner, D. 2005. 'An "Impossible" Transmission: Youth Religious Memories in Guinea-Conakry', *American Ethnologist* 32 (4): 576–92.

———. 2012. 'Multiple Nostalgias: the Fabric of Heritage in Luang Prabang (Lao PDR)', *Journal of Royal Anthropological Institute* 18 (4): 769–86.

Bissel, W. 2005. 'Engaging Colonial Nostalgia', *Cultural Anthropology* 20 (2): 215–48.

Casey, E. 2011. 'From Remembering: A Phenomenological Study', in J. Olick, V. Vinitzky-Seroussi and D. Levy (eds), *The Collective Memory Reader*. Oxford: Oxford University Press, pp. 184–87.

Davis, F. 1979. *Yearning for Yesterday: A Sociology of Nostalgia*. New York: Free Press.

Göbel, B. 2003. '"La plata no aumenta, la hacienda si": continuidades y cambios en la economía pastoril de Susques (Puna de Atacama)', in A. Benedetti (ed.),

Puna de Atacama. Sociedad, economía y frontera. Buenos Aires: Alcion Editora, pp. 199–242.

Grainge, P. 2002. *Monochrome Memories: Nostalgia and Style in Retro America*. Westport, CT: Praeger.

Guyer, J. 2004. *Marginal Gains: Monetary Transactions in Atlantic Africa*. Chicago: University of Chicago Press.

Jameson, F. 1991. *Postmodernism, or, the Cultural Logic of Late Capitalism*. Durham, NC: Duke University Press.

Harris, O. 1982. 'Labour and Produce in an Ethnic Economy, Northern Potosi, Bolivia', in D. Lehmann (ed.), *Ecology and Exchange in the Ande*s. Cambridge: Cambridge University Press, pp. 70–96.

———. 2000. *To Make the Earth Bear Fruits: Ethnographic Essays on Fertility, Work and Gender in Highland Bolivia*. London: Institute of Latin American Studies.

Herzfeld, M. 2005. *Cultural Intimacy: Social Poetics in the Nation-State*. New York: Routledge.

Karasik, G. 1984. 'Intercambio tradicional en la puna juvenal', *Runa* 24: 51–91.

Lehmann, D. (ed.) 1982. *Ecology and Exchange in the Andes*. Cambridge: Cambridge University Press.

Madrazo, G. 1981. 'Comercio interétnico y trueque reciproco equilibrado intraétnico', *Desarrollo económico* 21: 213–30.

Mayer, E. 2002. *The Articulated Peasant Household Economy*. Boulder, CO: Westview Press.

Murra, J. 1996. 'El control vertical de un máximo de pisos ecológicos y el modelo en archipiélago', 'Quince anos después: balance de la noción de archipiélago', in P. Morlon (ed.), *Comprender la agricultura campesina en los Andes centrales: Perú-Bolivia*. Lima: Institut Français d'Etudes Andines, pp. 122–36.

Parry, J. and M. Bloch. 1989. 'Introduction: Money and the Morality of Exchange', in J. Parry and M. Bloch (eds), *Money and the Morality of Exchange*. Cambridge: Cambridge University Press, pp. 1–32.

Pickering, M. and E. Keightley. 2006. 'The Modalities of Nostalgia', *Current Sociology* 54 (6): 919–41.

Platt, T. 1978. 'Symétries en miroir. Le concept de *yanantin* chez les Macha de Bolivie', *Annales ESC* 33: 1081–107.

———. 1987. 'Le calendrier économique des Indiens de Lipez en Bolivie au XXe siècle', *Annales ESC* 42 (3): 549–76.

Radcliffe, S. and S. Westwood. 1996. *Remaking the Nation: Place, Identity and Politics in Latin America*. London: Routledge.

Rivière, G. 1979. 'Evolution des formes d'échange entre altiplano et vallées. L'exemple de Sabaya, Bolivie', *Cahier des Amériques latines* 20: 141–58.

Rosaldo, R. 1989. 'Imperialist Nostalgia', *Representations* 26: 107–22.

Schudson, M. 1995. 'Dynamics of Distortion of Collective Memory', in D. Schacter (ed.), *Memory Distortion. How Minds, Brains, and Societies Reconstruct the Past*. Cambridge, MA: Harvard University Press, pp. 346–64.

Sturzenegger-Benoist, O. 2006. *L'Argentine*. Paris: Karthala.

Chapter 9

The Withering of Left-Wing Nostalgia?

Petra Rethmann

> The tradition of all the dead generations weighs like a nightmare on the
> brains of the living.
>
> Karl Marx, *The Eighteenth Brumaire of Napoleon Bonaparte*

In June 2010 at the People's Theatre (*Volksbühne*) in Berlin, I participated
in a conference with the provocative title *Kommunismus* (Communism).
Co-organized by the Rosa Luxemburg Foundation and one of Germany's
new political parties, die Linke (the Left), the workshop had been envisioned
as a follow-up to a conference that took place in 2009 in London under the
very same name, in an attempt to explore the lost grounds and possibilities
of communism (Douzinas and Žižek 2010). As invited speakers – including
Antonio Negri, Slavoj Žižek and Alain Badiou – battled over terms such
as communism, social welfare and social equality, and as a variety of
participants – many of whom had arrived from Hungary, Slovenia, Croatia,
former East Germany, Turkey and Russia – debated the merits of socialist
governance and The Party, it would have been easy to think that the Berlin
workshop was just one more symptom of the left's famed nostalgia for all
things socialist. And indeed, accusations of *Ostalgie*, *Yugonostalgia* and plain
old post-socialist nostalgia flourished in newspaper announcements and
reports. In fact, it appeared that if communism, along with its allegedly

official ideology, Marxism, could be imagined at all, then it was only in terms of nostalgic attachments to histories, states and political trajectories now lost. As if to echo a host of academic discussions that hold that any debate that does not immediately disavow some of the merits of (non-state) communism or its alleged ally, Marxism, could only produce an atmosphere of 'sentimental pastness' (Bewes 2002), nostalgic loss, or sadness (*acedia*), the mood anticipated for the Berlin meeting could only be imagined in terms of defensiveness, defeatism, or depression.

As if to defy the pessimism, at the meeting itself discussions were raucous, noisy and charged. Socialist, feminist, anarchist, autonomist and other kinds of Marxists were vying for a space to make their ideas clear, understood and heard. The questions that troubled many included not only doubts regarding assessments that today the rhetoric and term of communism could serve as a persuasive signifier for anti- and/or post-capitalist alternatives, but that – furthermore – as an idea communism could still generate a legible future-oriented vocabulary. Even if so, what kinds of futures could communism still name? What kind of communist idea, matter, thing – exactly – would it be that would still be able to generate a convincing future? A diluted version, reduced to the markers of social democracy and the welfare state? A utopian version in which the inequalities of work and capitalist-distributive systems of the fruits of labour could or would be redeemed through public ownership? In what follows, I take the polemical tone of these questions as my point of departure to interrogate one possible route of investigating these questions. However, instead of centring my discussion on, as Alain Badiou put it at the conference, 'properly communist matters', i.e., modes of organizing and The Party, I draw here on Wendy Brown's (2003) argument for the utopian imagination, as well as a brief discussion of what has recently reemerged in both political and academic discussions as the demand for basic income. While in the beginning I will discuss two registers through which nostalgia, especially 'left-wing nostalgia', articulates itself, my ultimate interest here is to suggest one possible analytical route that may help us to move beyond 'nostalgia's work of the negative' (Oushakine 2009: 5) or 'negativistic quiet' (Benjamin 1999: 425) to also move us beyond imaginations that can only conceive of political temporality and time as 'traumatic' (Stewart 2005), 'cynical' (Sloterdijk 1988), or in crisis.

My analysis of 'left-wing nostalgia' and one possible route to transcend its politically debilitating condition will necessarily be truncated and brief. To some extent this is so because each of the Marxist traditions that I reference here is so rich in history, struggle and thought that I cannot possibly hope to do full justice to them here. To another extent this is so because I am interested in sketching out some of the discussions of the Marxist

200 *Petra Rethmann*

imagination as they emerged at the Berlin meeting, including their philo-sophical and political tenets. While from an ethnographic standpoint that favours a look at the concrete and everyday workings of nostalgia on the ground this may seem strange, I treat the political theories and ideas that vied for attention in Berlin as ethnographic artefacts. It is in this sense that this essay resonates with anthropological genres that conceive of cultural and political analysis as a form of meditation (Povinelli 2011), rather than with those that trace nostalgia's anatomy through particular regional or material archives (Piot 2010, Scott 2004, Scribner 2005). Although like other anthropologists I am interested in (left-wing) nostalgia's mnemotic attach-ments to former political and socialist pasts (Berdahl 1999, 2001, 2005, Rethmann 2008, 2009), I use the term here to ask questions about routes of political analysis and understanding that have – at least from the perspec-tive of a more unorthodox left – depleted their meanings.

In this chapter I use the term 'left-wing nostalgia' in terms both specific and broad. Originally conceived by Walter Benjamin (1999) in a 1931 review essay on poet Erich Kästner, the term describes an individual or collective inability or refusal to come to terms with the particular character of one's own historical present or – to put it differently – understand political possibil-ity in terms other than temporal linearity or systemic critique. Furthermore, it also signifies a certain narcissism in regards to one's own political identity and attachments – a narcissism that hinders contemporary investments in thinking about forms of political mobilization, alliance or transformation dif-ferent from the ones that one may have known in the past. Finally, Benjamin also employs the term as an epithet for the revolutionary hack who is more attached to a particular analysis or idea – even to the failure of that idea – than to seizing possibilities for radical change in the present. Subsequently, the true curse of one's left-wing nostalgia are then not simply incapacitating sentiments of sadness and self-absorbed sorrow, but the fact that one's attach-ments to the object of one's loss supersede the desire to recover from this loss and seek possibilities for contemporary political transformations. It is in this vein that recently critical thinkers Kathy Weeks (2011), Jodi Dean (2009) and Wendy Brown (2003) have taken up the term as an expression of oppro-brium for those more beholden to certain long-term sentiments and possibly objects than to the possibilities of radical change in the present.

The first version of left-wing nostalgia that I sketch out here is perhaps most readily recognizable, resonating – as it does – with the myth of modern-ization. In this version, left-wing nostalgia appears in the shape of continuous and unabashed belief in economic productivism, growth and the unquestion-able value of labour as the primary mechanism of social achievement and cohesion. Although for many North American and West European readers this version may no longer carry a great deal of conviction, in contemporary East European and Russian contexts, for example, it continues to exert influence and meaning (Rethmann and Budratskys n.d). While I recognize the particular political, historical and economic circumstances that help to produce nostalgic attachments, I am not interested in lambasting East Europeans for their allegedly continuous backwards glance. Rather, I am interested in briefly sketching out a particular Marxist-oriented understanding that assists in producing left-wing nostalgia. Left-wing nostalgia's second version that I outline here is perhaps less recognizable, since it also echoes alternative dreams of collective welfare and health. What this version implies, I contend, is a nostalgia for an culturally and politically earlier time, a romanticization of non-alienated labour and craft production that – although it involves a more extensive critique of progress than the first version – nevertheless includes predictable social outcomes and a ready-made vision of what radical change could mean.

How can left-wing nostalgia wither? The analysis becomes more tricky once it moves into the realm of future-oriented temporalities and hope. In part three and four of my discussion I seek to make a case for what has variously been couched in terms of emergence or becoming. However, instead of following anthropological inquiries that advocate explorations of Deleuzian desire or Spinozean becoming (Biehl and Locke 2010, Povinelli 2011), here I examine the utopian imagination through a brief explication of Wendy Brown's (1995, 2003) analysis of how in at least some quarters of the left, the investment in critique has become attached to a set of affective states, including nostalgia, that are more attached to the past and its present than to the possibility and desire for different futures. However, instead of focusing on nostalgia's pastness and backward glance, what interests me here is its disavowal of a mode of imagination and critique that conceives political desires for radically different futures as its target. In building on Brown's impatience with left-wing nostalgic affects, I outline a Marxist route of thinking that embraces rather than disavows utopian desires and speculations. In then centring on what has recently become known as the demand for basic income – a form of unconditional income paid to individuals irrespective of their past, present, or future employments – I am interested in the ways in which the demand can offer a different, perhaps less nostalgic, route of temporality: one that is less concerned with a left politics of productivity and labour than the registers of life and freedom. That is, in taking seriously the demand's utopian tenets, here I am not so much concerned with the ways in which the demand appears as concrete democratic reform or route to greater distributive and economic justice (Birnbaum 2012, Ferguson 2009, Standing 2011), but as one necessary precondition for the articulation of liberatory futures.

A few last words before the analysis begins: although I neither have the space nor time to greatly expand on it, a considerable part of the analysis provided here has been written from the rather unorthodox perspective of squatters and autonomist Marxists that also participated in the meeting in Berlin. While the demise of many configurations of these movements has arguably produced its own forms of nostalgia, some of its critiques of Marxist (and capitalist) productivism continue to find an expression in, for example, Europe-wide anti-precarity movements that respond to the increasing precariousness of work not with a call for the restoration of stable work relations but with differently conceived relations between freedom, work and life. Second, in this chapter work constitutes a palpable if submerged register, and I do not spend much time discussing its configurations and roles. Although I am deeply aware of how a variety of analyses have shown that work does not always and necessarily involve forms of waged labour (Leacock 1982, Rediker 2005), work here refers to waged labour for the simple reason that waged work reflects the way in which 'work' was referred to at the Berlin meeting, and also because everybody I know largely knows and experiences work in its waged form. And third, in concert with other parts of the left, a significant part of my interest here is to rethink the terrain of the political not only in ethical but also politically collective terms (Duncombe 2007, Grauwacke 2007), including routes to both analytical and social change.

Left-Wing Nostalgia I

In a certain way, it may be unfair to criticize die Linke for what I am identifying here as left-wing nostalgia. After all, even though German liberals frequently mark die Linke as the effective successor of the former East German Party of Democratic Socialism (PDS) or even SED (Socialist Unity Party) (Müller 2009), it constitutes the outcome of the 2007 amalgamation of the PDS and the West German Electoral Alternative for Labour and Social Justice (WASG). In general, die Linke advocates workers' unions, progressive taxation, welfare justice and a minimum wage. Initially dismissed as an unswerving icon of commonplace representations of former East Germany as 'Stasiland' (Funder 2003) or Unrechtsstaat (a state of wrongs, as opposed to former West Germany as Rechtsstaat, a state of rights), in the last few years it has partially experienced significant electoral successes, especially in economically disadvantaged regions in Eastern and West Germany (for example, the Ruhr Valley) where unemployment rates of over 20 per cent constitute no longer the exception but the norm. On the one hand this is so because since the beginning of the millennium many of die Linke's policies and agendas have come to fill the political vacuum that emerged when in 2002 the SPD (Social Democratic Party), Germany's quintessential party of social democracy, began to support and push through a variety of neoliberal reforms (Haug 2005). On the other hand this is the case because die Linke continues to represent some of socialism's more easily recognizable ideals: the eventual eradication of private ownership of productive forces and the abolition of the private appropriation of surplus labour. While these ideals present a vision that continues to resonate across a large spectrum of social justice and left movements, within the context of die Linke they also continue to be steeped in an attachment to the glories of socialist modernization that from a perspective of precarity critics can only appear as nostalgic.

Although, as I said, the emergence of die Linke is largely associated with the political legacies of industrial state socialism, it also continues to resonate with some of the beliefs of socialist modernization. For example, in a published conversation with journalist Jürgen Elsässer, die Linke's key speaker Sahra Wagenknecht (Wagenknecht and Elsässer 1996) reflected on the purpose of socialist government and the state in which (in strong similarity to Lenin) she distinguishes two phases after the collapse of capitalism: a preliminary, socialist phase, in which a strict work discipline is extended over the whole of society; and the final phase of true communism. The socialist phase – a lengthy period of transition between capitalism and communism whose precise duration is unknown – requires a work-oriented ethics of 'perseverance', 'self sacrifice' and a commitment to the 'proper path of steady and disciplined labour'. To ensure that communism is achieved in the future, the offensive against capital must be partially suspended during the transition. Socialism thus involves a temporary intensification of capitalism, whereas communism is imagined abstractly as its pure transcendence. In the meantime, the task that a government must fulfil is to offer people – in all its scope – work. This includes the use of fierce competition, piece rates and an insistence on a work discipline that will combat petit bourgeois laziness, selfishness and anarchy. With its insistence on work perfected rather than transformed, this vision depends upon and revolves around an unquestioned valorization of the forces of labour, conceived in terms of economic expansion and social production.

From the perspective of radical precarity and German-centred autonomist movements, there exist two problems with the thesis of modernization as outlined above. First, there is the obvious problem that this particular socialist vision is founded upon an insufficient critique of capital; in short, that it preserves too many of capitalism's structures and values. In essence, what it involves is an endorsement of economic growth, industrial progress and a work ethic similar to the one found in capitalist and neoliberal economies, including the naturalization and celebration of the processes of development, expansion and growth. In this form, the critique of capitalist production does not extend, for example, to a critique of the labour process itself, and thus does not account adequately for – again, for example – Marx's many and pointed critiques of the mind-numbing and repetitive qualities of labour. What's more, this is a vision that limits communism to the transformation of property relations, leaving the basic form of industrial production – and even the mode of capitalist command over production – intact. Even if communism would still form part of a language that continues to resonate with parts of the left, according to the modernist logic the future alternative to capitalism is reduced to a new mode of politically administering and economically regulating the same industrial mode of production to which capitalism gave rise. In an ironic twist, then, communism can be understood as the rationalization of capitalism, the taming and mastery of its processes.

Left-Wing Nostalgia II

While die Linke continues to struggle with its attachments to socialist modernization, in Berlin a second version of left-wing nostalgia emerged when Maria Mies, a well-known professor of sociology and staunch critic of socialism's modernization thesis, offered her own vision of concrete and non-alienated labour. Perhaps best known from feminist discussions that have emerged out of and resonate with the Marxist-humanist paradigm, in Germany Mies' and other humanist-Marxists' visions gained popularity in the late 1960s and 1970s as one attempt to rescue Marxism from its inevitable association with then-existent socialist regimes, as well as from its more economistic tendencies. Firmly steeped in a Marxist tradition that opposes its model of modernization, Mies' and other humanist-Marxists' commitments revolve around political views that understand the creative individual as both the motor of history and unit of analysis. In the end, socialist humanism's cure for capitalism is not more work but better work. Its central theme is the transformation of alienated, meaningless labour into productive, pleasurable and enjoyable labour; in fact, this kind of labour is envisioned as one of the chief means by which 'we' can find and express our true humanity.

At the Berlin meeting, Maria Mies offered a critique of both capitalist and socialist modernization that harked back to her earlier understandings of alternative economies as a source of enjoyment and self expression. For example, the work of mothering, rural and peasant labour and artisanal and creative production is not completely bound by market logics and submerged in commodity production. What makes such forms of non-alienated (or less alienated) work especially fulfilling is that they are all involved in the direct and immediate production of life rather than in the production of things and wealth. In short, that they constitute forms of 'good work' in that they produce for use rather than for consumption. If we are to have a sense of necessity and purpose in our work, Mies argued, then we should produce useful products. The ultimate goal, she said, should be to envision forms of community in which work is once again integrated with life. Issues such as, for example, the intensity and length of the working day would then become irrelevant; and even a lifetime full of work would not be felt as a curse but as a potential source of happiness and fulfillment.

Steeped in a desire to rescue Marxism not only from its association with then-existent socialist regimes but also from some of its more economistic and determinist tendencies, in Germany Mies' vision is perhaps most closely associated with the emergence of the New Left, 1970s alternative culture and the Green Party, although recently it has also found strong resonances in ATTAC (Association for the Taxation of financial Transactions and Aid to Citizens), an international social movement and organization deeply critical of the neoliberal effects of globalization and invested in the work of devising economic and social alternatives to the current economic system. When I spoke with her, Mies told me that for her, as for others who strongly identify themselves with socialism's humanist values, ATTAC has become a new intellectual home. While she emphasized that within the movement her ideas are seen as important because they offer a critique of unsustainable patterns of consumption and of a commodity fetishism that works to deflect questions about the relationship between consumer goods and the conditions under which they are produced, she also admitted that many of her ideas are criticized for their latent romanticism – including a romanticization of craft production and concrete labour – and implied return to an earlier time. At the meeting, opposition to her proposals and ideas emerged principally from autonomist Marxists' conviction that even forms of concrete and non-alienated labour – no matter how attractive they may be – are still grounded in a model of productivist work, a productivism largely gleaned from pre-industrial modes of labour.

At the Berlin meeting there also emerged another critique levelled at the ways in which Mies draws on and fosters a discourse of alienation. Although many expressed their appreciation of her move against the dehumanization and automatization of humans inherent in the development of both socialist and capitalist modernization, it also produced discomfort precisely because quite a few associated it with a discourse on interiority, with the assumed loss and thus possible restoration of an essential human nature. The problem here then is not only that somebody like Mies offers a predictable narrative in terms of work and the organic unfolding of human nature but, even more, that it remains unclear how people can be empowered to act on feelings and desires looked upon as inauthentic. In the following two sections I hope to delineate a political vision and commitment that point beyond the left's attachment to a past and open up thinking about futurity in terms other than 'recuperation' or 'nostalgic regret'.

Future-Oriented Beginnings

What is it that Wendy Brown has to offer to us that could or would move us beyond some of the traps inherent in left-wing nostalgia? What kinds of future-directed approaches are inherent in her ideas? Admittedly, Marxism is both an unlikely and obvious source for utopianism. One the one hand, Marxism has ever so often served as the target of anti-utopian imaginations. On the other hand, Marxists themselves have so often repudiated the label that there is no little irony in the charge of utopianism being levelled at Marxism given that tradition's general hostility to the category. But just as there are traditions within Marxism that seek to establish the tradition's scientific and rational credentials, there are counter-traditions that also embrace rather than disavow utopian desire, speculations and demands. Currently Wendy Brown (2001, 2005) is perhaps one of the most notable examples, with her sustained effort to advocate a political philosophy that involves the affirmation of inventive imaginations. To offer a counterpoint to some of the nostalgic modes that suffused the meeting in Berlin, here I draw out one of the basic tenets of her thinking.

One of the lessons of both accounts of left-wing nostalgia that I briefly delineated above is that nostalgia hinges not only on our relationship to the past and present but also suggests a particular orientation to the future. As Wendy Brown (1995) describes it, a progressive (or left-wing) politics fuelled by wounded attachments to a particular identity or past continuously runs the risk of becoming deeply invested in its own impotence, even while it seeks to assuage the pain of its powerlessness through its vengeful moralizing, through its wide distribution of suffering, through its reproach to power as such. In this way critique can be misdirected and visions of change limited by the preoccupation with the preservation and vindication of existing identities and/or former pasts. As for left-wing nostalgia, in one iteration of this analysis, the left mourns its own (often idealized) past, its now-superseded forms of organizing and modes of political experience. In sum, left-wing-nostalgia is marked by a structure of desire that is more backward-looking than anticipatory: nostalgic subjects are more attached to their own forms of left critique than in the continuing possibility of social change. While this critique does not disavow history, certain attachments to history can overwhelm capacities for creating different futures.

An obvious problem from the perspective of the utopian imagination is the quality of the nostalgic subject's relation to a future-oriented temporality. Haunted by a past that tends to overwhelm the present, the forces of nostalgia also hollow out her or his visions of the future, frequently reducing them to either more or of the same or visions that could avenge the past. But the trouble with a nostalgic temporality encapsulated in Brown's portrait is not so much that the nostalgic subject tends to look backward and not forward. Even more troubling is the subject's relationship to the present, a mode of being in the moment that is disabling, an affective temporality that generates apathy and resignation. A future-oriented temporality as an affective disposition, however, requires a great deal more: an overcoming of a subject's possible fear of becoming different. Cultivating future-oriented temporalities as a political project of remaking the world involves the struggle to become not just able to think a different future but to become willing to lose one's (former) political attachments and become otherwise. 'What', Brown (2005: 107) asks, 'sustains a willingness to risk becoming different kinds of being, a desire to alter the architecture of the social world from the perspective of being disenfranchised in it . . .?' The project of a utopian imagination as conceived by her here requires an affirmation of what we have become as the constitutive ground from which we can become otherwise. Thus the project of the utopian imagination must struggle against both nostalgic sadness and a resentment of what has come to be and the fear of what might replace it, not because the future is settled but – far from it – because a different and perhaps better world remains a possibility.

Opening up the Demand

How and why does the demand for basic income constitute one possible route to think about an otherwise? As alluded to in the beginning, basic income is an income paid unconditionally to individuals regardless of their particular situation. Designed to establish a floor below which income cannot fall, the idea is that basic income would enable many to be independent of the wage system, but certainly less dependent on its present conditions and terms. The idea is not new to left politics. Currently, various proposals along these lines are debated with the current South African administration (Ferguson 2009), and in various European countries it is supported by radical welfare rights groups who see it as an alternative to the precariousness and invasiveness of the welfare system. In general, several aspects of the demand are debated by its advocates, including the amount of the income, what – if any – conditions should be attached to it, and the timing of its distribution. In fact, the level of income considered basic is the first and perhaps most significant point of debate, as the amount determines whether the income would merely subsidize low-wage jobs (as die Linke argues), or would provide individuals with the freedom to opt out of waged work. To be relevant to the politics of an utopian imagination, the income should be large enough to ensure that waged work is less a necessity than a choice. Defenders argue that it can be paid for by a variety of measures, including streamlined, more progressive and more effective systems of individual and corporate taxation.

For the purpose of my discussion here, the demand evinces a dual nature. As an economic perspective, it encourages critical reflection on the current wage system and distribution of labour, as well as a productivist ethics associated with the wage system. As a provocation to the present economic and social order of things, however, the demand does point towards the future that could or would be radically different from what we have right now: what could be different if wages were paid to everybody irrespective of work? As a mode of provocation, the demand's emphasis lies not so much on calling into questions the adequacy of the current wage system, but also emphasizes the collective and performative act of demanding: a political tactics that points beyond the particular scope of specific reforms. That is, exceeding the scope of a specific reform, as a provocation the demand can point to an 'otherwise': desire, freedom and even the possibility of 'getting a life'. And the latter, as Ludger, one of the associates of Berlin's autonomist-Marxist bookshop Schwarze Risse, argued, is something that many of us need to get: not as a commodity or individual possession, but as something that must be continually invented, not as a life that has always already been made for us, but as the one that we might want.

Seen in this light, the political project of the demand for basic income is both deconstructive and reconstructive, deploying at once negation and affirmation, simultaneously critical and utopian, generating estrangement from the present and provoking a different future. Or, to put it in Ludger's terms, it is a project that critically examines and even refuses many of the existing orders of politics, organizing and sociality that are given to us and demands alternatives. When Ludger spoke about the demand, he meant it as a way to gain some measure of distance from, for example, a current productivist ethics and work relations, and for creating some distance that might in turn create the possibility of a life no longer so thoroughly and relentlessly dependent upon (exploitative) work for its qualities. Therefore, somebody like Ludger might demand a basic income not so that he can have, do, or be whatever he already wants, does, or is, but because it might allow him to consider and experiment with different kinds of lives, with wanting, doing and being otherwise. The demand for a basic income could also be used as an occasion to contemplate the shape of a life beyond productivism and work: as not an individual but a collective endeavour, as a wealth of possibilities that non-future-oriented temporalities tend to diminish. It is in this way, for example, that the demand for basic income can serve as a provocation to imagine the possibilities of alternatives in which not only the structures, relations, values and meanings of social and political life might be substantially reconfigured.

Nostalgia and the Future

As a variety of authors have pointed out, nostalgia comes in many shapes: there exist progressive, reactive, reflective, restorative, reifying and hopeful nostalgias (Boym 2001, Flatley 2008), as well as nostalgias for emancipatory futures (Scott 2004). In fact, if it is true that nostalgia constitutes not only a historical but also a political problem (Jameson 2009), and if nostalgia does not only produce nostalgic but also fossilized subjects (Brown 2003), then what kinds of futures – apart from the 'resuscitation of old utopian hopes' – can particular forms of left-wing nostalgia engender? What kinds of conceptual, intellectual and political tools do we have at our disposal to produce an 'otherwise' or what Jodi Dean (2009: 20) would call 'new modes of dreaming'? Rather than arguing that, as a number of analysts at the Berlin meeting have suggested, we should be less resentful, nostalgic, or sad (which may be an unproductive argument to begin with), I have suggested here that a different approach to time and temporal orientation might constitute one route to move beyond some of the debilitating conditions of left-wing nostalgia. What, exactly, it is that may serve as resources for alternative conceptions of politics and time may be a matter of debate, but perhaps not that we are in need of them.

To return for one more second to the demand for basic income: in the current political climate, it is easy to dismiss the demand as 'merely utopian'. Rather than waste time on an impractical, continuously unfulfilled and untimely demand, both cynics and nostalgics might say, we should set our sight on more feasible goals. This well-known logic makes it easy to write the demand off as a naive daydream and unrealistic, and even as a potentially dangerous distraction from the always more important and necessary parameters of reform. That is, the supposed utopianism of this demand is not considered as an asset but a flaw. However, one could perhaps even contest the claim that the demand is only designated as utopian in these times, and I have pointed towards its practicality in relation to current economic trends.

Of course, part of what is in dispute here is the status of the notion of utopia or the utopian imagination. The idea of utopia that I have offered here is not teleologically conceived, and does not involve a political or philosophical blueprint of what a 'good society' should or would look like. Rather, with the notion of a utopian imagination I seek to indicate a more performative temporality: a concrete if partial glimpse of what could constitute an otherwise. Certainly, one problem with the idea of utopia, especially state-socialist utopias, is that it has almost always known too much too soon: that is, that in its more overdetermined configurations, a utopian future is frequently marked by a preconceived content and can be named. By contrast, the vision that I have put forward here offers a more fractional glimpse, offering an incitement towards the imagination and construction of alternatives. In this sense, the demand for basic income is able to prefigure a different world, a world in which the program or policy that the demand promotes would be considered as a matter of course both practical and reasonable.

Although throughout this chapter I have sought to make it clear that I agree with a variety of other analysts (Bewes 2002, Boyer 2006) who argue that the contemporary phenomenon of nostalgia seems to be less about the past than the future, I am, however, less convinced that a diagnostic focus on the redemptive values of sadness (Flatley 2008) or lost possibilities (Scott 2004) provides the best way out of nostalgia's potentially depressing function. In pitching an argument for different kinds of temporality, some of which might configure different relationships among past, present and future, I was also interested in thinking about political temporality and time as non-linear, multi-directional, simultaneous and certainly non-determined; that is, in ways that open up the possibility of thinking about futurity in terms both imaginative and real. Although I am not entirely sure if treating ideas and ideals as ethnographic artefacts here has always constituted a winning strategy, and although I am also convinced that on this front much work remains to be done, I would also argue that it behoves us to think about inventive affective temporalities in this now. Otherwise, a general left-wing mood of animosity not only against the past but also against this present will – to evoke Benjamin one last time – 'win'.

References

Benjamin, W. 1999. 'Left-Wing Melancholy', in M.W. Jennings, H. Eiland and G. Smith (eds), *Walter Benjamin: Selected Writings, Volume 2, 1927–1934*. Cambridge: The Belknapp Press of Harvard University Press, pp. 423–27.

Berdahl, D. 1999. '(N)ostalgie for the Present: Memory, Longing, and East German Things', *Ethnos* 64 (2): 192–211.

———. 2001. '"Go, Trabi, Go!": Reflections on a Car and its Symbolization over Time', *Anthropology and Humanism* 25 (2): 131–41.

———. 2005. 'Expressions of Experience and Experiences of Expression: Museum Presentations of GDR History', *Anthropology and Humanism* 30 (2): 156–70.

Bewes, T. 2002. 'An Anatomy of Nostalgia', *New Left Review* 14: 167–72.

Biehl, J. and P. Locke. 2010. 'Deleuze and the Anthropology of Becoming', *Current Anthropology* 51 (3): 317–51.

Birnbaum, S. 2012. *Basic Income Reconsidered: Social Justice, Liberalism, and the Demands for Equality*. Houndmills: Palgrave Macmillan.

Boyer, D. 2006. 'Ostalgie and the Politics of the Future in Eastern Germany', *Public Culture* 18 (2): 361–81.

Boym, S. 2001. *The Future of Nostalgia*. New York: Basic Books.

Brown, W. 1995. 'Wounded Attachments', in *States of Injury: Power and Freedom in Late Modernity*. Princeton: Princeton University Press, pp. 52–76.

———. 2001. *Politics out of History*. Princeton: Princeton University Press.

———. 2003. 'Resisting Left Melancholia', in D.L. Eng and D. Kazanjian (eds), *Loss*. Berkeley: University of California Press, pp. 458–65.

———. 2005. 'Untimeliness and Punctuality: Critical Theory in Dark Times', in *Edgework: Critical Essays on Knowledge and Politics*. Princeton: Princeton University Press, pp. 1–16.

Dean, J. 2009. *Democracy and other Neoliberal Fantasies*. Durham: Duke University Press.

Douzinas, C. and S. Žižek (eds). 2010. *The Idea of Communism*. London: Verso.

Duncombe, S. 2007. *Dream: Re-Imagining Progressive Politics in an Age of Fantasy*. New York: The New Press.

Ferguson, J. 2009. 'The Uses of Neoliberalism', *Antipode* 41 (1): 166–84.

Flatley, J. 2008. *Affective Mapping: Melancholia and the Politics of Modernism*. Cambridge: Harvard University Press.

Funder, A. 2003. *Stasiland: Stories from Behind the Berlin Wall*. London: Granta.

Grauwacke, A.G. 2007. *Autonome in Bewegung*. Hamburg: Assoziation A.

Haug, W. 2005. 'Untergang der Deutschen Linksregierung – Aufstieg der Linkspartei', *Das Argument* 47 (262): 451–58.

Jameson, F. 2009. *Valences of the Dialectic*. London: Verso.

Leacock, E. 1982. *Myths of Male Dominance: Collected Articles on Women Cross-Culturally*. New York: Monthly Review Press.

Müller, J.W. 2009. 'Just another Vergangenheitsbewältigung?: the Process of Coming to Terms with the East German Past', *Oxford German Studies* 38 (3): 334–44.

Oushakine, S. 2009. *The Patriotism of Despair: Nation, War, and Loss in Russia*. Ithaca, NY: Cornell University Press.

Piot, C. 2010. *Nostalgia for the Future: West Africa and the Cold War*. Durham: Duke University Press.

Povinelli, E. 2011. *Economies of Abandonment*. Durham: Duke University Press.

Rediker, M. 2005. *Villains of all Nations: Pirates in the Golden Age*. Boston: Beacon Press.

Rethmann, P. 2008. 'Nostalgie à Moscou', *Anthropologie et Sociétés* 32 (1–2): 85–102.

———. 2009. 'Post-Communist Ironies in an East German Hotel', *Anthropology Today* 25 (1): 19–42.

Rethmann, P. and I. Budraitskys. n.d. 'Russia's New Left and Other Evils'.

Scott, D. 2004. *Conscripts of Modernity: The Tragedy of Colonial Enlightenment*. Durham: Duke University Press.

Scribner, C. 2005. *Requiem for Communism*. Cambridge: The MIT Press.

Sloterdijk, P. 1988. *Critique of Cynical Reason*. Minneapolis: University of Minnesota Press.

Standing, G. 2011. *The Precariat*. London: Bloomsbury Academic.

Stewart, K. 2005. 'Trauma Time: A Still Life', in D. Rosenberg and S. Harding (eds), *Histories of the Future*. Durham, NC: Duke University Press, pp. 321–40.

Wagenknecht, S. and J. Elsässer. 1996. 'Vorwärts und Vergessen?: ein Streit um Marx, Lenin', in *Ulbricht und die Verzweifelte Aktualität des Kommunismus*. Hamburg: Konkret Literatur Verlag.

Weeks, K. 2011. *The Problem with Work: Feminism, Marxism, Antiwork Politics, and Postwork Imaginaries*. Durham: Duke University Press.

Afterword

On Anthropology's Nostalgia – Looking Back/Seeing Ahead

William Cunningham Bissell

A little more than a decade ago, around the turn of the millennium, I found myself struggling to make sense of what struck me as an ethnographic puzzle. While conducting research on sociospatial transformations in a rapidly changing East African city, I encountered many local interlocutors who spoke of the colonial urban past in explicitly nostalgic terms. To a US-trained African studies and anthropology scholar immersed in post-colonial critiques, these were not exactly the sort of sentiments I expected to hear – indeed, quite the reverse. Nor, at the time, did I know quite what to do with these discourses, at least initially: should I dismiss these claims? Simply ignore them? Certainly there was little historical evidence to support these evocations of the past in the colonial archives, which were them-selves filled with laments about urban disarray and decline. At the time, of course, studies of remembrance were undergoing a renaissance across the humanities, social sciences and cognitive fields, and the 'memory boom' within anthropology itself was well underway (Berliner 2005). Nostalgia, by contrast, had not quite yet come into its own within the discipline itself. One could find scattered references to 'resistant' or 'imperial' or 'structural' nostalgias (Herzfeld 1996, Rosaldo 1989, Stewart 1988), but a good deal of the anthropological discussion remained cast at the level of 'armchair nos-talgia', to give Arjun Appadurai's felicitous phrase a slightly different spin

(1996: 78). At the time, I could find very little in the ethnographic literature to guide me as I sought to interpret nostalgic expressions for the colonial period by Africans who had themselves been oppressed or marginalized by colonial rule – or their descendants, including youths who had no experience of colonialism at all. Something more was involved here than delusion, sloppy sentiment, or retrograde politics, and I wanted to develop a more nuanced understanding of the sociocultural implications of these statements. When the results of that work were published (Bissell 2005), my argument exactly hinged on trying to reposition nostalgia as an ethnographic conundrum: an analytic problem both *for* the field as well as *in* the field that took on strikingly different dimensions when framed anew.

*   *   *

In recent years, there has been a growing and more sophisticated anthropological engagement with nostalgia in its diverse forms and dimensions. The present volume certainly reflects and builds on these trends, taking precisely this ethnographic conjuncture as its point of departure. The diverse studies included here collectively work to establish connections between related domains, effectively linking 'ethnography as nostalgia' with 'ethnographies of nostalgia'. This is an important move for several reasons. First, it allows us to critically analyse the shaping of anthropology itself as a mode of modern knowledge confronted by a profound sense of dislocation and disruption – whether through colonialism, capitalism, or other forces of cultural change. The history of anthropology cannot be neatly severed from consideration of the subject positions and perspectives of specific ethnographers, including their sense of themselves, their place in the world, and their affective attachments to others. Second, raising these issues opens up the question of how anthropologists were motivated by divergent commitments to peoples, places, forms of community and cultural ways that appeared threatened or in need of preservation. And these questions are also intrinsically linked to how ethnographic subjects – our interlocutors in the field – theorize and practice their own understandings of the significance of ongoing processes of temporal and spatial change.

The recent proliferation of nostalgic discourses and practices in widely different sites and settings spread across the globe raises important questions – why now? How is it that nostalgia has spread so widely, seemingly cropping up everywhere? Is this a reflection of changes in the wider world that we are only just beginning to register? Or should the prominence of the concept be more correctly attributed to conceptual fashions or discursive shifts within the discipline itself? Even the mention of fashion in this instance might cause some scholars to squirm, believing that academics should not be influenced by trends or temporal fluff, swayed by the social herd. Fair enough. But fashion, like nostalgia, is an intensely social process as well as a phenomenon driven by the ebbs and flows of time. And in our current moment, one can think of all sorts of *fin de siècle* trends and tendencies that might help us account for the heightened salience of nostalgia: the dismantling of the Berlin Wall and the sudden collapse of the socialist world; the intensified space-time compression often characterized under the rubric of 'globalization'; millennial capitalism; climate change; and intensified waves of urbanization, especially in the megacities of China, India, the African continent and elsewhere, marking, for the first time in recorded history, that the majority of the world's population currently resides in cities, according to UN estimates just after the turn of the millennium (Davis 2006).

Of course, these epochal shifts might be seen as already old hat. Historically, the concept of nostalgia has almost invariably been linked to visions of turning points and temporal junctures. For some, of course, the recent prominence of nostalgia within anthropological discourse is a troubling sign of the times – evidence of conceptual fuzziness or incoherence in the field, on the one hand, or the rise of 'nostalgification' or a 'scholarly nostalgia industry' on the other (Boyer 2010, Lankauskas, this volume). But, as David Berliner argues, nostalgia is inevitably bound up with perceptions of crisis, problems of continuity and uncertainties about the viability of cultural transmission. These concerns have certainly been with us for quite some time, taking on different forms and operating with greater or lesser force in different moments and divergent milieu. But given nostalgia's relevance to visions of crisis and change, we can see how it remains especially apropos to engage a range of contemporary conditions both within the field and without.

* * *

Nostalgia is a sensibility keenly attuned to the problems and perils of modernity, and one can certainly see how it has haunted the course of social theory in the West, from Marx's 'all that is solid melts into thin air' to Weber's 'iron cage', Durkheim's 'mechanical solidarity', and much else besides (Frow 1997, Pickering and Keightley 2006, Robertson 1990). Modernity, as Bruce Berman observes, remains an incomplete project, an ongoing ordeal, and if its impact on Western social orders was destabilizing and disruptive in ways we are still seeking to contain, its destructive force elsewhere was far worse. In the African context, in particular, the encounter with modernity came through the violence and expropriation of European colonialism and capitalist extraction. This severe political and economic dispossession served to break down existing social orders and disrupt established moral economies, only incompletely reformulating them over time into something else. By contrast with Europe, capitalist incorporation of the continent never served to provoke a transformative counter-response leading to vigorous social movements, regulation in the common interest, social trust and more centralized bureaucratic welfare states guaranteeing basic social provisions for all citizens: precisely those elements of liberal orders in the West that have most come under attack since the rise of neoliberalism and globalization. To borrow Karl Polanyi's terms, in the African case no 'double movement' ever took place, with the result that far too many denizens of the continent were left to fend for themselves in the context of partial and imperfect markets, not to mention predatory or anti-democratic states. Especially in sprawling urban contexts, the majority of Africans found themselves in the post-colonial period struggling to make a living and make life without access to basic services, adequate infrastructure, social security, or clear paths to opportunity. As Berman argues, 'what was called "progress" in Malinowski's era and "development" in our own refers to global social processes that have not simply enriched a few and impoverished the many, but, more tragically, have generated intense moral and political crises in every society and led to the most destructive violence against humanity and nature in history' (2006: 1–2).

At the turn of the millennium, sustained attacks on labour, social welfare and public investment in the United States since the post-Fordist period have their complements elsewhere. There, neoliberal developments can be linked to the struggles unleashed within post-socialist societies by sudden alterations to the established terms of the social contract, or the convulsions now looming within Europe over unemployment, economic decline and the harsh politics of imposed austerity. From the developed world to the global south, we can discern multiple and intersecting threads of potential crisis: spiralling debt, sharply increased levels of socioeconomic inequality, rapid environmental degradation, rising seas, deleted natural resources, sprawling urbanization and doubtless more besides. In a wicked irony, the African modernity sketched so cogently by Berman may offer us a glimpse of a potential future we may all come to share, should these crises ripen and eventually come to pass.

*   *   *

In this sort of moment, we can certainly grasp why nostalgia might strike many observers as an apt discourse for our time. And anthropology itself has long had a privileged and intimate relationship with the idea of crisis as well as problems of cultural transmission – not only due to the fact that it was established as a field largely focused on peoples, languages, practices and ways of being that were deemed anything but stable, secure, or certain. To a certain kind of 'salvage' anthropology, linked ultimately to folklore and heritage studies, modernity made anthropological research possible while also threatening to make its subject dissolve or disappear. As Berliner wryly notes in this volume, 'losing culture is a nostalgic figure as old as anthropology' itself. Beyond this, the history of anthropology has also been periodically marked by its own internal sense of crisis, which has provoked recurrent debates over epistemology, the ethics of research and even the viability of ethnography itself, especially under post-colonial or post-structuralist conditions. In my own graduate training at Chicago not that long ago, I was still surprised to find some senior figures in the discipline waxing nostalgic about an easier time when 'we' still controlled the culture concept or ethnography was practiced relatively untroubled by other fields, other voices. Reveries for a better, simpler time, of course, can take many forms, even as youth may find the reminiscences of the elders altogether misplaced or mystifying. But I was struck by these sensibilities, even as I found myself bracketing them as intriguing pieces of ethnographic data. Crises can be productive as well as problematic, stimulating critical reflection and innovative change rather than blocking progress. As a budding anthropologist, I found myself more caught up in the creative ferment of my own moment, rather than harkening back to some golden age in the 1960s, or 1950s, or perhaps Boas or before. Looking forward, I learned to follow advice gleaned from the field: *Twende kwa wakati*, as the Kiswahili saying goes, 'we must move with the times', or perhaps more colloquially, 'go with the flow' – an orientation not at all out of place for a discipline focused on the consequences of sociospatial and temporal change, and seeking critical purchase on nostalgia as a particular orientation within and to the field.

Within the horizon of a particular Western-derived philosophical and literary tradition, nostalgia can assume certain known and comforting dimensions – appearing as something stable and secure (precisely what nostalgics ostensibly long for, oddly enough). From this perspective, when we refer to nostalgia it arrives infused with the aura of common sense, as if we already always know what the phenomena means: its quintessential dimensions and domain. This is precisely the point of departure where ethnographies of nostalgia take off, and the richest contribution that many of the essays in this volume make. Both in theory and in practice, the authors included here start out by posing some quite pointed questions about the meaning and form of nostalgia in divergent times and spaces. In varying ways, all of the authors refuse to take the term for granted or to assume they know what it means. And as these ethnographies document and dissect the proliferation of nostalgic discourses and practices in differing sites across the globe, they work to bring a distinctly anthropological edge to wider scholarly and public debates about commemoration and memory practices.

From the grounded and embodied perspective of field research, the essays caution us about treating nostalgia as a blanket concept or viewing it as a singular or uniform 'thing'. Olivia Angé's piece provides a striking case in point. The discourse of cambio versus negocio in Andean barter fairs might at first glance seem to conform to conventional understandings of nostalgia. The terms seem to invoke oppositions between the balanced reciprocity of exchange versus the cold calculations of the market, *Gemeinschaft* versus *Gesellschaft*, social relations versus self interest, the time of the elders and now. But, as she shows, more than simple 'lack, loss and longing' are involved in these invocations; nostalgic references to the past in this instance are strikingly decontextualized and unspecific, and have both performative and practical dimensions in the present. Indeed, these discourses seek to draw both parties in negotiations into a commensurate moral universe of values, while offering strategic advantages in the bargaining process. Without grasping these sociocultural subtleties in practice, the meaning of nostalgia can only remain elusive, decontextualized and disembodied, very much staying on the surface. Close ethnographic case study serves to open up new possibilities, complicating our sense of the myriad ways nostalgia operates on the ground in practice.

On a similar note, Maya Nadkarni and Olga Shevchenko, like others, warn about the risks of reifying nostalgia or believing that it carries a given content or stable properties. Historicizing nostalgia equally entails envisioning 'it' as a plural practice, with a multiplicity of meanings that have to be carefully explored and analysed in specific sociocultural contexts. Rather than attributing nostalgia from above or outside, critical ethnography begins with a rather different perspective: when informants invoke the past, what kinds of temporal contrasts or claims are being advanced, and to what ends? When people in the field give voice to longing or loss, what affective attachments and political projects are actually involved? How do they relate to counter-discourses or anti-nostalgic responses? Lankauskas touches on critiques of nostalgia as being sloppy or sentimental, emotive or retrograde, and then expresses a concern: nostalgia, he fears, 'tends to gloss over complexities, contradictions, and ambiguities of memorial practice in social life'. But is this really something that comes inherently with the conceptual terrain, or does the problem instead arise in the hands of particular interpreters? As he goes on to note, social memory is shifting, heteroglossic and multi-voiced, and nostalgia is very much part of this complex mix. Indeed, this volume itself provides eloquent testimony to that fact, offering

considerable evidence of the diversity and multiplicity of nostalgic practices, locating them within the intersecting, overlapping, cross-cutting, or
conflicting currents of a wider memoryscape.

*   *   *

Not all forms of nostalgia are the same nor do they point in similar directions –
far from it. Highlighting these differences entails emphasizing the need to
make careful analytic and ethnographic distinctions. Consider, for a moment,
just a few of the different modes and meanings of nostalgia debated in recent
work: 'bureaucratic', 'structural', 'armchair', 'imperial', 'colonial', 'resistant',
'post-communist', 'liminal', 'practical', 'consumerist', 'mass' and 'synthetic'.
Clearly, this is a polysemantic term, and one certainly sympathizes with
those scholars who warn about it becoming a catch-all phrase, lacking clear
analytic purchase. But at the same time, we should remain aware that nostalgia's currency within anthropological discourse is about more than just
fashion or intellectual trends. For in many ways, the topic emerges from the
intersection of some of the most important concerns of the field, at the end
of the twentieth century and as we head into the twenty-first.

First of all, it strikes me as no accident that nostalgia has become conceptually prominent precisely at a time when questions of space, place, landscape and geographic concerns have returned to the fore of the discipline.
Nostalgia, in fact, serves as a powerful means of connecting space with time –
something that makes it significant for scholars as well as the folk with whom
we work in the field. Indeed, in many of these papers we can readily see how
nostalgic discourses often serve to link sociospatial changes with temporal
processes, using specific sites as a point of departure for ruminations about
history, the passage of life, and the flow of time. The end of the Cold War,
post-socialism, post-colonialism, late capitalism, neoliberalism, globalization:
all of these epochal terms mark out moments of intense spatial reconfigura-
tion, and these changes in borders and boundaries have sparked intense
debates in different parts of the world about imagined pasts and hoped-for
futures, alternatively desired or cast in doubt, but with significant implications for social forms and cultural life in the here and now.

To take but one example, few regions of the world have been as inten-
sively or radically reshaped in the last decades as emergent cities in China,
undergoing dramatic growth and shock modernization in a very short time
span. Charting these processes in Kunming, in south-western China, Li
Zhang gives us a powerful sense of the stakes involved. Even though the
city was officially designated as 'historical cultural', and hence deserving of
preservation, it was instead being remade to overcome a sense of lateness
and being left behind, 'just one of many Chinese cities undergoing massive

demolition of the old and hasty construction of the new in the effort to become modern' (Zhang 2006: 461). She movingly describes setting off one day with her parents in search of the old Kunming teahouse where they had been married long ago. They had not been back for years and feared it might have already been swept away, insofar as it was located in an older district slated for demolition. By luck they found the building still stood, and her father moved through the courtyard, touching the wooden framework of the structure and recalling the celebration in embodied (and evocative) detail. The nostalgia sparked by touch and the inhabitation of place was neither simply romantic nor sentimental, but instead 'had a transformative power that created a material link with the past through specific spatial objects' (ibid.).

And so it is in many sites elsewhere. The built environment can serve as a mnemonic touchstone or a portal to the past; in urban contexts especially, architecture in stone or steel is built to last, being both capital and labour intensive, and can stand as tangible markers of change over the course of a life or longer. While individual structures may change, the broader shape of the neighbourhood or the cityscape is more durable, serving as a potent horizon point for narratives of fluctuation and flow. Nor is this just true for the built fabric of the city. Indeed, many of the chapters here reflect the diverse ways that nostalgia is sparked or stimulated by material culture, objects, or goods. The text by Joseph Lévy and Inaki Olazabal captures this dimension beautifully with the suggestive figure of *la llave*: the key to a house long ago left behind, carried by the Jews of Spain into exile following the expulsion in 1492. These keys stand as remnants and material reminders of a lost world, objects that open the past, later refigured into heirlooms to be passed down – material and symbolic touchstones for family history and cultural identity. Nostalgia in this sense is rarely ideal, but instead more commonly defined in relation to an entire object world of evocative 'things'. Nor need this be the case solely with the stuff of 'heritage' – heirlooms, antiques, hand-crafted goods and the like. As Jonathan Bach shows, nostalgia can seize on just about anything, from kitsch to kids toys or mass consumer ephemera, providing insight into the ways that commodities take on new meanings as they circulate and shift between regimes of value (and inflected by temporality, acquiring new patina over time). By drawing attention to how everyday objects acquire new value through temporal shifts, Bach highlights how nostalgia works 'to create a popular-cultural form of knowledge transmission' – often by reworking precisely the stuff of popular culture. Nostalgia's popularity within the field can be attributed to its capacity to open up significant subjects of disciplinary concern for creative rethinking: on the one hand, linking up with concerns about commodities, consumption and circulations of value; on the other, directly connecting with long-term anthropological interests in memory, museums, monuments and especially material culture.

Well over a century ago, Georg Simmel argued that any inquiry into the nature of modern life must start with 'the equation which structures like the metropolis set up between the individual and the super-individual contents of life' (1950 [1903]: 409). In an older world, he wrote, humans faced a more brute struggle for subsistence and survival, pitted against the forces of nature. But in the space of the city, humanity has shifted to confront a 'social-technological mechanism'. As Simmel observes, 'the deepest problems of modern life derive from the claim of the individual to preserve the autonomy and individuality of his existence in the face of overwhelming social forces, of historical heritage, of external culture, and of the technique of life' (ibid.). As this suggests, modernity at least in part entails the production and proliferation of objective culture, in waves that threaten to overwhelm or encompass us. As both cultural subjects and social analysts we seek to come to grips with this burgeoning domain. More than a century later, Simmel's observation carries even greater weight now, with the tremendous growth of material goods, artefacts and collections, the proliferation of museums, mass commodity culture, consumption and the capacity of diverse media to document and disseminate all these things (not to mention, discourses on classification, connoisseurship and the need for conservation of objects).

As this last point suggests, nostalgia remains a protean concept, linked in crucial ways to arenas of cultural life that have long provoked the anthropological imagination, as memory opens up issues of embodiment, everyday practice and cultural performance. Nostalgia rarely exists as an idealized text, but instead is most often ritually enacted, displayed and staged. Rebecca Bryant captures this quite well in her text on the re-presentation of the Turkish Cypriot past, exploring forms of new nostalgia sparked by festivals, museums and other collective, ritualized performances. We see a similar kind of staging in heritage sites globally, as Berliner (2012) has shown in his work on Luang Prabang, where quite different orientations to the Orient, to the exotic and to the historic past circulate and collide among very different actors and institutions in a city undergoing profound change. And in the present volume, there is also Lankauskas' subtle ethnographic analysis of how participants read or respond to the 'Survival Drama' in the reconstructed Soviet-era Bunker, so aptly (perversely? ironically?) named 'The House of Creativity'. Rather than kitsch or comedy, staged socialist spectacle operates to spark popular discourse about history, blurring the ethnographic lines between education and entertainment in intriguing ways.

Along these lines, nostalgia raises important questions about the mediation and mobility of cultural production. Many anthropologists grapple with distance and displacement, and most of us work in worlds where culture is no longer so neatly contained within recognizable or delimited boundaries. Nostalgia is all about cultural worlds that are evoked from a distance in space and time: put on display in museums, commemorated in photographs or archival fragments, represented in ruins or remnants, or recreated and then maintained on the web and other forms of new media.

Lastly, nostalgic discourses also serve as a means to connect 'affect' and everyday life, putting together emotion and embodiment in a single analytic frame. In their various ways, the essays in this volume reflect on the 'field' in a dual sense: critically considering the role of nostalgia in the discipline's past and reflecting on our own attachments or commitments to communities, places, and social lives – placing them in counterpoint or tension with the engagements, visions and voices of the people with whom we work. Ultimately this serves to remind us of the value of sustaining generous scholarly engagements with the world beyond the academy – for nostalgia, as I have argued, represents much more than just academic fashion. Its prominence as a topic, I would argue, has a great deal to do with its salience in providing critical purchase on the unfolding and uneven dynamics of modernity. If something like a memory industry has arisen, it is largely because dynamics of cultural spectacle and display, of images and the imaginary, have played such an increasingly central role in late capitalist cultural dynamics – undergirding mass tourism, museums, media, the marketing of culture and the uses of heritage in a wider economy of space and social life. In future these dynamics will undoubtedly shift, but that does not mean that nostalgia's place in the field will necessarily diminish. Attachments to the past and anguish about the future will assume new guises. But so long as intimations of crisis and change continue, the kinds of critical energies unleashed in this volume will guarantee that anthropologists will still have much to say about diverse ethnographic deployments and dimensions of nostalgia.

References

Appadurai, A. 1996. *Modernity at Large*. Minneapolis: University of Minnesota Press.

Berliner, D. 2005. 'The Abuses of Memory: Reflections on the Memory Boom in Anthropology', *Anthropological Quarterly* 78 (1): 183–97.

———. 2012. 'Multiple Nostalgias: The Fabric of Heritage in Luang Prabang (Lao PDR)', *Journal of the Royal Anthropological Institute* 18 (4): 769–86.

Berman, B. 2006. 'The Ordeal of Modernity in an Age of Terror', *African Studies Review* 49 (1): 1–14.

Bissell, W. 2005. 'Engaging Colonial Nostalgia', *Cultural Anthropology* 20 (2): 215–48.

Boyer, D. 2010. 'From Algos to Autonomos: Nostalgic Eastern Europe as Postimperial Mania', in M. Todorova and Z. Gille (eds), *Post-Communist Nostalgia*. New York: Berghahn, pp. 17–28.

Davis, M. 2006. *Planet of Slums*. London: Verso.

Frow, J. 1997. *Time and Commodity Culture: Essays in Cultural Theory and Postmodernity*. Oxford: Oxford University Press.

Herzfeld, M. 1996. *Cultural Intimacy: Social Poetics in the Nation-State*. London: Routledge.

Pickering, M. and E. Keightley. 2006. 'The Modalities of Nostalgia', *Current Sociology* 54 (6): 919–41.

Robertson, R. 1990. 'After Nostalgia? Willful Nostalgia and the Phases of Globalization', in B.S. Turner (ed.), *Theories of Modernity and Postmodernity*. London: Sage.

Rosaldo, R. 1989. *Culture and Truth: The Remaking of Social Analysis*. Boston: Beacon Press.

Simmel, G. 1950 [1903]. 'The Metropolis and Mental Life', in K.H. Wolff (ed.), *The Sociology of Georg Simmel*. Glencoe, IL: Free Press.

Stewart, K. 1988. 'Nostalgia – A Polemic', *Cultural Anthropology* 3: 227–41.

Zhang, L. 2006. 'Contesting Spatial Modernity in Late-Socialist China', *Current Anthropology* 47 (3): 461–84.

Notes on Contributors

Olivia Angé obtained her PhD in Anthropology at the Université Libre de Bruxelles. After being a postdoctoral fellow at the University of Oxford, she is currently a postdoctoral fellow at the Quai Branly Museum, as well as an associate researcher at the ULB and at the Ecole des Hautes Etudes en Sciences Sociales. She specializes in the study of economic exchanges and cultural transmission in the Argentinean Andes, where she has performed extensive fieldwork since 2005. Her research has been published in *The Journal of Latin American and Caribbean Anthropology*, *Terrain* and *Social Anthropology*, among others.

Jonathan Bach is Associate Professor and chair of the interdisciplinary Global Studies Program at The New School in New York City. His present research explores the intersection of memory, materiality and identity and he is working on a book on the material legacies of the GDR. Recent articles have appeared in *Cultural Anthropology*, *Theory, Culture & Society* and *Public Culture*.

David Berliner is Associate Professor of Anthropology at Université Libre de Bruxelles, and the coeditor of Social Anthropology/Anthropologie Sociale. He has conducted ethnographic research in Guinea-Conakry and Laos. His areas of theoretical expertise include the anthropology of cultural heritage and social memory as well as the study of gender and sexuality. Some of his articles have been published in *American Ethnologist*, *Cahiers d'Études Africaines*, *JRAI*, *Gradhiva*, *Terrain*, *L'Homme*, *RES Anthropology and Aesthetics* and *Anthropological Quarterly*.

William Bissell is Associate Professor of Anthropology and Sociology at Lafayette College. He is working in Zanzibar. His latest book *Urban Design, Chaos, and Colonial Power in Zanzibar* (Bloomington: Indiana University Press,

2010) is a portrait of a cosmopolitan African city and an exploration of colonial irrationality. His previous publications include articles and book chapters on colonial nostalgia, cinema, and the politics of development in contemporary African cities.

Rebecca Bryant is A.N. Hadjiyannis Senior Research Fellow in the European Institute at the London School of Economics. She is a cultural anthropologist who has conducted extensive research on both sides of the Cyprus Green Line, as well as in Turkey. She is the author of *Imagining the Modern: The Cultures of Nationalism in Cyprus* (London: I.B. Tauris, 2004) and *The Past in Pieces: Belonging in the New Cyprus* (Philadelphia: University of Pennsylvania Press, 2010), as well as coeditor of *Cyprus and the Politics of Memory: History, Community, and Conflict* (London: I.B. Tauris, 2012). Her current research concerns politics and society in the Turkish Cypriot community between 1963 and 1974 as well as a comparative analysis of unrecognized states.

Chris Hann is Director and leads the Department of Resilience and Transformation in Eurasia at the Max Planck Institute for Social Anthropology, Halle. A pioneer of field research in Eastern Europe in the socialist era, he has explored related themes in economic and political anthropology comparatively in Turkey and China (Xinjiang). His publications include *Not the Horse We Wanted! Postsocialism, Neoliberalism, Eurasia* (Berlin: Lit Verlag, 2006) and *Economic Anthropology: History, Theory, Critique* (with Keith Hart; Cambridge: Polity, 2011).

Gediminas Lankauskas is Associate Professor of Cultural Anthropology at the University of Regina, Canada. He holds a BA from Vilnius University, a Master's degree from Trent University, and a PhD from the University of Toronto. He was a Postdoctoral Fellow at Concordia University in Montréal. His research interests include post-socialist transformation in Eastern Europe, 'modernity', religiosity, morality, as well as nationalism and the state. He is also interested in remembrance of the recent socialist past in the European East via consumer practices, visual representations, discourse and performance. Dr Lankauskas' work has been published in *Ethnos*, *The Senses and Society*, *Anthropologie et sociétés*, *Lietuvos etnologija (Lithuanian Ethnology)*, *Focaal: European Journal of Anthropology, Journal of Contemporary European Studies* and in edited volumes.

Joseph J. Lévy has a PhD in Anthropology and teaches at the Faculty of Social Sciences, Université du Québec à Montréal (Canada). He has published several books and articles on the Sephardi Jewish community in Montréal and on the Jewish memory in Spain and Morocco. Among them, *Identités Sépharades et modernité* (coedited with J.-C. Lasry and Y. Cohen; Laval: Presses de l'Université Laval, 2007) and papers in *Theoros* and *Les cahiers Espaces*.

Maya Nadkarni is Visiting Assistant Professor of Anthropology in the Department of Sociology and Anthropology at Swarthmore College. Her previous publications include articles and book chapters on post-communist nostalgia, monumentality, and spectacles of criminal and celebrity culture in post-socialist Hungary. Currently she is completing a book manuscript titled *Remains of Socialism: Memory, Nation, and the Future of the Past in Postsocialist Hungary*.

Inaki Olazabal has a PhD in Anthropology and is an Associate Professor at the School of Social Work at the Université du Québec à Montréal. He has published several books and articles on the Achkenazi community in Montréal and on the Jewish memory in Spain, among them *Khaverim. Les Juifs ashkénazes de Montréal au début du XXe siècle. Entre le Shtetl et l'identité citoyenne* (Quebec: Nota Bene, 2006). He has also published articles, coauthored with J. Lévy, in *Annals de l'institut d'estudis Gironins* and *Les Cahiers Espaces*.

Petra Rethmann is Professor of Anthropology at McMaster University in Canada, a faculty member in the Cultural Studies and Critical Theory programme, and a member of the Institute on Globalization and the Human Condition. She writes and teaches on the relationship between history, memory and politics, as well as on aesthetics, art, political possibility and imagination. She is currently working on a book that examines the politics of revolution, memory and nostalgia by looking at museum and institutional sites in Russia, Germany and Mexico. She is the author of *Tundra Passages* (Pennsylvania: Penn State University Press, 2001), coeditor of *Global Autonomy: Frictions and Connections* (with Imre Szeman and Will Colemen; Vancouver: University of British Colombia Press, 2010) and the author of numerous articles that have appeared in edited volumes and in journals such as *American Anthropologist*, *American Ethnologist*, *Anthropologica*, *Cultural Critique* and *Anthropologie et Société*.

Olga Shevchenko is Associate Professor of Sociology at Williams College where she teaches courses on socialism and post-socialism, culture, consumption, images and identity. She is the author of *Crisis and the Everyday in Postsocialist Moscow* (Bloomington: Indiana University Press, 2009) and a range of articles and book chapters on the contemporary Russian popular culture, everyday political discourse, memory and nostalgia. Presently, she is working on an edited volume entitled *Double Exposure: Memory and Photography*, and a collaborative ethnographic project on Soviet family photography and generational memories of socialism, provisionally entitled *Snapshot Histories*.

Index